To Patricia Wismer,
friend and colleague,
"May the angels sing you into Paradise."

IN THE EMBRACE OF GOD

Feminist Approaches to Theological Anthropology

Ann O'Hara Graff, editor

ORBIS BOOKS
Maryknoll, New York 10545

The Catholic Foreign Mission Society of America (Maryknoll) recruits and trains people for overseas missionary service. Through Orbis Books, Maryknoll aims to foster the international dialogue that is essential to mission. The books published, however, reflect the opinions of their authors and are not meant to represent the official position of the society.

Published by Orbis Books, Maryknoll, NY 10545-0308
Manufactured in the United States of America

Library of Congress Cataloging-in-Publication Data

In the embrace of God : feminist approaches to theological
    anthropology / Ann O'Hara Graff, editor.
        p.   cm.
    Includes bibliographical references and index.
    ISBN 1-57075-029-7 (alk. paper)
    1. Man (Christian theology) 2. Feminist theology. 3. Catholic
Church—Doctrines.   I. Graff, Ann Elizabeth O'Hara, 1950—   .
BT745.15   1995
233'.082—dc20   95-24228
                                                              CIP

Contents

Introduction

Embedded deep in the Christian tradition is the insight that human beings live, and move, and have our being in the embrace of God. From a theological point of view the very project of our self-examination is carried out in relation to God. Concomitantly, our access to God is gained through ourselves. We have only our own lives with our experiences. This is our medium and reality. This is where theological anthropology begins. We seek understanding of ourselves in the context of our inevitable and primal relationship to God.

To point to ourselves appears simple but quickly emerges as more complex. Our own persons grow out of and participate in the life of the physical world, our families, societies, cultures, and histories. We are individuals who are inextricably social beings in every sense. We are each a distinct realization of our ecology. Thus to refer to ourselves throughout the essays in this book is not simply to reflect on us as individuals, as if we were each isolated in our uniqueness. However unique we are, we human beings belong to one another, to our peoples, and to this planet. Thus theological anthropology attends to *anthropos* in a sense that locates our personal selves in wider webs without which we would not be or be who we are. It is theological anthropology because we recognize that *theos* is present and participates in every moment of our experience, ultimately, creator, sustainer, and eschatological hope of all that we are, of our histories, and of the cosmos.

The recognition that we come from God and are going to God, that we belong to God, that we dwell within the embrace of God and are capable of being the dwelling place of God who may dwell in us—these recognitions of our intimacy with our creator are ancient in Christianity. They are written in the letters of Paul and the Gospel of John, figured in the theologies of Origen and Athansius, the passionate *Confessions* of Augustine, and reconfigured over the centuries, whether in the work of Catherine or Teresa, Bernard, Bonaventure, Thomas, Karl Rahner, or Elizabeth Johnson. It is this relational context that invites exploration within the broad area of theological anthropology. The questions about where we come from and where we are going immediately arise. Thus theological anthropology entails some forms of attention to our place in creation as well as to issues of eschatology (the last things). Traditionally, theologians have also

1

explored issues about human identity, notably the claim that we are made in the image and likeness of God, as well as those dimensions of our relational contexts that we have labeled sin and grace. This ties us into questions about the person and work of Jesus the Christ.

In all of this, the sensibilities of this book are particularly Catholic, because we are grounded in a sense of the immediate, immanent presence of God in and through our experience. The very realities of our experience, however ambiguous or even sinful, nevertheless can be a bearer, a sacrament, of the Divine. It is this very insight, grounded in creation and incarnation, that turns and returns us to our experience to seek new theological vision.

What makes a book like this an opening into renewed and reconstructive theological conversation about what it means to be human is that feminist theologians are re-examining the field of human experience, especially the diversity of women's experience. Attention to the real lives of women, ourselves and others, raises new questions and provokes new explorations; it also raises old questions but with new insights or concerns. Therefore, the essays in this book, which have grown out of eight years of conversation in the theological anthropology seminar of the Catholic Theological Society of America, augmented by the conversation in the women's seminar on constructive theology, represent voices and directions being taken in this recent research.

Moreover, since these essays are specifically informed by the searchings of women in conversation with and about women, the multiple experiences of women—especially as these are engaged in multilateral conversations both within and among diverse groups of women—have been our teachers. Their voices guide this research. Many of the contributors to this book are white feminists who are committed to search out the experiences of women of their own race and class but are also committed to learning from and supporting dialogue with women different from themselves. They do this aware of histories and contemporary practices of racism and classism that continue to wound and divide, and in the hope that we are engaged in the long processes of reconciliation and healing. Other contributors include María Pilar Aquino, whose roots are in Mexico and whose identity is drawn from Latin American feminists; Ada María Isasi-Díaz, a Cuban immigrant to the U.S. who identifies herself with the concerns of the Latinas and indeed, her wider people, as a *mujerista* theologian; a third contributor is an Asian man, a leader in interreligious dialogue between East and West, as well as a recent key thinker in the area of eschatology, Peter Phan. Our book is richer for the ongoing conversation our project members have had with a womanist member of our writing group, but also poorer for the loss of her essay due to unforeseen circumstances. However, it has especially been in the context of many formal and informal conversations in the Catholic

Theology Society of America that our thinking has been shaped. There we have been aided by the generous leadership of John Farrelly and have learned much from senior scholar Mary Aquin O'Neill. To the many people who have joined us, criticized us, and contributed to our work, we all owe thanks.

The book opens with an introduction to steps taken in feminist theory that have provided entry points and background for many areas of feminist thought. Mary Ann Zimmer explores the area of feminist theory in order to indicate the backdrop it provides for feminist theological anthropology today. Her essay is followed by Mary Ann Hinsdale's account of the very recent history of developments in Catholic theological anthropology, which locates the reconstructive efforts of this book and provides extensive bibliography. In fact, the notes throughout the text are intended to provide a sense of what to read and where the present conversation is in the discipline.

Following these introductions, the essays move into the foundational area of the turn to experience. This begins with María Pilar Aquino's painstaking map of the way toward the inclusion of women's experience in the anthropological conversation taking place in the Latin American church, including the exponents of "liberation." Women in Latin America, in the United States, and around the world have had to struggle to become visible and have their voices heard and engaged. My essay provides a sense of the difficulty of naming women's experience, the complexity of experience, and the implications for theology once women's experiences are taken seriously. Ada María Isasi-Díaz then offers an entry point into the experience of Latina women and a sense of how that lays a foundation for a *mujerista* theological anthropology.

The essays then move into the way particular explorations of women's experiences both critique and reconstruct Christian theology. Susan Ross offers a complex and critical reappropriation of women's bodies and sexuality. I offer a review of recent work in feminist psychology and its potential to deepen our understanding of several issues in theological anthropology. Patricia Wismer examines the diverse realities of women's suffering and asks how suffering might be rethought theologically.

Much feminist work has arisen in situations of pain. The issues of the many faces of suffering and the experience of sin have generated a great deal of attention in feminist theology, as they do in any liberation theology. Thus, as the text turns to very specific theological connections that have already been indicated repeatedly in the earlier essays, the problem of sin re-emerges in Sally Ann McReynolds' article. From there we move to the need to reawaken connections between humans and our dwelling place, the earth. Anne Clifford outlines a much needed ecofeminist ethic of solidarity that is grounded in rethinking our place in creation. In that creation, we have been made according to the image and likeness of God. Mary Catherine Hilkert reopens the theology of *imago Dei* as it functioned in the tradition and can be rethought today in light of feminist research. Finally, Peter Phan reviews feminist efforts in eschatology and indicates both what has been suggested and where our thinking might continue to develop. Both the Hilkert and Phan essays take us into the language of grace, which has been raised throughout. The fact, however, that the reopening of experience has been linked with the dis-covering of so much pain makes both the attention to that pain and the retrieval, for example, of such fundamental realities as our embodied selves as good and holy (see Ross), markers of the state of the rethinking of this area of theology. Most of the essays demonstrate the movement into experience, through suffering and sin, toward hope, recreation, and renewal of human life and well-being. Ultimately, the discipline is about understanding, setting to rights, and offering avenues toward whole-making, grounded in a renewal of our understandings of what being human is all about.

As questions of identity, value, meaning, and hope emerge for us in this search, we re-encounter God. Theological anthropology engages this complex struggle to understand ourselves, aware that in its depth this is a sacred dilemma, ultimately open to God. Here Jacob— and Rachel—wrestle with the angel. This is no God of rules, submissive to churches, at our beck and call, or who provides quick and easy answers. Rather, in our depths we have no alternative but to wrestle with the truth of ourselves and the God who is absolutely God.

Consider these essays the journey, perhaps more truly the wanderings, of diverse people committed to etching new maps on the charted and uncharted territory of human and Divine. Our maps and meanderings are written for ourselves and for you, our readers, in the hope that we might all find some insights that will help us live more truthfully and more carefully together in and into the kin-dom of God.

Finally, let me personally thank the members of the CTSA who contributed to this book. Their intelligence, patience, and good will are deeply appreciated. I also owe many thanks to Howard Linz, who generously gives of his time and computer skills to the Institute of Pastoral Studies at Loyola in Chicago. Without his abilities to translate computer languages, this book would not have been possible. Similarly, my graduate assistant, Mary Louise Jones, whose pastoral skills already serve many, used her considerable computer capabilities to aid the editing process in almost magical ways. Finally, I want to thank Susan Perry of Orbis Books for her enthusiasm, patience, and confidence in the helpfulness of this project for the ongoing endeavor of theological conversation in service of all God's people.

Ann O'Hara Graff

Part I

THE FRAMEWORK

1

Stepping Stones in Feminist Theory

Mary Ann Zimmer

Some feminists live with a husband and children in a nuclear family; some live in exclusively female communities. Some feminists believe that a career should be every woman's aspiration; some think that close involvement with our present business system can only destroy women's innate preference for cooperation and community. Despite their differences, however, these varied feminists all share a common conviction that something is badly amiss with women's current place in this world.[1] In this essay I offer a sense of the range of feminist theories that have developed in order to explain women's situation of disadvantage and to propose remedies for it. After a brief orientation to feminist theory and theology, I will provide an overview of several major strands of feminist theory. Then I will focus on three issues that have particular relevance for theological anthropology.

Feminist Theory and Theology

As Anne Carr describes it, feminist theology engages in a twofold critique, "not only a Christian critique of sexist or patriarchal culture but a feminist critique of Christianity."[2]

Any time a faith community reflects on its beliefs and practices in order to articulate, for a particular historical present, the meaning of this tradition, a whole range of assumptions colors that reflection. These are what Francis Schüssler Fiorenza calls background theories, "those implied theories that impact upon considered hypotheses and judgments."[3] These include theories about "the self, society, and the world," as well as "the means and methods of interpreting past tradition and present experience."[4] While not necessarily directly theological, one's background theories shape the questions, evaluations and choice of resources that operate in one's theology.

One's background theories tend to be part of one's taken-for-granted view of the world, but when beliefs and practices are contested or when there is a significant level of change going on within the faith community or the cultural context, it becomes important to examine the implicit assumptions that undergird explicit claims.[5] The questions that feminism addresses to Christian theology and practice require such an examination. At the same time feminist theology's own assumptions need to be as clear as possible. Thus, some initial understanding of the range of feminist theory will help make explicit the background theories that underlie the critique that feminist theologians raise and the constructive proposals they make.

Defining Feminism

Feminism is a complex movement with many branches and streams.[6] Most feminists, though, would agree with the definition of the feminist project as it is laid out by bell hooks. Feminism, hooks asserts, can best be defined as "the struggle to end sexist oppression."[7] According to this definition, feminism is not merely a personal label but a commitment to action in the real world. hooks describes herself as seeking an understanding of feminism that is suitable for a broader group than the white, middle and upper class, liberal women whose agenda, she argues, has shaped the feminist movement of the last three decades.[8] Thus she is adamant about the need for women to actively repudiate not only sexism but also the racism, homophobia and class divisions by which some women are both oppressors and oppressed.[9] In order to emphasize the importance of being alert to these interacting sources of oppression, I would expand hooks' definition to add that feminism is the *self-critical* struggle to end sexist oppression.

Just as hooks is clear about the fact that the struggle to end sexist oppression will mean different things to different groups of women in the U.S., resistance to the oppression of women also has different concrete manifestations in other parts of the world. Economic and cultural differences will affect the goals, priorities and strategies of feminism in different parts of the world and for different groups within any one nation.[10] Within each context, however, feminist theorists contribute to the struggle to end sexist oppression by analyzing women's situations. The work of feminist writers, literary critics, historians, sociologists, theologians, artists, ethicists, psychologists, scientists, etc. helps construct a broader and more complex picture of women's oppression, as well as of women's accomplishments and strengths and of the dynamics that keep current systems in place. Thus feminist theorists open up new awarenesses of both the strengths and the vulnerabilities of systems of oppression and provide building materials for strategies that work toward full human flourishing.[11]

Feminist Theory as Critical Theory

From the above description, one can see that feminist theory is not theory in Aristotle's sense of *theoria,* the contemplation of universal truth for its own sake, but is, rather, an instance of *critical theory.*[12] As Raymond Geuss describes it, critical theory aims at "emancipation and enlightenment, at making agents aware of coercion and putting them in a position to determine where their true interests lie."[13] As critical theory, feminist theory does not aim at a dispassionate observation of what already exists or what is universally true but offers a critique of false notions about women's interests and situations with the goal of freeing women from deception. Feminist theory, then, has a political purpose in the sense that feminist theorists are working toward a redistribution of power that will be emancipatory for women. As we shall see, even questions about the nature of the human person in her/his relationship to God, the subject matter of theological anthropology, can be asked and answered in ways that are either emancipatory or oppressive for women.

Analyzing Oppression

The oppression of women is a complex phenomenon requiring an analysis that can do justice to its pervasiveness, its variety and its vulnerabilities. Iris Marion Young describes five dimensions that operate in different combinations in situations of oppression: exploitation, marginalization, powerlessness, cultural imperialism and violence.[14] *Exploitation* refers to the systematic transfer of the benefit of one person or group's work to the advantage of another. *Marginalization* is the unwillingness or inability of the economic system to use the capabilities of a person or group of persons. *Powerlessness* is the position of being the recipient of direction from others but being unable to give orders or exercise control over one's situation. *Cultural imperialism* is the universalization of one group's culture to the exclusion of all others. *Violence* names the dimension of institutionalized or socially permissible violence against persons or groups.

To Young's dimensions of oppression, Black feminist theorist Patricia Hill Collins adds analysis of the levels on which oppression operates: the individual, cultural and social/structural.[15] Collins argues that one must locate the variety of sites where oppression functions in order to know where resistance can be mounted. She gives particular emphasis to the location of oppression and resistance on the level of self-definition. From her experience in the dominated subculture of Black women, Collins points out that it is an important act of resistance for women at least to claim their own *understanding* of themselves in situations where there is little else they can control. By highlighting resistance on all these levels Collins raises for all oppressed groups the question of whether the dominant culture and the structures and institutions that undergird it are as pervasively successful in their domination as is often assumed. With the dimensions and levels of oppression in mind, we turn now to an examination of how different strands of feminist thought have located the sources of and remedies for women's pervasive disadvantage.

Varieties of Feminist Theory

Different branches of feminist theory have understood women's oppression as stemming from different causes and requiring different strategies of resistance and transformation. In a very general way, feminist theories can be grouped under the categories liberal, existentialist, gynocentric, socialist, and postmodern.[16] Each grows out of particular practical questions about how to understand and eliminate the oppression of women. Each strand of theory encourages us to question certain assumptions, be wary of certain pitfalls, focus on particular desired outcomes; each is more useful for addressing some concerns than others.

Although feminist historical studies have discovered women in every era who objected to and acted against enforced female inferiority, the roots of feminism as a modern Western movement are found in the late eighteenth century.[17] The Enlightenment produced a number of writers who rejected the notion of women's inferiority and developed a *liberal* feminism that located the source of women's oppression in the lack of *equality* between women and men. These early liberal thinkers argued for women's equality by applying to women the Enlightenment theories of the person that hold up rational thinking as the natural, universal human ability that undergirds the dignity and rights of the individual and the equality of persons.[18]

Enlightenment thought, in general, did not apply its emancipatory theories to women because it portrayed them as less rational than men and, on these grounds, unable to claim the rights granted to full persons.[19] Liberal feminism, however, argued that women are not *naturally* different from men but continue to be at a disadvantage because they are socialized to act differently than men, are permitted only restricted opportunities and are channeled into social roles that are less respected, rewarded, and self-developing than those of men.[20]

What is often called the "first wave" of feminism as a movement in the United States dated to the Seneca Falls Convention of 1848 and was basically a liberal movement that argued from an Enlightenment perspective and focused on obtaining equal rights for women, e.g., the right to vote, to own property, to speak in public.[21] Religious arguments for equality were also widely used. As Sarah Grimkè put it, "All I ask of our brethren is that they will take their feet from off our necks and permit us to stand upright on that ground which God designed us to occupy."[22] What progress was made at this stage was applicable chiefly to middle-class and wealthy white women, since these were the people whose situation was most improved by changes in property and inheritance laws.[23]

By the late eighteenth century, the movement had split into several factions, the strongest of which attended almost entirely to the issue of suffrage and argued its case from a *gynocentric* point of view. Focusing on women's uniqueness or difference rather than their equality, it put particular emphasis on women's moral superiority and the importance of women using their maternal skills to create a positive moral climate in the public as well as the domestic arena.[24] The dominant branch of the movement, the National American Woman Suffrage Association, was reluctant to support Black, working class, and immigrant women for fear of losing the support of more powerful groups, even refusing membership to Black women.[25] After women's suffrage was obtained in 1920, this stage of the movement lost its momentum.

"Second wave" feminism in the United States began in the 1960s with a revival of the liberal argument for women's equal rights.[26] This liberal feminism focused on obtaining access for women to the roles, privileges, and opportunities of the adult, rational human person. They have been especially vigilant about obtaining equal treatment of women in education, the workplace and the legal system.

What is problematic about the liberal approach is that the admission of women to situations and characteristics that have traditionally been the realm of men does not necessarily help women (and men) become more fully human but actually upholds the cultural stereotype of masculine roles and values as normative humanity for all. In other words, the roles and characteristics traditionally assigned to women continue to be devalued while women are encouraged to gain advantage by adopting roles and characteristics that had traditionally been male. In addition, the liberal perspective gives little attention to the fact that not even all men are treated as equal and that both women and men continued to be oppressed (by both men and women) on the grounds of class, nationality, religion, race, etc. Finally, as Italian feminist theorists have emphasized, liberal feminism, by denying any difference between women and men, does not recognize how this focus on equality eliminates public consideration of the concrete consequences of women's difference.[27] This approach leaves no space, then, for asking whether women might be different, in what ways this might be true and how might important differences be acknowledged and supported rather than penalized in the social, political, and cultural mainstream. In addition, this model of equality eliminates any opportunity for women to define themselves for themselves.

By the 1970s, liberal feminism was under heavy critique by those who argued that liberal feminism perpetuates women's inferior status because it does not critique the implicitly male norm that is held up as the goal of human equality. Women's contacts with one another in consciousness-raising groups placed new emphasis on women's experience as a source of knowledge and political unity and gave rise to a new period of woman-centered feminism. At the same time, women who had participated in radical social movements, e.g., the civil rights and antiwar movements and New Left groups like the Students for Democratic Society, had begun to organize on behalf of women's liberation as they experienced their own oppression by men in radical organizations.

The turn to woman-centered or *gynocentric* feminism raised up women's experience as a source of positive value and the norm by which to critique the male-dominated systems of value, meaning, identity, and social organization that liberal feminism leaves in place.[28] This strand of theory locates the source of women's oppression in the cultural system of patriarchy, a system of differential power based on the assumption that male gender identity is normative. It points to the destructive tendencies of this system and looks for relief for women in a reformed, transformed, or even separate culture shaped by women's experience and the values developed by women.[29]

Some gynocentric feminists do not believe that the current cultural system is redeemable at all. These advocate separatism, the withdrawal of women from male-dominated society into exclusive communities of women where women can develop their identity and values away from the oppressive reach of patriarchy and the necessity of pleasing males. Even those who do not advocate separatism do recognize a need for temporary places or times of separation. Alice Walker, for example, describes a womanist as "[c]ommited to survival and wholeness of entire people, male and female. Not a separatist, except periodically for health."[30]

Issues of sexuality, reproduction, and motherhood are key concerns for this strand of feminism. Can marriage and motherhood be anything other than institutions of patriarchal oppression? Does motherhood have value for women themselves, or is it merely one more way for women to serve a society built on men's interests?[31] Can heterosexual relationships be positive, or are they inevitable situations of domination? Can women really be themselves if they are mothers and/or wives? Can women really be themselves if they are not mothers?

U.S. women from nondominant racial groups have been among those who are articulating the positive riches of women's experience. At the same time, they have been critical of the tendency of white, middle-class women to talk about "woman's" experience as though all women share the same experiences, status or values.[32] The opportunity to work outside the home, for example, is, for some women, perhaps especially those of the white middle and upper classes, a major goal of feminism. For others their deepest desire is to be free to care for their own children rather than being forced by economic necessity to work long hours in someone else's home, which has often been the situation of poor Black women whose job options have been domestic labor.

Another major criticism of an oversimplified gynocentric theory is that it tends to ignore women's capacity for evil by romanticizing women's experience and relationships as entirely positive. This romanticization prevents feminist analysis from including a picture of women as whole persons. It particularly does not provide for analysis of the fact that some women are oppressors of other women because of difference in race, class, nationality, sexual orientation, etc. Finally, gynocentric feminism, rejecting as patriarchal many forms of organizational structure, tended toward withdrawal rather than engagement in political and structural change.

Both liberal and gynocentric feminism have drawn on the insights of *existentialist* feminism, best exemplified by Simone de Beauvoir's classic work, *The Second Sex*. Existential feminism locates the source of women's disadvantage in the difficulty women have in claiming their own subjectivity. Because of its pervasive influence in later theory, I will give extended attention to de Beauvoir's analysis of the categories *self* and *Other* as descriptive of the social relations of men and women.[33]

The notion of the Other has its roots in Sartre who described the individual's efforts to establish a self in a world in which physical existence is given but one's subjectivity must be self-created. One establishes a self by making someone else an object, the Other.

> If in general there is an Other, it is necessary above all that I be the one who is not the Other and it is in this very negation effected by me upon myself that I make myself be and that the Other arises as the Other. This negation which constitutes my being and which, as Hegel said, makes me appear as the Same confronting the Other, constitutes me "Myself."[34]

Thus the object has the positive function of enabling the self to experience itself as subject. The constituting of the Other-as-object also ensures that the Other is not a threat, i.e., not a subject able to objectify.[35]

De Beauvoir argued that the social and cultural positions of men and women are so unequal because men have assumed the role of the self and maintain women in the role of Other, as object rather than subject. In this fundamentally asymmetrical relationship "... relation of the two sexes is not quite like that of two electrical poles, for man represents both the positive and the neutral, as is indicated by the common use of *man* to designate human beings in general; whereas woman represents only the negative, defined by limiting criteria, without reciprocity."[36] Thus woman "is not regarded as an autonomous being. . . . She is defined and differentiated with reference to man and not he with reference to her. He is the Subject, he is the Absolute—she is the Other."[37]

De Beauvoir acknowledges that this view of woman is not always a negative one; the female may, for example, be worshiped as a deity. Even when the female is worshiped, however, it is as Other, outside the realm of the human.[38] When she is admired for human qualities, she is valued precisely as Other, a foil for man. She is "all except herself."[39]

The opposition of the self and the Other functions to secure the position of the self by keeping before the individual the proof of his or her own subjectivity and ensuring that the Other will remain an object rather than a subject able to objectify in turn. In the case of man and the female Other, a set of oppositional characteristics define their respective positions. Man is transcendent, woman immanent.[40] Woman is identified with nature, man with culture.[41] Woman is involved with the particular, domestic, and private, man with the universal and public.[42]

Numerous feminist theorists since de Beauvoir have explored the implications of her insight for explaining the virtually universal (at least in modern Western cultures) lesser valuation of the feminine. As an influential example, cultural anthropologist Sherry Ortner, writing in the 1970s, analyzed the implications of the identification of the male with the sphere of culture and the female with the sphere of nature. Ortner's colleague, Michelle Rosaldo, used the dichotomies of public/male and private/female to analyze the situation of women's devaluation. Both Ortner and Rosaldo (and de Beauvoir, for that matter) framed their original arguments as descriptive of universal, cross-cultural characteristics of societies. Since the 1970s, much of feminist theory has become more critical of such universalizing because feminist activists and thinkers are recognizing the oppressive results of any one group assuming that its experience defines all women.[43] One resource that challenges the tendency to universalize is socialist attention to women's concrete conditions.

Socialist feminists link the problem of women's oppression with the general economic disadvantage that is the lot of the working class in a capitalist economic system. They criticize feminist theories for failing to give adequate weight to the effects of women's material situation but, at the same time, they also fault socialism for its failure to attend to the specific disadvantages of women and its tendency to unquestioningly subsume women into their husband's class. Socialist ideals, they argue, seem to assume that women's situation will improve automatically with the end of capitalism, but no adequate account of women's true class situation or of domestic labor is given in classical socialist theory. Socialist feminists understand the disadvantaged situation of women to be caused by their absence (as mother and household worker) from socialist theory or by their compulsory participation in reproduction as a specialized system of production.[44] As Seyla Benhabib and Drecella Cornell point out, however, trying to fit women into a Marxist model "subsumes typically female activities under the model of work, narrowly understood as the producing and formation of an object."[45] Thus the very categories of analysis available to socialist thought can mask important elements of the experience that feminist theorists are trying to articulate.

The repeated openings of feminist theory to the differences of gender, race, culture and class locations are key markers of what is now termed *postmodern*. The modern era, inaugurated with the "Enlightenment" of the seventeenth century and the struggles of the eighteenth century to create democratic Western governments, rested on dramatic recognitions of the powers, limits, and rights of individual and collective "man" and "his" detached autonomous reason. The postmodern serves as a marker of the recognition of the impossibility of universalizing that "man." We are female and male, actors within cultures, subcultures, societies, racial groups, classes based on heritage or wealth, and much more. The article by Graff in this volume on the effort to name women's experience sorts this out further than I can attend to here. However, each of these has clearly arisen in what we have already examined.

Perhaps what is critical to note is that postmodern feminist theorists attend to difference. Here there is a broad range of bases for that articulation.[46] A word of caution is in order, however. Some feminists are convinced that if women are defined only by very different and changing identities, feminism's ability to produce convincing criticism of existing sources of oppression and engage in effective political organization is greatly weakened. [47]

Moreover, among some male postmodern theorists, the demise of the subject has been announced. Feminists have been quick to note that this interesting death has been proclaimed just as the voices of women and peoples who have long been denied public voice have finally become speakers in the international conversation about human life, its meaning, and politics.[48]

Among the key speakers in this present postmodern conversation are those concerned with language itself. I am only able to offer two brief glimpses into their concerns.

Post-structuralist theorists regard language not as a means by which a self can *represent* reality, nor as a means of *self-expression,* but as a system by which one's sense of reality and subjectivity are *constructed.*[49] Because language is not tied to representation of a reality outside itself, meaning can be slippery, differing according to context. The same is true of the self constructed by language. This emphasis on the mobility and contextuality of both self and meaning highlights the possibility of change and the vulnerability of existing ideas, practices, and systems. What is constructed (rather than given by nature) can be deconstructed.

Postmodern French feminist theorists locate women's disadvantage in the entire language/symbol system, which is the means by which a dominant identity or meaning (the phallocentric) defines itself in contrast to what it is not (the feminine). Thus the feminine has no status, identity or language of its own but functions to provide the boundary against which a perpetually threatened language/meaning system can define itself. Here, again, are echoes of de Beauvior. As marginal, women are always a threat to the order of the system, a system in which they are both entrapped and resistant. Resistance is located particularly in the female body, which expresses (without language) a source of identity and difference for women. Positive change for women comes not in aspiring to the stability of dominant meaning but in appreciating and exploiting women's own marginal position.[50]

While these remarks can only offer a starting point, it is clear that each type of feminist theory that we have examined raises particular questions and calls on unique resources. A few of the many questions that they present to Christian theology of the person are examined below.

KEY ISSUES: FEMINIST THEORY AND THE HUMAN PERSON

Nature and Nurture

Although it is probably impossible, finally, to draw the line precisely between nature and nurture as forces in shaping our selves and our social arrangements, feminist theory has tended to distinguish the biological consequences of being male or female (according to one's bodily configuration and hormone levels) from the socially constructed norms for femininity or masculinity, i.e., one's gender. This interest in learned identities and behaviors and in the structures that keep them in place is particularly strong in feminist theory because of its commitment to *change*.[51] Further questions that might be asked include whether the socially constructed identities and behaviors are imposed on a person, chosen by her/him, or negotiated in some complex combination of accommodation and resistance. What can be considered "natural" about being human? Is this nature the same for men and women? for each man and woman?

Body, Mind, Gender

When feminist theory examines our understandings of being human, questions about the significance of the body are key to the discussion. This is true partly because women have often been identified with the bodily aspects of being human while men have been assigned the project of transcending the body through culture and thought. According to de Beauvoir, primitive man was able to dominate woman because "the human male . . . remodels the face of the earth, he creates new instruments, he invents, he shapes the future," while woman is "biologically destined" because in "maternity woman remained closely bound to her body like an animal."[52] Feminist analysis criticizes the devaluation of the body that takes place when the essence of humanity is identified with the ability to reason. At the same time the assumption that women's nature is essentially defined by their body or reproductive capacity is also problematic. What difference does it make that human persons are embodied? What difference does it make that bodies are gendered? These issues have formed a starting point for further research, and much of this is detailed in Ross's essay in this volume.[53]

Content and Process

Most varieties of feminism critique both the *content* of what we have heretofore taken to be accurate knowledge about humanity and the *process* by which reliable knowledge has been justified. What is the role of our own concrete experience and social location in shaping how we understand our humanity? How do we sort out cultural stereotypes from biological necessity? Is detached, abstract generalization the goal of knowledge? Who has participated in defining the knowledge that we have? Who has not? Crucial to this issue is the effort to name and think about the experiences of women. As this volume explicates, both experiential content and the process of naming and working with it are the basis of the present rethinking of theological anthropology.

CONCLUSION

Even a survey as brief as this demonstrates the rich array of questions and resources that feminist analysis brings to our efforts to understand and change women's situation. It also shows that any approach that attributes women's oppression to a single cause is inadequate by itself because such a theory is usually guilty of universalizing the experience or position of one limited group of women. Adequate feminist theory must be able to account for the position of some women as both oppressor and oppressed, be able to think about women as significantly different from men as well as having commonalities, e.g., rights, abilities, that are equal to those of men, and to recognize that gender oppression alone does not constitute the most salient problematic for all groups of women. Yet even when race, sexual orientation, or class distinguish some women from others, their specific situation of sexist oppression cannot be overlooked. Feminist theologians draw on the resources offered by all the strands of feminist thought as they critique the sexist elements of Christian tradition, bring a Christian critique to bear on contemporary culture, and construct new understandings of the human person in relationship to God.

NOTES

1. I will use *feminine* to refer to the culturally assigned characteristics and roles of women. I will use *feminist* for those persons and positions that argue that at least some aspects of women's traditional role are oppressive.

2. Anne E. Carr, *Transforming Grace: Christian Tradition and Women's Experience* (San Francisco: Harper & Row, 1988), p. 99.

3. Francis Schüssler Fiorenza, "Systematic Theology: Task and Methods," in Francis Schüssler Fiorenza and John P. Galvin, eds., *Systematic Theology: Roman Catholic Perspectives*, vol. 1 (Minneapolis: Fortress Press, 1991), p. 74.

4. Ibid., p. 75.

5. For a description of the role of culture during contested times, see Ann Swidler, "Culture in Action: Symbols and Strategies," *American Sociological Review* 51 (April 1986): 273-86.

6. For an overview of the theoretical streams within current feminist thought, see Josephine Donovan, *Feminist Theory: The Intellectual Traditions of American Feminism* (New York: Continuum, 1991); Patricia Hill Collins, *Black Feminist Thought: Knowledge, Consciousness and the Politics of Empowerment* (London: HarperCollins Academic, 1990); Gisela Bock and Susan James, eds., *Beyond Equality and Difference: Citizenship, Feminist Politics and Female Subjectivity* (New York: Routledge, 1992).

7. bell hooks, *Feminist Theory from Margin to Center* (Boston: South End Press), p. 40.

8. Ibid., p. 18.

9. Ibid., pp. 49-55.

10. For a description of differences between European and U.S. feminism, see Karen Offen, "Defining Feminism: A Comparative Historical Approach," *Signs: Journal of Women in Culture and Society* 14 (Autumn 1988): 119-57. Brief information on feminism in a wide range of countries can be found in Robin Morgan, ed., *Sisterhood Is Global: The International Women's Movement Anthology* (Middlesex, England: Penguin Books, Inc., 1984).

11. I owe this phrase to Rebecca Chopp. See her *The Power to Speak* (New York: Crossroad, 1989), p. 9.

12. Aristotle, *Nicomachean Ethics* 10.1; esp. 1172b.

13. Raymond Geuss, *The Idea of Critical Theory: Habermas and the Frankfurt School* (Cambridge: Cambridge University Press), p. 54.

14. Iris Marion Young, "The Five Faces of Oppression," in *Justice and the Politics of Difference* (Princeton, NJ: Princeton University Press, 1990), p. 40.

15. Collins, p. 227.

16. Various classification systems can be found. See, for example, Donovan.

17. It must not be supposed that women outside the North Atlantic region either historically or currently share precisely the situation or particular issues of North American and European women. See Morgan, *Sisterhood Is Global*; and Rosalyn Terborg-Penn, Sharon Harley, and Andrea Benton Rushing, eds., *Women in Africa and the African Diaspora* (Washington, DC: Howard University Press, 1987).

18. On the Enlightenment roots of contemporary liberal feminism, see Donovan, pp. 1-21. For a contemporary critique of this approach, see Iris Marion Young, "Impartiality and the Civic Public," in Seyla Benhabib and Drucilla Cornell, eds., *Feminism as Critique: On the Politics of Gender* (Minneapolis: University of Minnesota Press, 1987).

19. Teresa Brennan and Carole Pateman, "'Mere Auxiliaries to the Commonwealth': Women and the Origins of Liberalism," *Political Studies* 27 (June 1979): 183-200.

20. See, for example, Mary Wollstonecraft, *A Vindication of the Rights of Woman* (New York: Norton, 1967).

21. "Declaration of Sentiments and Resolutions, Seneca Falls," in Miriam Schneir, *Feminism: The Essential Historical Writing* (New York: Random House, 1972), pp. 77-82.

22. Sarah M. Grimké, "Letter to Mary S. Parker, 183" in Schneir, p. 38.

23. Janet Saltzman Chafetz and Anthony Gary, *Female Revolt: Women's Movement in World and Historical Perspective* (Totowa, NJ: Rowman and Allanheld, 1986), p. 108.

24. Ibid., p. 110.

25. Ibid.; Terborg-Penn, p. 77.

26. Friedan, Betty, *The Feminine Mystique* (New York: Norton, 1963).

27. See Silvia Vegetti Finzi, "Female Identity between Sexuality and Maternity," in Bock and James, *Beyond Equality.*

28. Gynocentric feminist theory includes those approaches often called radical feminism and cultural feminism. Radical feminism, which developed in reaction to leftist political movements, should not be confused with the use of *radical* to mean "extreme."

29. For a range of approaches to gynocentric feminism, see Mary Daly, *Gyn/Ecology: The Metaethics of Radical Feminism* (Boston: Beacon Press, 1978); Alice Walker, *In Search of Our Mothers' Gardens: Womanist Prose* (New York:

Harcourt, Brace, Jovanovic, 1983); and Margaret Fuller, *Woman in the Nineteenth Century* (New York: Norton, 1971 [1845]).

30. Walker, p. xi.

31. See Adrienne Rich, *Of Woman Born: Motherhood as Experience and Institution* (New York: W. W. Norton & Co., 1976).

32. See Cherrie Moraga and Gloria Anzaldua, eds., *This Bridge Called My Back: Writings by Radical Women of Color* (Watertown, MA: Persephone Press, 1981).

33. For a concise but nuanced description and critique of de Beauvior's position and its relationship to existentialism, see Rosemarie Tong, *Feminist Thought: A Comprehensive Introduction* (Boulder: Westview Press, 1989), pp.195-216.

34. Jean-Paul Sartre, *Being and Nothingness: An Essay on Phenomenological Ontology*, trans. Hazel E. Barnes (New York: Philosophical Library, 1956), p. 283.

35. Ibid., p. 268.

36. Simone de Beauvoir, *The Second Sex*, trans. H. M. Parshley (New York: Bantam, 1961), p. xxvi.

37. Ibid., p. xxviii.

38. Ibid., p. 71.

39. Ibid., p. 237.

40. Ibid., pp. 429-30.

41. Ibid., pp. 63-65.

42. Ibid., p. 448. For an excellent discussion of the ways these divisions have appeared in feminist theory and some of the problems with them, see Sandra Harding, "The Instability of the Analytical Categories of Feminist Theory," *Signs: Journal of Women in Culture and Society* 11 (1986): 645-64. Alice Jardine traces how the concept of the Other has been used in post-structuralism and in French feminism in *Gynesis: Configurations of Woman and Modernity* (Ithaca, NY: Cornell University Press, 1985), pp. 105-117.

43. Rosaldo herself has criticized the universalism of her earlier position. See M. Z. Rosaldo, "The Use and Abuse of Anthroplolgy: Reflections on Feminism and Cross-Cultural Understanding," *Signs* 5, (Spring 1980): 389-417. For a cross-cultural critique of Ortner's use of the nature-culture categories, see the response to her in Carol MacCormick and Marilyn Strathern, *Nature, Culture, and Gender* (Cambridge: Cambridge University Press). Her critics basically argue that this dichotomy holds up for Western cultures but cannot be defended when applied to others, though it has commonly been *projected* onto a wide variety of situations by Western social scientists.

44. See Christine Delphi, *Close to Home* (Amherst, MA: University of Massachusetts Press, 1984).

45. See Seyla Benhabib and Drucilla Cornell, "Introduction," in *Feminism as Critique: On the Politics of Gender*, p. 2.

46. This is especially true for postmodern feminist theories, which include a far wider range of methodological basis and resources than I am able to indicate in so brief an essay.

47. For a primarily positive reading of feminism and postmodernism, see Jane Flax, "Postmodernism and Gender Relations in Feminist Theory," and Nancy Fraser and Linda J. Nicholson, "Social Criticism without Philosophy: An Encounter between Feminism and Postmodernism," in Linda J. Nichol-

son, ed., *Feminism/Postmodernism* (New York: Routledge, 1990). A more negative assessment can be found in Seyla Benhabib, "Epistemologies of Postmodernism: A Rejoinder to Jean-Francois Lyotard," in Nicholson, *Feminism/Postmodernism.*

48. Barbara Christian, "The Race for Theory," *Feminist Studies* 14 (Spring 1988): 67-79.

49. For a description of the ties of post-structural feminism to psychoanalysis, see Chris Weedon, *Feminist Practice and Poststructuralist Theory* (Oxford: Basil Blackwell, 1987).

50. Included in this group are Julia Kristeva, Hélène Cixous, and Luce Irigary. These theorists do not all describe themselves as feminist, either because they want to distinguish themselves from particular interpretations of feminism to which they object or because they reject the notion that *any* generalized statements can be made about women as a group, or even about an individual woman, since the very language being employed makes her a contrast category for *man's* self-understanding. See, for example, Julia Kristeva, "Women's Time," in Roril Moi, ed., *The Kristeva Reader* (New York: Columbia University Press, 1986), pp. 188-213.

51. On the question of the social construction of sexual difference, see Judith Butler, "Variations on Sex and Gender: Beauvoir, Wittig and Foucault," in Benhabib, *Feminism as Critique.*

52. de Beauvoir, pp. 64-65.

53. See Rosi Braidotti, "On the Female Feminist Subject or: From 'She-Self' to 'She-Other'" in Bock and James, *Beyond Equality,* p. 184.

2

Heeding the Voices

An Historical Overview

Mary Ann Hinsdale

Theological anthropology is a foundational discipline in Christian theology. It is concerned with understanding the meaning of human existence within the context of Christian revelation. Particularly since "the turn to the subject,"[1] reflection on "human nature," or "person-hood," has become a natural corollary in theological reflection on the doctrines of God, creation, sin, the person and work of Jesus Christ (incarnation and redemption), grace and eschatology.[2] Moreover, theological anthropology provides important underpinnings for worship, spirituality, ethics, and pastoral care—disciplines that heavily depend upon implicit theories of what it means to be human and how human beings relate to the divine.[3] In the curriculum of some theological schools, the topics treated in this book are discussed under the rubric "Christian anthropology." In this essay I use the more general formulation, "theological anthropology," in order to include feminist[4] theoretical reflection about the nature of human subjectivity and knowing, embodiment and suffering, in addition to the traditional anthropological doctrines of creation, sin and grace.

In general, feminist work in theological anthropology has followed the three hermeneutical pathways of feminist theology: 1) critique, 2) recovery, and 3) reconstruction.[5] It should be noted that these feminist hermeneutical tasks are not necessarily sequential or chronological, nor are they ever completely "finished." Feminist theological anthropology agrees with Karl Rahner's observation: ". . . the actual mode in which this one [human] nature is objectively realized in the concrete is stamped and conditioned by the special circumstances of history which correspond to the plurality of types and situations justifiably existing in the Church."[6] Thus, just as becoming human is a task that always rests with human beings themselves, so too do the tasks of critique, recovery, and reconstruction undertaken by feminist hermeneutics remain ongoing projects.

Critique of malestream theological anthropology has been a constant feature of feminist theology since the late 1960s.[7] In terms of a "corrective," feminist theological anthropology has always insisted on more than a remedial inclusion of women in patriarchal theological reflection; rather, it has been concerned to lift up "women's voice,"[8] not simply as critic, but as shaper of theological anthropology. Nevertheless, the ensuing debates surrounding "difference" and "equality" in feminist theory have made terms such as "women's voice" or "women's experience" problematic.[9] While reacting to the universalizing tendencies of masculinist/patriarchal theological anthropology, white, academic, feminist theology has had to acknowledge its own tendency to speak of "women's voice/experience" in a universalist sense, from an unacknowledged perspective of the privileged, dominant culture (viz., white, Eurocentric, middle-class, heterosexual, etc.).[10] Thus, feminist theological anthropology itself has had to become self-critical in order to come to terms with the fact that the pluralism of the human situation demands greater consciousness of the variety of social locations represented among women and the implications this has for feminist theological reflection.[11]

In re-imaging theological anthropology from the diverse experiences of women, feminist scholars of religion have also contended with the liability of rarefied, abstract theological language. The very language of patriarchal theology can mute, if not silence altogether, women's voices. European feminist theologian Ursula King has commented on the necessarily experimental and experiential character of feminist theology that is evident in its language and style:

> Much of traditional theology is too abstract, too reified, too divorced from real life. Feminist theologians try to mediate their theological thinking through a less abstract, more contextual language often woven around stories, experiences and events. They are suspicious of the false abstractions and overly rationalistic conceptualizations of traditional theologies. Out of their experience of oppression they recognize the suppression of experience in much theological thinking which often also implies an unwholesome separation of theology from a truly transforming and life-giving spirituality.[12]

Here feminist theology faces a particular challenge in keeping alive the concrete experiences of women (which, after all, comprise its starting point) in articulating a feminist theological anthropology. On the one hand, the final theological "product" must be recognizable as experiential, or "located" enough in the particular in order for grass-roots women to feel their voices/experiences have received a real hearing. On the other hand, academic theological discourse requires that the stories or descriptions of experience be analyzed in the light of the authentic faith tradition of the community if they are to move beyond mere narrative.[13]

Along with the critique of androcentric anthropology, the task of *historical recovery and retrieval* seeks out the "lost voices" of women in order to restore them to the communal tradition. Just as the "new history"[14] has begun to focus on the ordinary, everyday experiences of people (as opposed to the history made by generals, kings, popes and bishops), feminist theology focuses on the experience of women, both past and present, in their ordinary, everyday lives. This has meant using the experience and language of ordinary women as a basis for feminist theology, not simply the experience and language of academic theologians.[15] It has also meant acknowledging the androcentric and patriarchal nature of the biblical, patristic, and conciliar texts, while at the same time challenging them by reclaiming the sufferings and struggles of women "through the subversive power of the 'remembered past.'"[16]

According to some feminist theologians, the search for an alternative tradition from the past as yet has yielded rather meager and fragmentary results.[17] A call has gone out for feminist exegetes and historians to read the "silences" of androcentric texts and engage in an imaginative reconstruction of historical reality. This has led to the third hermeneutic task, *reconstruction*, which is the site of the most recent endeavors in feminist theological anthropology.[18] In the words of Rosemary Ruether,

> Feminist theology does not stop at . . . [the] unmasking of sexist bias. . . . Feminist theology becomes possible only when it is perceived that the basic foundations of theology itself, that is, the reflection on human experience in relation to God, cannot only be rescued from sexist bias, but can be reconstructed as the authentic base from which to critique this sexist bias. Feminist theology starts with the affirmation that God, the ground of being and new being, underlies, includes, supports, and promotes female personhood as much as male personhood. Woman is not subordinate or "included under," but equivalent as imago dei.[19]

Since it is the major intention of *In the Embrace of God* to present examples of constructive feminist scholarship in theological anthropology, I will confine my remarks here to an important clarification about the hermeneutic strategy of reconstruction: in keeping with the self-critical awareness noted above, feminist theological anthropology seeks to avoid a new false universalism that would create a theological anthropology based on female experience alone.[20] At the same time, attending to the variety of women's past and present experiences presents a real challenge for constructive feminist theological anthropology: is it possible to avoid falling into complete relativism or such utter fragmentation that any sense of common human identity and purpose is lost?[21] It seems clear from the work that has been accomplished so far that feminists attempting to construct theological anthropology believe that hierarchy and dominance can be overcome only when the differences and multiplicities of knowers and known are acknowledged and taken seriously.[22] An overarching, unified, objective "synthesis" of the meaning of being human is not the goal to which feminist anthropology aspires. At the same time, feminist theological anthropology does well to be reminded that self-defining movements of marginalized persons are often greeted with suspicion and hostility by those who have held the power of definition. Feminist theological anthropology (and feminist theology in general) must remain ever vigilant lest multiplicity tumble into such fragmentation that it plays into the hands of those who benefit from keeping patriarchal/kyriarchal[23] patterns of repression in place.

What follows is an overview of the development of feminist theological anthropology as it has been undertaken from all three hermeneutical vantage points. It is hoped that such a "state of the question" will provide a backdrop for understanding how the voices and experiences of women have been (or might yet be) heard in an emerging feminist theological anthropology.

CRITIQUE OF ANDROCENTRIC THEOLOGICAL ANTHROPOLOGY

In a 1960 essay in *The Journal of Religion,* Valerie Saiving first raised the question of gender in theological anthropology, asserting that the sex of the theologian played a role in the way one construed the doctrines of sin and grace.[24] Saiving's article received scant attention until it was reprinted nearly twenty years later in a collection of feminist theological essays.[25] Although it would take until 1968 for the first major book-length critique of Catholic theological anthropology to appear, Rosemary Radford Ruether was already reflecting on Christian anthropology from a feminist perspective in the mid 1960s.[26] In 1967 Ruether assessed the secular women's liberation movement, concluding that its opposition to dualism and domination offered the possibility of "a doctrine of humanity and a doctrine of the salvation appropriate to humanity that stands as a critique of classical Christian spirituality."[27]

Ruether, trained in classics and patristics, argued that the early church fathers' appropriation of Platonic dualism in interpreting the creation story resulted in an intermingling of anti-body and anti-female prejudices that has been at the heart of a deep-seated dualism in classical western thought ever since.[28] In Ruether's analysis western dualism is not limited to sexuality but is further projected sociologically as class, race, and ethnic domination. Each subjugated group is made to bear stereotypical features of the "lower self" ("fickle, bestial, passionate—yet at the same time—passive, irrational, contemptible, dangerous"[29]). These projections eventually become internalized, so that a fixed social order of relationships and roles results. Though her examples have changed over the years, Ruether has held fast to a critical analysis that sees hierarchical dualism as the fundamental fatal flaw in traditional Christian anthropology.[30]

In 1968 Mary Daly's *The Church and the Second Sex*[31] chronicled the misogynist treatment of female personhood in Christian thought by presenting a thorough examination of the classic sources and traditions of Judaism and Christianity. Daly also singled out Greek philosophical dualism as the culprit for the androcentric/patriarchal view of women as the second—and therefore, lesser—sex. Her book marked the beginning of a long line of feminist critiques of the traditional doctrines of Christian anthropology. Although this was to be Daly's last book written as a Catholic, like Rosemary Ruether, the early Daly called for a return to a more authentic view of human personhood, one rooted in the vision of humanity contained in Jesus' prophetic preaching of the "reign of God."[32]

Throughout the 1970s and 1980s, Catholic feminist theological anthropology continued to use the insights of critical theory and ideological criticism to ferret out those elements in the tradition that explicitly or implicitly undermined women's full human personhood. However, feminist critique of androcentric theological anthropology seems to have crested with the Sacred Congregation for the Doctrine of the Faith's 1977 publication of *Inter Insignores* ("The Declaration on the Admission of Women to the Ministerial Priesthood"). Though subsequent church pronouncements have continued to reflect a basically dualistic, androcentric anthropology, *Inter Insignores* presented a watershed for understanding the development of critical feminist theological anthropology.[33]

The CDF declaration evoked a number of scholarly commentaries.[34] One of these studies, undertaken by the leading North American professional theological organization, the Catholic Theological Society of America, attempted a thoroughgoing examination of the declaration's underlying anthropology.[35] In its comprehensive study of *Inter Insignores,* the CTSA report used an heuristic of anthropological "models" to critique the understanding of male and female personhood reflected in the document (i.e., how biological (sex) difference is related to what is meant by "human being").

Using typological analysis, the report built upon a 1975 article by Mary Aquin O'Neill that described the faces of secular feminism and their corresponding "visions of humanity." O'Neill found three models of humanity operative among feminist thinkers: "polarity," "androgyny" and "unisex." The polarity vision (held mainly by feminist separatists) held that men and women are human beings in essentially different ways. The androgynous vision recognized "different" ways of being human for men and women, but claimed these differences were merely cultural. The unisex vision held that there existed only a single way of being human, insisting that biology was simply accidental.[36] In its adaptation the CTSA report collapsed O'Neill's androgynous and unisex visions into one category, arriving at two fundamental models of theological anthropology: 1) the *dual-nature model* (a "different-but-equal" model that stressed the complementarity of the sexes, seeing sex-role duality as part of the created order, "the divine plan"; in short, a biological determinism) and 2) the androgynous *single-nature model* (neither sex has any pre-ordained roles, biology is "accidental," important for reproduction but not constitutive of personhood). Henceforth these two models became the chief analytical tools used by theologians engaged in critical reflection on the underlying theological anthropology of church teaching and praxis.[37]

At the 1979 CTSA meeting, Mary Buckley responded to the Research Report's two models.[38] Explaining that she was employing a methodology that "makes use of women's experience today and of insights from the social sciences,"[39] Buckley pointed out that both the dual-nature and single-nature models were imbedded in a social context.[40] They both reflect individualistic and idealistic orientations: the dual-nature model reflects an hierarchic-elitist social pattern that accepts stratification for "right ordering"; the single-nature model is the product of a "one-dimensional society" and is basically assimilationist. Buckley was especially cautious about the single-nature model (which the CTSA report seemed to prefer). As she reflected, "all seem equal, but in reality women are told to assimilate to the norm of the human which is male."[41] In her view, "equality" constituted too much of an abstraction. Moreover, "single-nature" suggested that only *one* idea of personhood in the male/female relation is the paradigm for being human. As Buckley pointed out, such paradigms usually turn out to resemble the group in power (white, Western, male, etc.).

Buckley's antidote for these limitations was to propose a "transformative, person-centered" model. This model aimed at the transformation and transcendence of the old gender roles and, in effect, the transformation of social structures. She dreamed of:

> a non-authoritarian, non-competitive, non-hierarchical society
> in which leadership is fully accountable to the people . . . a
> society organized around human needs, a society in which
> nurture and care is a priority, a society in which wisdom and
> skill is shared . . . in which leadership is shared and responsible
> while at the same time fulfilling its true function.[42]

Buckley recognized that such qualities were often referred to as
so-called "womanly" or "feminine" virtues. But since they embody
the praxis and witness that Jesus gave, she argued that they must
therefore belong to the whole human race. This third anthropological
model entailed a liberating vision of a more human world, a vision of
a "kingdom of justice and peace which leads to the questioning of
oppressive structures and relationships, whether sexist, racist or classist."[43]

A year later, in an article entitled "Theological Anthropology and
the Experience of Women,"[44] Anne Carr summarized the reflection
which had emerged up to this point concerning how women's experience affected the formulation of theological anthropology. She
sought to correlate O'Neill's theological responses to the "three faces
of feminism" and Karl Rahner's theological anthropology. Rahner,
noted Carr, always repudiated any idea of "nature" as static essence.
She found his emphasis on freedom and decision making quite appropriate to what Buckley had proposed: the possibility of fashioning
a "third" model that would be *critical* of the hidden social bias present
in any model of being human while insisting at the same time on social
transformation. Thus the transformative model became the preferred
model of feminist theological anthropology in the early 1980s, holding
that both men and women are able to become "genuinely moral
subjects in their own right . . . [with] full participation in both the
public and private world of Church and society, so that the world may
be more human for everyone."[45]

Anthropological models (as presented by the CTSA report, O'Neill,
Buckley, and Carr) have been helpful in drawing attention to the
confusion of the categories of "sex" and "gender" and for articulating
the basis of disagreement that surrounds several doctrinal and church
praxis issues, but of late, they have come in for some criticism.

Tiina Allik, for example, is concerned that the two basic models,
each in its own way, devalue human finitude. In her estimation, since
the goodness of creation is a basic premise of Christian theology, both
"single anthropology" and "dual anthropology" proponents distinguish too sharply between culture and nature.[46] The dual-anthropol-
ogy model implicitly believes that women have access to an
unmediated experience. It fails to see that women's experience is
always mediated by cultural concepts. But the single anthropology
model, thinking of full humanity as "the development of capacities

which escape the conditioning of human bodiliness and finitude," also denies the full scope of human finitude. In Allik's view, finitude is not a limitation but an important qualification of human being: "human finitude is not only human limitedness, but also an openness and receptivity to the world, a basis for the creativity and spontaneity of human existence."[47]

Another analytical approach in feminist theological reflection on anthropology is trying to rethink "difference" in a manner that does not focus exclusively on sex.[48] Thus, Elizabeth Johnson draws upon Edward Schillebeeckx's six "anthropological constants"[49] in her proposal for a more adequate model of anthropology. Johnson's main interest is to find a way through the impasse which the "effective history" of the maleness of Christ has worked upon the whole Christian community and the dilemma it has posed for theology (especially anthropology and christology) and church praxis.[50] She argues that all the constants are intrinsic to human identity, not just sexuality. In order to create a holistic, interdependent vision of human personhood: 1) corporeality (which includes one's sexuality and the ecological environment); 2) relationship to other persons as the formative context of our own individuality; 3) relationship to social, political and economic structures; 4) conditioning by time and space; 5) the dynamic of theory and praxis experienced as culture (as opposed to instinct); and 6) orientation to the future are all part of what it means to be human. Thus, her recommendation is for a multi-polar anthropology:

> [An] anthropological model of one human nature instantiated in a multiplicity of difference [that] moves beyond the contrasting models of either sex dualism or the sameness of abstract individuals towards the celebration of diversity as entirely normal. The goal is to reorder the two-term and one-term systems into a multiple-term schema, one which allows connection in difference rather than constantly guaranteeing identity though opposition or uniformity.[51]

Still other feminist theologians have proposed models based upon "partnership," "relationality" or "mutuality," as paradigmatic of both human limitation and human possibility.[52] Mary Aquin O'Neill, for example, has rethought the way the anthropological models have been used:

> I now think that for the Christian theologian the issue is not whether one adopts a two-nature or a one-nature anthropology ... The issue is rather how to imagine the oneness that is to obtain between the sexes. Is it, in other words, a unity to be realized in an individual way or one that can be realized only in a commu-

nity of persons? . . . The model of the person is not the autonomous and isolated individual but the covenanted one who is free because bound to others and to God. It demands an anthropology of mutuality in which the male/female difference becomes paradigmatic of human limitation and possibility and in which being like God can be achieved only by the gift of self to others and the reception of the gift of self from others.[53]

Finally, there have been attempts since the mid-1980s to flesh out the "transformative, person-centered" model,[54] which rested upon the critical notion that conceptualizations of "the human" have social consequences. Although Buckley's reflection on the unisex or person-centered (the single-nature model) revealed that it simply proposed assimilation to the image of humanity as white, male, elite, holders of power, recent versions of a "third model" have pointed out the anthropocentric limitations of this vision. The transformative model fails to analyze the human domination of animal and nonsentient nature. Thus the question was raised: is it possible to create a theological anthropology that does not put the human being at the pinnacle of creation but stresses ecological interdependence, an ecological (or "creation-centered") theological anthropology?[55]

Recognizing that human beings, under the influence of modern science, have lost their interdependent relationship with nature, ecological and ecofeminist theologians have been calling for an anthropology that retrieves humanity's partnership with God in cocreation.[56] They reject the "kingship" model, where human beings dominate and subdue the earth, as well as the biblical model of stewardship, because both fail to do justice to the mutual relatedness of human beings, earth, and the Creator Spirit. As Elizabeth Johnson points out, the stewardship model calls for human beings to be caretakers, but it keeps the structure of hierarchical dualism. Stewardship is an improvement over the model of domination, but it is blind to the fact that human beings are also dependent upon the earth, not merely its protectors.[57]

What is needed, say ecofeminist theologians, is an anthropological model that is both non-dualistic and non-instrumental. If human beings could incorporate a respect for difference into their mode of knowledge building, then we would have "a principle for ordering the world radically, theologically, in an all-encompassing compassion and respect, content with multiplicity."[58] Scientist Barbara McClintock called such a principle "a feeling for the organism," a description which suggests that, with human relationships as well as with plants, a respect for difference "constitutes a claim not only on our interest but on our capacity for empathy—in short, the highest form of love: love that allows for intimacy without the annihilation of difference."[59]

McClintock's principle is very similar to what Elizabeth Johnson calls
the "kinship" model:

> If separation is not the ideal but connection is; if dualism is not
> the ideal but the relational embrace of diversity is; if hierarchy
> is not the ideal but mutuality is; then the kinship model more
> closely approximates reality. It sees human beings and the earth
> with all its creatures intrinsically related as companions in a
> community of life. Because we are all mutually interconnected
> the flourishing or damaging of one ultimately affects all. This
> kinship attitude does not measure differences on a scale of
> higher or lower ontological dignity but appreciates them as
> integral elements in the robust thriving of the whole.[60]

Despite their usefulness, the analytical framework of models in and
of itself cannot put theologians in touch with women's actual experience. As analytical tools, models help problematize theological anthropology for feminist theology. They provide a helpful heuristic for
critically approaching texts and/or symbols with a hermeneutics of
suspicion in order to critique androcentric bias. By themselves, however, they cannot accomplish the second and third hermeneutical
tasks of feminist theology, thus we must turn to the other two hermeneutic tasks, the recovery/retrieval of women's experience and the
reconstruction of theological anthropology as inclusive of the full
humanity of women.

THE RECOVERY OF WOMEN'S EXPERIENCE

Recovering women's experience for feminist theological anthropology reflects the broader shift that has occurred in theological
method: the use of experience as a starting point for theological
reflection.[61] Yet, as Ellen Leonard has pointed out, this hermeneutical
task is not simply a matter of "adding the experiences of those who
have been previously ignored."[62] Rather, the historical retrieval of
hitherto invisible women and contextualized approaches to the concrete experiences of women have contributed to the formation of a
new epistemology that "enables us to recognize the pluralism of
women's experience across different cultures, races and classes."[63]
Thus, the work of recovering women's experience for theological
anthropology aims both to de-center the concept of "universal man"
and draw attention to the interstitial character of women's experience
with respect to such differences as age, culture, race, class, and sexual
orientation.
Since the beginnings of feminist theology, women have attempted
to counteract the use of the Bible to legitimate societal and ecclesiastical definitions of "woman's place."[64] Over the last twenty years

feminist biblical scholars and historians of early Christianity have unearthed information about the role of women in the Jesus move-ment and the incipient church that has great import for theological anthropology. Significant research in the 1960s and 1970s focused upon new readings of the creation accounts in Genesis, the prophetic actions of Jesus toward women, the greater fidelity of the women disciples in comparison to the male disciples, and the ambiguous statements of Paul (i.e., Gal 3:28 compared with 1 Cor 11:11-12).[65] Much of this research was aligned with reformist feminist ideals which sought to distinguish the prophetic, liberating *content* of bibli-cal anthropology from its androcentric, patriarchal *form.*

In 1983 Elisabeth Schüssler Fiorenza criticized this approach to feminist interpretation as "neo-orthodox," since it failed to take seri-ously the way the tradition (including the Bible) and church structures have legitimated and perpetuated the bondage of women.[66] She likewise critiqued the postbiblical feminist rejection of the Bible which, in her estimation, promoted a dehistoricized and disembodied vision of feminist "Selves" who have escaped patriarchal "non-being" in order to live in a "gynocentric life-center on the fringes of andro-centric culture and history." Although Schüssler Fiorenza advocated remaining in dialogue with goddess feminists such as Carol Christ, "in order to come to a fuller understanding of the liberating biblical impulses for women's struggle against patriarchal biblical sexism,"[67] she saw Mary Daly's qualitative leap into a new (and separate) feminist Time/Space only as reinforcing "the androcentric reality construction of Western culture according to which male existence and history is the paradigm of human existence and human his-tory."[68]

Schüssler Fiorenza's hermeneutics, which 1) claims the contempo-rary community of women struggling for liberation as a locus of revelation and 2) moves from the androcentric biblical context to the social-historical context of our "foresisters as victims *and* subjects participating in patriarchal culture," has influenced much of feminist biblical scholarship since the mid-1980s. Borrowing a phrase from poet Adrienne Rich, it is an approach that calls for a "reconstituting" of the historical world of Christian beginnings which not only ana-lyzes the historical oppression of women but also seeks to change the social reality of the Christian churches in which this oppression takes its specific historical patriarchal forms.[69]

Recent examples of reconstitutive biblical retrieval that are signifi-cant for theological anthropology can be seen in the work of feminist exegetes who have focused on the creation texts of Genesis 2-3,[70] the prophetic women in the Jesus movement,[71] the reconstruction of women's voices in Pauline texts,[72] the formative role that Greco-Ro-man household codes (especially in Colossians, Ephesians, the Pas-torals and 1 Peter) have played in creating androcentric anthropology, and the possibility that they constitute a "defensive" reaction against women who "preach, teach, prophesy, travel, preside at worship . . .",[73] and the recovery of women's leadership and autonomy that is preserved in "non-canonical" biblical literature such as the Gospel of Mary (Magdalene), the Acts of Thecla, and the infancy gospels, Proto-James and Pseudo-Matthew.[74]

The post-biblical history of Christian thought has been mined by feminist historians and has proved helpful for unearthing hitherto hidden viewpoints on such anthropological themes as embodiment, subjectivity, sin, and grace. The rediscovery of "early church mothers" such as Perpetua and Felicitas, Macrina, Paula, Egeria, Leoba, Dhuoda, and Hrotsvit of Gandersheim,[75] as well as the burgeoning research into the female mystical tradition represented among the beguines and other holy women of the Middle Ages, have been especially fruitful in this regard.[76] The writings of Hildegard of Bingen, Hadewijch of Antwerp, Gertrud of Helfta, Mechthild of Magdeburg, Marguerite Porete, Angela of Foligno, Clare of Assisi, Catherine of Siena, and Julian of Norwich, to name but a few,[77] prove that medieval women need not be relegated to either the "pit or the pedestal"[78] but have contributed important resources for feminist theological anthropology. As Elizabeth Petroff argues, their importance does not derive only from their enlargening of the canon of medieval literature but because

> they derive from a different experience of the body, a different epistemology, and a different relationship to language. I see these texts as a window onto a lost world of experience of thousands of women from late antiquity until just before the Renaissance, an experience that is recuperable by us only if we radically challenge prevailing ideas of what constitutes literature and what is the nature of reality.[79]

The history of women in Christianity from the Reformation through the mid-twentieth century also provides valuable resources for feminist theological anthropology. Teresa of Avila, Jane de Chantal, Sor Juana, Jeanne Guyon, Susanna Wesley, Ann Lee, Jarena Lee, Phoebe Palmer, Lucretia Mott, Hannah Whitall Smith, Amanda Berry Smith, Elizabeth Cady Stanton, Pandita Ramabia, and Georgia Harkness represent but a selection from the "litany" of women whose varied experiences of self and the divine offer new resources for articulating Christian anthropology.[80]

In the United States, the history of women's religious orders and the post-industrial history of laywomen have also yielded important data (albeit mostly from the social location of white educated women) regarding women's spirituality and leadership.[81] Of special note in their retrieval work is the attention feminist historians have given to the rhetorical style of women writers during certain periods. Amy Oden, for example, reminds us that "self-deprecation was a literary device that would no more be left out than good grammar."[82] In other cases, what may sound like meek putting down of self, in fact, may be a deliberate strategy of self-preservation.[83]

From this brief survey it is clear that historical retrieval of women's experience is still only ancillary to the articulation of an inclusive feminist theological anthropology. In particular, the limitations of social location *and* the revision necessitated by the discovery of *new* social locations necessitate that historical resources must be revisited and reread continually in order to bring newly discovered perspectives to bear on past interpretations. Thus, historical retrieval, like critique, soon leads to the third vantage point of feminist hermeneutics: reconstruction.

FEMINIST RECONSTRUCTION

Since the whole aim of *In the Embrace of God* is to present reconstructive work in theological anthropology from a feminist perspective, this section will be comparatively brief. Rebecca Chopp and Mark Lewis Taylor, editors of the anthology *Reconstructing Christian Theology,* describe the task of theological reconstruction as

> reworking theology's symbols and doctrines in various ways and . . . a continual re-engaging of the diverse communities that Christians address and with whom they must work today for an emancipative restoration of personal and social flourishing.[84]

A large part of the work of reconstruction is to develop the links between doctrinal symbols (in this case, theological anthropology) and structural problems (for example, violence against women and the ecological crisis). Reconstruction must also take into consideration the discursive shifts that have altered theology today.[85] According to Chopp and Taylor, these include: 1) the replacement of the "melting pot" myth with the metaphor of collage; 2) the crises of survival and loss of flourishing that call for the denouncement of sin and the announcement of grace in new ways; 3) the ambiguities of postmodern culture, especially the debunking of foundational truth and the openness of texts to a variety of meanings; 4) a postcolonial sensibility which searches out nonexploitative structures of living together on the planet; and 5) a shift to mutual critique and dialogue with other world religions.[86]

Although each of these shifts needs to be considered in the reconstruction of theological anthropology from a feminist perspective, because such an anthropology is still in an embryonic stage, some of the shifts have admittedly received more attention than others. Thus, in my reading, feminist anthropology has so far been particularly engaged with the first three shifts more than the last two (although much of such an assessment depends upon how narrowly one defines the discursive shifts). For example, attention has begun to be paid to contextuality and social location in the reconstruction of what it means "to be human," but there has been little exploration of how theological anthropology might be approached constructively in dialogue with feminist perspectives from other religions.[87]

Much of the reconstructive work in feminist theological anthropology derives from two sources: the reflection that arises from diverse women's contextual experience (i.e., "womanist," "*mujerista*" and other contextual feminist theologies[88]) and from women's own historical, embodied experience as it bears on the significance of sexuality and human relationships. Often this work does not label itself "theological anthropology" and is found as such only implicitly in writings classified as "ethics" or "christology" or "mariology." Thus, for example, Christine Gudorf, in her book, *Body, Sex and Pleasure,* provides a theological anthropological framework for reconstructing Christian sexual ethics.[89] Similarly, rethinking theological anthropology provides the starting point for a recent revision of mariology in a book by Ivone Gebara and Maria Clara Bingemer.[90] Susan Brooks Thistlethwaite's *Sex, Race, and God: Christian Feminism in Black and White,* entails an anthropology in her discussion of nature and the fall.[91] Both Carter Heyward and Rita Nakashima Brock critique androcentric theological anthropology to move to a recovery of "erotic power" as a central symbol for Divine love and for revisioning christology.[92]

Finally, reconstructive theological anthropology also has begun to take up the traditional symbols and doctrines of Christian anthropology: creation,[93] sin,[94] and grace.[95] By and large, however, one still struggles to find much mention of feminist reconstructive or even feminist critical work in theological anthropology in the most recent textbooks in the field.[96] It is to be hoped that *In the Embrace of God* is at least a first step in filling that void.

NOTES

1. The "turn to the subject" refers to the paradigm shift that displaced "revealed truth" and made human reason the final court of appeal for the interpretation of reality. Enlightenment philosophers such as Descartes, Locke, Hume, and Kant all contributed to this shift. Kant, in particular, argued that objects as we know them do not have their own objectivity as a "given"; rather, they are largely constituted by the knowing consciousness which organizes sense experience into an intelligible field. For further background, see David Kelsey, "Human Being," in Peter C. Hodgson and Robert H. King, eds., *Christian Theology: An Introduction to Its Traditions and Tasks,* new rev. ed. (Minneapolis: Fortress Press, 1994), p. 178-82; and Francis Schüssler Fiorenza,

"Systematic Theology: Task and Methods," in Francis Schüssler Fiorenza and John Galvin, eds., *Systematic Theology: Roman Catholic Perspectives* (Minneapolis: Fortress Press, 1991), pp. 36-40.

2. David Kelsey's excellent essay discusses the development of theological anthropology as a discipline, as well as its chief concerns. See David H. Kelsey, "Human Being," pp. 167-93.

3. For general overviews of the topic see Michael Downey, ed., *The New Dictionary of Catholic Spirituality* (Collegeville, MN: Liturgical Press, 1993), s.v. "Anthropology, theological," by Janet K. Ruffing; Joseph A. Komonchak, Mary Collins, Dermot A. Lane, eds., *New Dictionary of Theology* (Wilmington, DE: Michael Glazier, 1987), s.v. "Anthropology, Christian," by Michael Scanlon; and Edward Farley, "Toward a Contemporary Theology of Human Being," in J. William Angell and E. Pendleton Banks, eds., *Images of Man* (Macon, GA: Mercer University Press, 1984), pp. 57-78.

4. In using the term *feminist* in this essay, I am employing Rosemary Ruether's criterion of "the promotion of the full humanity of women" as the critical principle of feminist theology. See her *Sexism and God-Talk: Toward a Feminist Theology* (Boston: Beacon Press, 1983), pp. 18-20. As has been made evident by its many practitioners, there is more than one "feminist" perspective at work in "feminist theology," which is, as Amanda Porterfield suggests, a "pluralistic but ultimately holistic movement" ("Feminist Theology as a Revitalization Movement," *Sociological Analysis* 48 [1987]: 234-44). This essay will concentrate mainly on feminist theologies that have emerged from the Jewish and Christian and biblical traditions, in dialogue with insights from feminist theory and feminist religious movements that have developed outside established religious institutions.

5. This description of tasks is borrowed from June O'Connor, "Feminist Religious Thought," *Religious Studies Review* 12 (1986): 202. In biblical studies, a similar process emerges as the feminist exegete either 1) judges the text in light of its patriarchal bias (and compares it with an ideal "prophetic-liberating" tradition), 2) tries to retrieve texts overlooked or distorted by such bias, or 3) turns to the reconstruction of biblical history in "an attempt to show that the actual situations of the Israelite and Christian religions allowed a greater role for women than the codified writings suggest." For a complete discussion of these tasks as they belong to the reformist branch of feminist biblical scholarship, see Mary Ann Tolbert, "Defining the Problem: The Bible and Feminist Hermeneutics," *Semeia* 28 (1983): 113-26. Another approach speaks of "the hermeneutics of suspicion, proclamation, retrieval (remembrance and historical reconstruction) and creative actualization" as comprising the major elements of feminist scholarship. See Elizabeth Schüssler Fiorenza, *In Memory of Her: A Feminist Theological Reconstruction of Christian Origins* (New York: Crossroad, 1983), pp. 3-93.

6. "The Church Finds Herself," *Theological Investigations,* vol. 8 (New York: Seabury Press, 1971), p. 75.

7. See, for example, these early feminist theological works: Kari Elisabeth Børresen, *Subordination et équivalence. Nature et rôle de la femme d'après Augustin et Thomas d'Aquin* (Subordination and Equivalence: The Nature and Role of Woman in Augustine and Thomas Aquinas), trans. Charles H. Talbot (Washington, DC: University of America Press, 1981; Oslo: Universitetsforlaget, 1968); Sheila D. Collins, *A Different Heaven and Earth: A Feminist Perspective on Religion* (Valley Forge, PA: Judson Press, 1974); The Cornwall Collective, *Your*

Daughters Shall Prophecy: Feminist Alternatives in Theological Education (New York: Pilgrim Press, 1980); Mary Daly, *The Church and the Second Sex* (New York: Harper and Row, 1968); Sarah Bentley Doely, ed., *Women's Liberation and the Church* (New York: Association Press, 1970); Rosemary Ruether, ed., *Religion and Sexism: Images of Women in the Jewish and Christian Traditions* (New York: Simon and Schuster, 1974); idem, *New Woman, New Earth: Sexist Ideologies and Human Liberation* (New York: Seabury Press, 1975).

8. The idea of "women's voice" comes from the field of socio-linguistics, which studies male and female patterns of discourse, sex-linked language, and sex differences in conversational patterns. In the late 1970s feminist sociologists, historians and developmental psychologists began to write about the "different voice" of women in comparison with men. See, for example, Carol Gilligan, *A Different Voice* (Cambridge, MA: Harvard University Press, 1982). Mary Belenky, Blythe Clinchy, Nancy Goldberger, and Jill Tarule argued that women become alienated and "voiceless" when expected to operate according to "male models of knowing," which establish "truth" by dispassionate methods. Based on extensive interviews, they claimed that women "know" in at least five different ways and concluded that until these ways are acknowledged as legitimate, women cannot claim the power of their minds or "find their voice." See *Women's Ways of Knowing* (New York: Basic Books, 1986).

9. See, for example, M. C. Lugones and E. V. Spelman, "Have We Got a Theory for You: Feminist Theory, Cultural Imperialism and the Demand for Women's Voice," *Women's Studies International Forum* 6 (1983): 573-81; Joan Scott, "Deconstructing Equality-Versus-Difference," *Feminist Studies* 14 (Spring 1988): 33-50; and Sandra Harding, "Reinventing Ourselves as Other: More New Agents of History and Knowledge," in Linda Kaufman, ed., *American Feminist Thought At Century's End: A Reader* (Cambridge, MA: Blackwell, 1993), pp. 140-64.

10. A classic illustration is the letter that black feminist Audre Lorde wrote to Mary Daly after Daly's *Gyn/Ecology* appeared. Lorde critiqued Daly's assumption that all women suffer the same oppression simply because they are women. To hold this, according to Lorde, "is to lose sight of the many and varied tools of patriarchy. It is to ignore how those tools are used by women without awareness against each other." See Audre Lorde, "An Open Letter to Mary Daly," in *Sister Outsider* (Trumansburg, NY: The Crossing Press, 1984), pp. 66-71.

11. On the issue of social location, see the insightful article by Ann O'Hara Graff, "The Struggle to Name Women's Experience: Assessment and Implications for Theological Construction," chapter 7 of this volume. Though it is impossible to generalize about "women's experience," a foothold is gained in Anne Carr's appropriation of David Tracy's notion of "the interpreted meaning of the contemporary situation" as a way of understanding what is meant by "women's experience." Experience would include personal experience and cultural creations, doing justice to specific social-scientific studies, as well as to other religious and theological interpretations of women's experience. Cf. "Theological Anthropology and the Experience of Women," *Chicago Studies* 19 (1980): 114-15. The problem, however, is not so much *whether* one can speak of such experience, but how can one avoid losing the *specificity* of the experience which forms the basis of anthropological reflection?

12. Ursula King, "Voices of protest and promise: Women's studies in religion, the impact of the feminist critique on the study of religion," *Studies in Religion* 23 (1994): 322.

13. On the question of how one moves from experience to theology, see Patricia O'Connell Killen and John de Beer, *The Art of Theological Reflection* (New York: Crossroad, 1994).

14. For a helpful introduction to the "new history," see Peter Burke, ed., *New Perspectives on Historical Writing* (University Park, PA: The Pennsylvania State University Press, 1992). For its application to women, see Carroll Smith-Rosenberg, "The New Woman and the New History," *Feminist Studies* 3 (1975): 185-98. For an example of how this method impacts women's religious history, see Jo Ann Hackett, "In the Days of Jael: Reclaiming the History of Women in Ancient Israel," in Clarissa W. Atkinson, Constance H. Buchanan, and Margaret Miles, eds., *Immaculate and Powerful: The Female in Sacred Image and Social Reality* (Boston: Beacon Press, 1985), pp. 15-38.

15. For examples of this kind of methodology, see Ada María Isasi-Díaz and Yolanda Tarango, *Hispanic Women: Prophetic Voice in the Church* (San Francisco: Harper and Row, 1988); Ada María Isasi-Díaz, *En la Lucha: A Hispanic Women's Liberation Theology* (Minneapolis, MN: Fortress Press, 1993); and Mary Ann Hinsdale, Helen M. Lewis, S. Maxine Waller, *'It Comes from the People': Community Development and Local Theology* (Philadelphia: Temple University Press, 1995).

16. Schüssler Fiorenza, *In Memory of Her*, p. 31.

17. Although she is not entirely pessimistic about this hermeneutic approach, see Rosemary Ruether's review of its problems in "Feminist Theology and Spirituality," in Judith L. Weidman, ed., *Christian Feminism: Visions of a New Humanity* (San Francisco: Harper and Row, 1984), pp. 12-13.

18. A continuing difficulty in reconstructing theological anthropology from a feminist perspective is that the inherited language and structures derive from patriarchal theology. Thus, even the very *concepts* that are employed in traditional theological anthropology are brought into question. Feminist theologians have continually reminded one another, in the words of the late poet Audre Lorde, that they "can not dismantle the master's house using the master's tools." Nevertheless, some women appear to have begun to do precisely that. A nonexhaustive litany of pioneers in the hermeneutics of reconstruction includes: Rita Nakashima Brock, Katie Cannon, Rebecca Chopp, Chung Hyun Kyung, M. Shawn Copeland, Mary Rose D'Angelo, Mary Daly, Ada María Isasi-Díaz, Ivonne Gebara, Carter Heyward, Elizabeth A. Johnson, Mercy Amba Oduyoye, Kwok Pui-lan, Sallie McFague, Rosemary Ruether, Elizabeth Schüssler Fiorenza, Delores Williams and now, I dare say, the contributors of this book!

19. Ruether, "Feminist Theology and Spirituality," p. 11.

20. On the danger of "false universalism," see Ursula King's comments in "Voices of protest and promise," pp. 328-29.

21. The dangers of fragmentation that can result from an over-emphasis on different social locations was discussed recently by a panel of feminist theologians from diverse perspectives at the College Theology Society's 1993 annual meeting. See Mary Ann Hinsdale and Phyllis Kaminski, eds., *Women and Theology: The Fortieth Annual Volume of the College Theology Society* (Maryknoll, NY: Orbis Books, 1995). For an excellent comprehensive discus-

sion of this issue, see Mary McClintock Fulkerson, *Changing the Subject: Women's Discourses and Feminist Theology* (Minneapolis: Fortress Press, 1994), pp. 355-93.

22. Janice Capel Anderson makes this point in her review of feminist biblical criticism. See her "Mapping Feminist Biblical Criticism: The American Scene," *The Critical Review of Books in Religion* (Atlanta: Scholars Press, 1991), pp. 21-44.

23. The term *kyriarchal* has been coined by Elisabeth Schüssler Fiorenza to highlight that Western patriarchy is "ruling power . . . in the hands of elite, propertied, educated, freeborn men." See her "Introduction" in Elisabeth Schüssler Fiorenza and Mary Shawn Copeland, eds., *Violence Against Women* (Maryknoll, NY: Orbis Books, 1994), pp. xxi-xxii, n. 1.

24. Valerie Goldstein Saiving, "The Human Situation: A Feminine View," *Journal of Religion* 40 (1960): 100-12.

25. Carol Christ and Judith Plaskow, eds., *Womanspirit Rising: A Feminist Reader in Religion* (New York: Harper and Row, 1979), pp. 25-42.

26. In 1964, Ruether reviewed Franz Arnold's *Woman and Man: Their Nature and Mission* (Freiburg: Herder, 1963) for *Cross Currents.* Although she extolled Arnold's "sensitive analysis of the genuine dignity and equality of the feminine with the masculine person," she complained that he was "somewhat less acute . . . when he attempts to show that negative attitudes toward women belong primarily to paganism and cannot be found in the biblical tradition" (p. 398). Using the review as a platform, Ruether then proceeded to critique the sources for the perpetualization of women's inferiority to men in the Old Testament and the church's inherited Hellenistic worldview. She was especially critical of Arnold's defense of the exclusion of women from ministry on account of their "natures," as "historically very dubious" and his contention that Protestant denominations that do ordain women thereby express contempt for them. This was "a blatant *non sequitur*" in Ruether's estimation. Finally, she excoriated Arnold for his patriarchal understanding of family that allows woman no rights to roles outside the home, and in an extended rebuttal of his "head" and "heart" typology, goes on to critique hierarchical notions of marriage, arguing that "in the modern fluid family each couple must find their own particular balance [of roles]" (p. 400). For Ruether, this certainly includes the possibility that a woman can be a wife and mother *as well as* an artist, musician, scientist, or scholar. Ruether's discussion in 1964 presaged many of the conversations that engage contemporary feminists today. See "Woman and Man," *Cross Currents* 14 (1964): 398-400.

27. Rosemary Radford Ruether, "Women's Liberation in Historical and Theological Perspective," in Sarah Bentley Doely, ed., *Women's Liberation and the Church* (New York: Association Press, 1970), p. 26. In this article Ruether located the source of male dominance in the emergence of the self-conscious, individualized ego and a corresponding objectification of the world as "other." She further connected this "alienation within the human psyche" with the development of the notion of "private property" and the general alienation of human beings from nature and all that is identified with it (i.e., women). See "The Becoming of Women in Church and Society," *Cross Currents* 17 (Fall 1967): 418-26.

28. According to Ruether, both Gregory of Nyssa and Augustine taught that "God created an original archetypal spiritual humanity, and the advent

of bodiliness, femaleness, and sexuality occurs only as a result of the Fall."
See Ruether, "Women's Liberation," p. 28.

29. Ibid., p. 29.

30. For example, see Rosemary Ruether, *Sexism and God-Talk: Toward a Feminist Theology* (Boston: Beacon Press, 1983) and idem, *Gaia and God: An Ecofeminist Theology of Earth Healing* (San Francisco: Harper San Francisco, 1992).

31. (New York: Harper and Row, 1968).

32. Daly's *Beyond God the Father* (Boston: Beacon Press, 1973) marked her exit from Catholicism. Daly traces her own feminist intellectual journey in the various prefaces and afterwords to *The Church and the Second Sex* (see "A new feminist postchristian introduction" in 1975 and "New archaic afterwords" in 1985) as well as her memoir, *Outercourse* (San Francisco: Harper San Francisco, 1992).

33. See, for example, Pope Paul VI, "Address on the Role of Women in the Plan of Salvation," *Insegnamenti* 15 (1977); Pope John Paul II, "Apostolic Letter 'Mulieris Dignitatem' on the Dignity and Vocation of Women on the Occasion of the Marian Year," *Origins* 18 (1988): 261-83; "Priestly Ordination" (*Ordinatio sacerdotalis*), Apostolic Letter on Ordination and Women of Pope John Paul II, *Origins* 24 (1994): 50-52.

34. See, for example, Leonard and Arlene Swidler, eds., *Women Priests. A Commentary on the Vatican Declaration* (New York: Paulist Press, 1977) and Carroll Stuhlmueller, ed., *Women and Priesthood: Future Directions, A Call to Dialogue from the Faculty of the Catholic Theological Union at Chicago* (Collegeville, MN: The Liturgical Press, 1978).

35. Catholic Theological Society of America, *Research Report: Women in Church and Society*, ed. Sara Butler (Mahwah, NJ: Darlington Seminary, 1978). Along with Butler, the committee included Anne Carr, Margaret Farley, Frederick Crowe and Edward Kilmartin.

36. See Mary Aquin O'Neill, "Toward a Renewed Anthropology," *Theological Studies* 36 (1975): 725-36. Reprinted in Walter Burkhardt, ed., *Woman: New Dimensions* (New York: Paulist Press, 1977).

37. For example, Anne Carr, *Transforming Grace: Women's Experience and Christian Tradition* (San Francisco: Harper and Row, 1988), pp. 117-33; and Elizabeth A. Johnson, "The Maleness of Christ," in Anne Carr and Elisabeth Schüssler Fiorenza, eds., *The Special Nature of Women? Concilium* (1991/6): 108-16, make use of these models. Another usage (not derived from the CTSA report) is that presented by Karl Lehmann, "The Place of Women as a Problem in Theological Anthropology," *Communio* 10 (1983): 219-39; idem, "Mann und Frau als Problem der theologischen Anthropologie: Systematische Erwägungen," in Theodor Schneider, ed., *Mann und Frau: Grundproblem theologischer Anthropologie*, Questiones Disputatae, v. 121 (Freiburg: Herder, 1989), pp. 53-72.

38. Mary Buckley, "The Rising of the Woman is the Rising of the Race," *CTSA Proceedings* 34 (1979): 48-63.

39. Ibid., p. 48.

40. Ibid., p. 58. "As one reflects on the constant interrelationships of the personal and the public, it becomes clear that the anthropological models are not merely formal, conceptual and individualistic, but are from the first

embedded in and related to a social context, however imperfectly or summarily that social context can be described."

41. Ibid., p. 59.

42. Ibid.

43. Ibid., p. 61.

44. *Chicago Studies* 19 (1980): 113-28.

45. Buckley, pp. 62-63.

46. Tiina Allik, "Human Finitude and the Concept of Women's Experience," *Modern Theology* 9 (1993): 67-85. It is important to realize that Allik uses the terms "single anthropology" and "dual anthropology" in a slightly different frame of reference than the CTSA models discussed above. Her usage derives from Jean Grimshaw, "Human Nature and Women's Nature," in *Philosophy and Feminist Thinking* (Minneapolis: University of Minnesota Press, 1986), pp. 104-38. This is important because she is discussing the "dual anthropology" often espoused by so-called radical feminists who see women's experience as unique, privileged and even superior. Despite Fergus Kerr's desire to make French radical feminist theorist Luce Irigaray a standard-bearer for John Paul II's "eternal feminine" anthropology in *Mulieris Dignitatem* and *Ordinatio Sacerdotalis* (an incredible feat of patriarchal logic!), I see the dual anthropology espoused by radical feminist theory as different from that held by the opponents of women's ordination. The "freeing of the radically other, feminine, voice" that Irigaray champions is hardly the same as limiting women to specific roles in the Christian community based upon an "ontic" difference. Irigaray's celebration of the self-sufficient pleasure of female sexuality, her resistance toward any fixed and hierarchical opposition, the fluidity of her language (like women's bodies themselves) all serve to convince me that the affinity Kerr finds between her metaphors and the pope's are but wishful thinking. See Fergus Kerr, "Discipleship of Equals or Nuptial Mystery?" *New Blackfriars* 75 (1994): 344-54.

47. Ibid., p. 82, n. 1. This positive evaluation of human finitude is shared by Jane Kopas in *Sacred Identity: Exploring a Theology of the Person* (Mahwah, NJ: Paulist Press, 1994), pp. 110-26. See also Kathryn Tanner, "The Difference Theological Anthropology Makes," *Theology Today* 50 (1994): 567-79.

48. Elizabeth Johnson, "The Maleness of Christ," in Anne Carr and Elisabeth Schüssler Fiorenza, eds., *The Special Nature of Women?*: 108-16. The tendency to focus on biological sex as the major *discrimen* in theological anthropology also is critiqued by Roger Haight in "Women in the Church: A Theological Reflection," *Toronto Journal of Theology* 2 (1986): 116, n.5.

49. See Edward Schillebeeckx, *Christ: The Experience of Jesus as Lord* (New York: The Seabury Press, 1980), pp. 731-43.

50. For example, conceptualizations of what it means to be "human" undergird the debates around such issues as whether women can be ordained, what is the redemptive efficacy of Jesus' maleness, and whether homosexuals are "disordered" by nature.

51. Johnson, p. 111.

52. On "partnership," see Letty Russell, *The Future of Partnership* (Philadelphia: Westminster, 1979); idem, *Growth in Partnership* (Philadelphia: Westminster, 1981); Elisabeth Moltmann-Wendel, "Partnerschaft," in Claudia Pinl et al., eds., *Frauen auf neuen Wegen: Studien und Problemberichte zur Situation der Frauen in Gesellschaft und Kirche* (Berlin: Burckharthaus, 1978), pp. 271-301. But

see the critique of this model by Catharina J. M. Halkes, *Suchen was ver-lorenging: Beiträge zur feministiche Theologie* (Gutersloh: Mohn, 1985), pp. 100-30. Endorsing a model of "relationality" are Denise Ackermann, "Defining Our Humanity: Thoughts on a Feminist Anthropology," *Journal of Theology for Southern Africa* 79 (1992): 13-23; Isabel Carter Heyward, *The Redemption of God: A Theology of Mutual Relation* (Washington, DC: University of America Press, 1982). For a model of "mutuality," see Marjorie Suchocki, "Openness and Mutuality in Process Thought and Feminist Action," in Sheila Greeve Dava-ney, ed., *Feminism and Process Thought* (New York: Edward Mellen Press, 1981), pp. 62-82; Mary Grey, *Feminism, Redemption and the Christian Tradition* (Mystic, CN: Twenty-Third Publications, 1990) and Mary Aquin O'Neill, "The Mystery of Being Human Together," in Catherine M. LaCugna, ed., *Freeing Theology: The Essentials of Theology in Feminist Perspective* (San Francisco: Harper Collins, 1993), pp. 139-57.

53. O'Neill, "Mystery of Being Human," pp. 150-51.

54. In addition to Mary Buckley, Dermot Lane similarly referred to a "transformative, subject-centered" model of anthropology in order to stress that human identity resides in personal subjectivity, a differentiation that transcends sexuality. See "Women and the Question of Anthropology," Un-published lecture given at St. Michael's College, Winooski, VT (Summer 1981).

55. This question occupies Thomas Berry, *The Dream of the Earth* (San Francisco: Sierra Club Books, 1988); Lois K. Daly, "Ecofeminism, Reverence for Life, and Feminist Theological Ethics," in Charles Birch, William Eakin, Jay B. McDaniel, eds., *Liberating Life: Contemporary Approaches to Ecological Theology* (Maryknoll, NY: Orbis Books, 1990); Matthew Fox, *Original Blessing* (Santa Fe, NM: Bear and Co., 1983); Douglas John Hall, *Imaging God: Dominion as Stewardship* (Grand Rapids, MI: W. B. Eerdmans Pub. Co., 1986); Sallie McFague, *The Body of God: An Ecological Theology* (Minneapolis: Fortress Press, 1993); Jürgen Moltman, *God in Creation: An Ecological Doctrine of Creation* (London: SCM Press, 1985); Rosemary Ruether, *Gaia and God: An Ecofeminist Theology of Healing* (San Francisco: Harper San Francisco, 1992); and Dorothy Soelle with Shirley Cloyes, *To Work and To Love: A Theology of Creation* (Phila-delphia: Fortress Press, 1984).

56. In addition to the works mentioned in n. 55 above, see Carol Adams, ed., *Ecofeminism and the Sacred* (New York: Continuum, 1993); idem, *The Sexual Politics of Meat: A Feminist Vegetarian Critical Theory* (New York: Continuum, 1990); David G. Hallman, ed., *Ecotheology: Voices from South and North* (Maryknoll, NY: Orbis Books, 1994); Catharina J. M. Halkes, *New Creation: Christian Feminism and the Renewal of the Earth* (Louisville: Westminster/John Knox Press, 1989); John Haught, *The Promise of Nature: Ecology and Cosmic Purpose* (New York: Paulist Press, 1993); Elizabeth Johnson, *Women, Earth, and Creator Spirit*, 1993 Madeleva Lecture in Spirituality (New York: Paulist Press, 1993); Jay B. McDaniel, *Of God and Pelicans: A Theology of Reverence for Life* (Louisville: Westminster/John Knox, 1989); Sean McDonaugh, *To Care for the Earth: A Call to a New Theology* (Santa Fe, NM: Bear and Co., 1986); Anne Primavesi, *From Apocalypse to Genesis: Ecology, Feminism and Christianity* (Min-neapolis: Fortress Press, 1991); and Eleanor Rae, *Women, the Earth, the Divine* (Maryknoll, NY: Orbis Books, 1994).

57. Johnson, *Women, Earth, and Creator Spirit*, p. 30.

58. Anne Primavesi, "A Tide in the Affairs of Women?" in *Ecotheology: Voices from South and North*, p. 196.

59. Ibid., p. 197. For a discussion of McClintock's views, see Evelyn Fox Keller, *A Feeling for the Organism: The Life and Work of Barbara McClintock* (New York: W. H. Freeman, 1983). See also Keller's *Reflections on Gender and Science* (New Haven, CN: Yale University Press, 1985).

60. Johnson, *Women, Earth, and Creator Spirit*, p. 30.

61. In addition to the references to "the turn to the subject" noted above, see Anne Carr, *Transforming Grace: Christian Tradition and Women's Experience* (San Francisco: Harper and Row, 1988); Dermot Lane, *The Experience of God: An Invitation to Do Theology* (New York: Paulist Press, 1981); Gerald O'Collins, *Fundamental Theology* (New York: Paulist Press, 1981), and René Latourelle, ed., *Dictionary of Fundamental Theology* (New York: Crossroad, 1994), s.v. "Experience," by Gerald O'Collins.

62. On this question, in addition to Graff's article cited above, see Ellen Leonard, "Experience as a Source for Theology," *Proceedings of the Catholic Theological Society of America* 43 (1988): 44-61; and Monika Hellwig, "Whose Experience Counts in Theological Reflection?" (Milwaukee: Marquette University Press, 1982).

63. Leonard, p. 48. See also Lisa Sowle Cahill, "Feminist Ethics and the Challenge of Cultures," *CTSA Proceedings* 48 (1993): 65-83.

64. The most famous example, of course, is Elizabeth Cady Stanton, *The Original Feminist Attack on the Bible: The Woman's Bible* (facsimile ed., New York: Arno, 1974). For an astute evaluation of the political significance of Cady Stanton's biblical interpretation, see Elisabeth Schüssler Fiorenza's discussion in *In Memory of Her*, pp. 7-14.

65. See, for example, Phyllis Trible, "Eve and Adam: Genesis 2-3 Reread," [1973], reprinted in Carol P. Christ and Judith Plaskow, eds., *Womanspirit Rising* (San Francisco: Harper and Row, 1979), pp. 74-83; Phyllis Bird, "Images of Women in the Old Testament," in Rosemary Ruether, ed., *Religion and Sexism*, pp. 41-88; Constance F. Parvey, "The Theology and Leadership of Women in the New Testament," idem., pp. 117-49; Krister Stendahl, *The Bible and the Role of Women: A Case Study in Hermeneutics* (Philadelphia: Fortress Press, 1966); Elisabeth Schüssler Fiorenza, "Women in the Early Christian Movement," [1976], reprinted in *Womanspirit Rising*, pp. 84-92; Leonard Swidler, "Jesus Was a Feminist," *Catholic World* 212 (1971):177-83; Madeleine Boucher, "Some Unexplored Parallels to 1 Cor 11:11-12 and Gal 3:28: The New Testament on the Role of Women," *Catholic Biblical Quarterly* 31 (1969): 50-58; Rachel Wahlberg, *Jesus According to Woman* (New York: Paulist Press, 1975); Evelyn and Frank Stagg, *Woman in the World of Jesus* (Philadelphia: Westminster, 1978).

66. Letty Russell, Rosemary Ruether, and Phyllis Trible, in different ways, are judged to have taken a neo-orthodox hermeneutical stance in *In Memory of Her*, pp. 14-21.

67. Ibid., p. 18.

68. Ibid., pp. 28-29.

69. Ibid., pp. 30-31. Note here the liability of too neatly categorizing feminist hermeneutics into "stages" of critique, retrieval, and reconstruction. It is clear that those who perform "reconstitutive" exegesis are already into the work of reconstruction. In addition to Schüssler Fiorenza, see Bernadette

Brooten, "Early Christian Women and their Cultural Context: Issues of Method in Historical Reconstruction," in Adela Yarbro Collins, ed., *Feminist Perspectives on Biblical Scholarship* (Chico, CA: Scholars Press, 1985), pp. 65-91.

70. Mieke Bal, *Lethal Love: Feminist Literary Reading of Biblical Love Stories* (Bloomington, IN: Indiana University Press, 1987); Susan S. Lanser, "(Feminist) Criticism in the Garden: Inferring Genesis 2-3," *Semeia* 41 (1988): 67-84; Carol Meyers, *Discovering Eve: Ancient Israelite Women in Context* (New York: Oxford University Press, 1988).

71. This research argues that placing the gospel accounts about women into the overall story of Jesus and his movement reveals a subversive element and thus recognizes women's centrality in the Jesus movement. See E. Schüssler Fiorenza's discussion in *In Memory of Her*, pp. 105-59. See also Joanna Dewey, "The Gospel of Mark," in Elisabeth Schüssler Fiorenza with the assistance of Ann Brock and Shelly Matthews, *Searching the Scriptures: A Feminist Commentary* (New York: Crossroad, 1994), pp. 470-509; Elaine Wainwright, *Toward a Feminist Critical Reading of the Gospel of Matthew*, Beihefte zur Zeitschrift für die Neutestamentliche Wissenschaft 60 (Berlin: DeGruyter, 1991). Mary Rose D'Angelo's approach seeks to "re-member" Jesus as a prophet within a prophetic movement where "women as prophets share fully in the same spirit that empowered Jesus and the other men of the prophetic movement." See her "Re-membering Jesus: Women, Prophecy, and Resistance in the Memory of the Early Churches," *Horizons* 19 (1992): 199-218: 208.

72. See Antoinette Clark Wire, *The Corinthian Women Prophets: A Reconstruction through Paul's Rhetoric* (Minneapolis: Fortress, 1990).

73. This is the view of Linda M. Maloney in her commentary "The Pastoral Epistles," in *Searching the Scriptures*, pp. 361-80, esp. p. 362. See also, idem, Mary Rose D'Angelo, "Colossians," pp. 313-24; Sarah Tanzer, "Ephesians," pp. 325-48; Kathleen E. Corley, "1 Peter," pp. 349-60. See also Joanna Dewey, "1 Timothy," "2 Timothy," "Titus," in Carol A. Newsome and Sharon Ringe, eds., *The Women's Bible Commentary* (Louisville: Westminster/John Knox, 1992); Dennis R. MacDonald, *The Legend and the Apostle: The Battle for Paul in Story and Canon* (Philadelphia: Westminster Press, 1983); and Clarice J. Martin, "The *Haustafeln* (Household Codes) in African American Biblical Interpretation: 'Free Slaves' and 'Subordinate Women,'" in Cain H. Felder, ed., *Stony the Road We Trod: African American Biblical Interpretation* (Minneapolis: Fortress Press, 1991), pp. 206-31.

74. See Karen L. King, "The Gospel of Mary Magdalene," in *Searching the Scriptures*, pp. 601-34; idem, Sheila McGinn, "The Acts of Thecla," pp. 800-28; Jane Schaberg, "The Infancy of Mary of Nazereth," pp. 708-27; and Jane Schaberg, *The Illegitimacy of Jesus: A Feminist Theological Interpretation of the New Testament Infancy Narratives* (New York: Crossroad, 1990).

75. Important collections of primary texts include Peter Dronke, *Women Writers of the Middle Ages: A Critical Study of Texts from Perpetua to Marguerite Porete* (Cambridge: Cambridge University Press, 1984); Amy Oden, ed., *In Her Words: Women's Writings in the History of Christian Thought* (Nashville: Abingdon Press, 1994); Elizabeth Alvilda Petroff, *Medieval Women's Visionary Literature* (New York: Oxford University Press, 1986); Katharina M. Wilson, ed., *Medieval Women Writers* (Athens: The University of Georgia Press, 1984), and Patricia Wilson-Kastner, et al., eds., *A Lost Tradition: Women Writers of the Early Church* (Lanham, MD: University Press of America, 1981). Other important

works on women's experience and subjectivity in the so-called patristic period and early Middle Ages include Frances Beer, *Women and Religious Experience in the Middle Ages* (Rochester, NY: Boydell Press, 1992); Jo Ann McNamara and Suzanne F. Wemple, "Sanctity and Power: The Dual Pursuit of Medieval Women," in Renate Bridenthal and Claudia Koonz, eds., *Becoming Visible: Women in European History* (Boston: Houghton Mifflin, 1977), pp. 90-118; Rosemary Ruether, "Mothers of the Church: Ascetic Women in the Late Patristic Age," in Rosemary Ruether and Eleanor McLaughlin, eds., *Women of Spirit: Female Leadership in the Jewish and Christian Tradition* (New York: Simon and Schuster, 1979), pp. 71-96; Joyce E. Salisbury, *Church Fathers, Independent Virgins* (New York: Verso, 1992); Elisabeth Schüssler Fiorenza, "Word, Spirit and Power: Women in the Early Christian Communities," in Ulrike Wiethaus, ed., *Women of Spirit*, pp. 29-70; *Maps of Flesh and Light: The Religious Experience of Medieval Women Mystics* (Syracuse, NY: Syracuse University Press, 1993); and Richard Woods, "Women and Men in the Development of Late Medieval Mysticism," in Bernard McGinn, ed., *Meister Eckhart and the Beguine Mystics* (New York: Continuum, 1994).

76. A standard work on the beguines is Ernest W. McDonnell, *The Beguines and Beghards in Medieval Culture* (New Brunswick, NJ: Rutgers University Press, 1953; New York: Octagon, 1969). Elise Boulding has written on their economic practices and characterized them as an incipient women's movement. See *The Underside of History* (Boulder: Westview Press, 1976), pp. 415-49. See also Edmund Colledge, ed. and trans., *Mediaeval Netherlands Religious Literature* (New York: London House and Maxwell, 1965); Carol Neel, "Origins of the Beguines," *Signs* 14 (1989): 321-41; and Elizabeth Aloida Petroff, "A New Feminine Spirituality: The Beguines and Their Writings in Medieval Europe," in *Body and Soul: Essays on Medieval Women and Mysticism* (New York: Oxford University Press, 1994), pp. 51-65.

In addition to the anthologies of primary texts mentioned in n. 75, mention should be made here of Emilie Zum Brunn and Georgette Epiney-Burgard, *Women Mystics in Medieval Europe*, trans. Sheila Hughes (New York: Paragon House, 1989) and the Classics of Western Spirituality Series published by Paulist Press.

Finally, the work of Carolyn Bynum, Margaret Miles, and Elizabeth Alvilda Petroff deserve special mention. See Carolyn Bynum, *Fragmentation and Redemption: Essays on Gender and the Human Body in Medieval Religion* (New York: Zone Books, 1991); *Holy Feast and Holy Fast: The Religious Significance of Food to Medieval Women* (Berkeley: University of California Press, 1982); *Jesus as Mother: Studies in Spirituality of the High Middle Ages* (Berkeley: University of California Press, 1982); Margaret R. Miles, *Carnal Knowing: Female Nakedness and Religious Meaning in the Christian West* (Boston: Beacon Press, 1989).

77. The literature on medieval women mystics is simply too vast to recount here. Some selected examples, in addition to those already mentioned, include: on Hildegard of Bingen: Barbara Newman, *Sister of Wisdom: St. Hildegard's Theology of the Feminine* (Berkeley: University of California Press, 1987) and Sabina Flanagan, *Hildegard of Bingen: A Visionary Life* (London: Routledge, 1989); on Hadewijch, Mechtild and other beguines: Fiona Bowie, ed., and Oliver Davies, trans., *Beguine Spirituality: Mystical Writings of Mechtild of Magdeburg, Beatrijs of Nazareth, and Hadewijch of Brabant* (New York: Crossroad, 1989); Elizabeth Dreyer, *Passionate Women: Two Medieval Mystics* (New York:

Paulist Press, 1989); on Gertrude: Carolyn Bynum, *Jesus as Mother,* pp. 170-209; Gertrud Jaron Lewis and Jack Lewis, "Introduction," *Gertrud the Great of Helfta: Spiritual Exercises* (Kalamazoo, MI: Cistercian Publications, 1989), pp. 1-18; on Marguerite Porete: Ellen Ross, "'She Wept and Cried Right Loud for Sorrow and for Pain': Suffering, the Spiritual Journey, and Women's Experience in Late Medieval Mysticism," in *Maps of Flesh and Light,* pp. 45-59; and Robert Lerner, *The Heresy of the Free Spirit in the Later Middle Ages* (Notre Dame, IN: University of Notre Dame Press, 1972), pp. 68-78; 200-208; on Angela of Foligno: Elizabeth Petroff, "Writing the Body: Male and Female in the Writings of Marguerite d'Oingt, Angela of Foligno, and Umiltà of Faenza," in *Body and Soul,* pp. 204-24; on Clare of Assisi: Elizabeth Petroff, "A Medieval Woman's Utopian Vision: The Rule of St. Clare of Assisi," in *Body and Soul,* pp. 66-79; on Catherine of Siena: Carolyn Bynum, *Holy Fast and Holy Feast,* pp. 165-218; and Suzanne Noffke, "Introduction," Catherine of Siena, *The Dialogue,* trans. Suzanne Noffke (New York: Paulist Press, 1980), pp. 1-22; on Julian: Robert Llewelyn, *Julian: Woman of Our Day* (London: Darton, Longman and Todd, 1985) and Joan Nuth, *Wisdom's Daughter: The Theology of Julian of Norwich* (New York: Crossroad, 1994).

78. The phrase is Eileen Power's, "The Position of Women," in C. G. Crump and E. F. Jacob, eds., *The Legacy of the Middle Ages* (Oxford: Oxford University Press, 1938), p. 401.

79. Petroff, *Body and Soul,* p. ix.

80. Oden's anthology, *In Her Words,* includes selected writings by all of these women. Her extremely helpful bibliography gives a complete listing of primary sources for all of their writings.

81. On women religious see Mary Ewens, *The Role of the Nun in Nineteenth Century America* (New York: Arno Press, 1978) and Margaret Susan Thompson, "Women, Feminism, and the New Religious History: Catholic Sisters as a Case Study," in Philip R. Vandermeer and Robert P. Swierenga, eds., *Belief and Behavior: Essays in the New Religious History* (New Brunswick, NJ: Rutgers University Press, 1991), pp. 136-63; on laywomen (but only from the U.S.A.), see the essays in Karen Kennelly, ed., *American Catholic Women: An Historical Exploration* (New York: Macmillan, 1988).

82. Oden, p. 13.

83. This is the argument of Alison Weber in the case of Teresa of Avila. See her *Teresa of Avila and the Rhetoric of Femininity* (Princeton, NJ: Princeton University Press, 1990).

84. Rebecca S. Chopp and Mark Lewis Taylor, eds., *Reconstructing Christian Theology* (Minneapolis: Fortress Press, 1994), p. 21. This anthology, which represents the latest fruit of theological reflection from the "Workgroup on Constructive Theology," sees the task of reconstruction as one of three dynamics which make up the entire enterprise of theological interpretation: analysis, reconstruction, and envisioning emancipatory praxis. Although entering into a detailed explanation here is not possible, in my view, these dynamics are parallel to the hermeneutical tasks of feminist theological anthropology which inform this essay. It is important to point out (as do Chopp and Lewis) that "emancipatory praxis" is not simply a final step of theological reflection but is also the vision that grounds analysis and reconstruction.

85. Again, the frame of reference is to shifts occurring in the United States primarily.

86. Chopp and Taylor, pp. 3-11.

87. Maura O'Neill and Ursula King have noted the paucity of feminist voices in interreligious dialogue. See King, "Voices of Protest and Promise," pp. 323-26; and O'Neill, *Women Speaking, Women Listening: Women in Interreligious Dialogue* (Maryknoll, NY: Orbis Books, 1990). Arvind Sharma and Katherine K. Young, eds., *The Annual Review of Women in World Religions* (Albany: State University of New York Press, 1991-) and Denise Carmody, *Women in World Religions* (Englewood Cliffs, NJ: Prentice-Hall, 1989) are helpful, but they are more descriptive than constructive theological works.

88. See Susan B. Thistlethwaite and Toinette M. Eugene, "A Survey of Contemporary Global Feminist, Womanist, and Mujerista Theologies," *Critical Review of Books in Religion* (Atlanta: Scholars Press, 1991), pp. 21-44, and Ursula King, ed., *Feminist Theology From the Third World: A Reader* (Maryknoll, NY: Orbis Books, 1994).

89. (Cleveland, OH: The Pilgrim Press, 1994).

90. Ivone Gebara and Maria Clara Bingemer, *Mary: Mother of God, Mother of the Poor,* trans. Phillip Berryman (Maryknoll, NY: Orbis Books, 1989), pp. 1-19. See also the section "An Egalitarian Anthropological Perspective," by María Pilar Aquino, in *Our Cry for Life: Feminist Theology from Latin America,* trans. Dinah Livingstone (Maryknoll, NY: Orbis Books, 1993), pp. 82-97. Ada María Isasi-Díaz discusses *mujerista* anthropology in *En la Lucha,* pp. 168-71.

91. (New York: Crossroad, 1989).

92. See Rita Nakashima Brock, *Journeys By Heart: A Christology of Erotic Power* (New York: Crossroad, 1991) and Carter Heyward, *Touching Our Strength: The Erotic as Power and Love of God* (San Francisco: Harper and Row, 1989).

93. See, for example, Anne Clifford, "Creation," in Francis Schüssler Fiorenza and John P. Galvin, eds., *Systematic Theology: Roman Catholic Perspectives,* vol. 1 (Minneapolis: Fortress Press, 1991), pp. 195-248; idem, "Feminist Perspectives on Science: Implications for an Ecological Theology of Creation," *Journal of Feminist Studies in Religion* 8 (1992): 65-90.

94. Mary Grey, "Falling into Freedom: Searching for New Interpretations of Sin in a Secular Society," *Scottish Journal of Theology* 47 (1994): 223-43; Mary McClintock Fulkerson, "Sexism as Original Sin," *Journal of the American Academy of Religion* 59 (1991): 653-75; Christine Smith, "Sin and Evil in Feminist Thought," *Theology Today* 50 (1993): 208-19; Delores Williams, "Sin, Nature and Black Women's Bodies," in *Ecofeminism and the Sacred,* pp. 24-29; idem, "A Womanist Perspective on Sin," in Emilie M. Townes, ed., *A Troubling in My Soul* (Maryknoll, NY: Orbis Books, 1993), pp. 130-49.

95. There has been comparatively little constructive feminist theological reflection on grace. One exception is Elizabeth Dreyer, *Manifestations of Grace* (Wilmington, DE: Michael Glazier, 1990). Though in many ways this is a textbook that reviews the history of the theology of grace, her inclusion of Julian of Norwich and a very short section on "Grace in Women's Experience," which draws upon the writings of Adrienne Rich, Alice Walker, and Toni Morrison, represents an important corrective for the way traditional seminary courses on grace are taught.

96. See, for example, Roger Haight, "Sin and Grace," in *Systematic Theology: Roman Catholic Perspectives,* vol. 2 (Minneapolis: Fortress Press, 1991), pp. 75-141; Alister E. McGrath, *Christian Theology: An Introduction* (Cambridge,

MA: Blackwell, 1994), pp. 369-404; Stephen J. Duffy, *The Dynamics of Grace: Perspectives in Theological Anthropology* (Collegeville, MN: The Liturgical Press, 1993). Both John R. Sachs and Peter C. Hodgson include some mention of feminist critique and a few bibliographical references in their books, but neither presents any constructive anthropological reflection from a feminist perspective. See Peter C. Hodgson, *Winds of the Spirit: A Constructive Christian Theology* (Louisville: Westminster/John Knox Press, 1994) and John R. Sachs, *The Christian Vision of Humanity: Basic Christian Anthropology* (Collegeville, MN: The Liturgical Press, 1991).

Part II

FOUNDATIONS IN EXPERIENCE

3

Including Women's Experience

A Latina Feminist Perspective

María Pilar Aquino

(Translated from the Spanish by Colette Joly Dees)

> *In order to progress in our praxis, we feminists have had to*
> *struggle for the autonomy of our organizations. . . . Autonomy*
> *is supported by the conviction that the liberation of women is*
> *mostly our own responsibility. Men are not likely to bring up*
> *our claims since these would run counter to their privileges that*
> *have been internalized in their consciences for centuries.*[1]
> —Virginia Vargas Varela
> Peruvian feminist

Feminist studies have demonstrated that the theoretical models on which the foundations of contemporary anthropological sciences are based have been constructed by men. Intellectually, these men have worked on the premise of a Western, white, European, heterosexual androcentric culture.[2] In addition to these factors, feminist theology has pointed out the clerical and hierarchical nature of the theological anthropology that underlies the Christian discourse. Thus today, the anthropological concepts at the foundations of the theological task are under rigorous scrutiny.[3] Moreover, the nonwhite feminist currents from the North and from the geopolitical South are pointing to the need to create and incorporate in feminist critical epistemology those

I want to express my thanks to Sue Perry, editor at Orbis Books, for encouraging me to write this chapter.

anthropological categories that move beyond the Eurocentric and racist vision of white discourse.

Today, the very notion of "anthropology," in both its historical genesis as well as in its subsequent conceptual developments, is found to be in an open process of revision and reformulation. Feminist critique has shown that the formal subject matter of that notion contains social interests and that it has been formulated to respond to questions rooted in the experience of white men. As a social group, these thinkers established theoretical principles to interpret and explain human existence. For that reason, since their European beginning, anthropological sciences have often made nonwhite cultures and people of the Third World an object of their study, arranged according to their own principles.

As a result, these people never appear in their own right, but only insofar as they fit within Western scientific categories. Moreover, these sciences do not show any concern to examine the symbolic configurations built on sexual asymmetry or the cultural framework of social, racial and gender relations that affect women. The experiences and knowledge of women as a social group only acquired analytical and epistemological relevance with the emergence of the suspicion about the peripheral character conferred on women in androcentric conceptual settings and with the development of specifically feminist disciplines of critique. In the area of Third World theologies, women's lives have acquired cognitive importance beginning with the emergence of the theologies of liberation—whose identity is governed by the epistemological primacy of history's impoverished and marginalized—and then with the incorporation of new analytical concepts that restore the work and the knowledge of women giving rise to the feminist theology of liberation.

The conceptual tenuousness of both the notions of anthropology and theological anthropology becomes more evident in the presence of the methodological advances of feminist theories and theologies. While androcentric scholars strive to decipher the codes of the invisible labyrinth in which the myth of "universal man" is found, feminists are constructing new theoretical instruments that explain and activate the practices of women as protagonists in socioreligious transformation, in the actual locations in which we women find ourselves.

In this article, I intend to examine and to show the theoretical categories used in some collective documents produced by Third World theologians. These documents also involve a theological language patterned according to social gender, as is the case of all written, verbal or symbolic expressions. Consequently, these documents not only reflect the anthropological models at work in Christian discourse but also have a share in the intellectual and symbolic construction of social relations, with direct implications for women's lives. But what are these implications? The possible answers to this question can only be formulated in a critical way if we establish the main thrust of this work beforehand. My objective is to find those intellectual elements that can help us confront and advance the struggles of women for social transformation leading to justice, or in the words of Ivone Gebara, for "a reorganization of society as a whole."[4]

At this point, I have to explain why I have used the term *les teologues* in the original Spanish version of this article. The structurally sexist nature of the Spanish language is becoming more and more of an essential obstacle when we women seek to express our own vision of things. No one can deny the evidence that the Spanish language uses concepts and meanings of gender as "universal" terms referring to women and men. However, this universal assumption is always androcentric. The myth of the "masculine" being generic only shows the point of view of those who have established the rules of the language. Given that, historically speaking, women have been excluded from the formal construction of the language, the meaning of words contains only the experience of men. This is the source of the androcentric nature of the Spanish language. The limitations of a language to express the self-understanding of those who use it can be changed.

This is why I suggest a neutral neologism. I have used "*les* [men and women] theologians" when I am referring to women and men, instead of "*men [los]* theologians" as the generic and androcentric term. The same can be done in the case of "*les* niñes [children]" for boys and girls and "*les* ancianes" [elderly] for elderly men and women. I must also indicate a serious problem that I find in translations of documents or books from Spanish into English, notably those of liberation theology. The authors of these translations eliminate, probably in good faith, the sexist language contained in Spanish theological works. For example, they translate *hombres* [men] as "person," *los hombres* [men in general] as "the people," *los hijos* [sons] as "the children," and so on. By proceeding in this fashion, they present works as if they reflected a conscious attitude on the part of their authors concerning the role that social gender plays in their consciences. However, this is not the case with most of the theologians of the Third World, including the best of the Latin American theologians. These translations have not even explained the sexist nature of the original works. On one hand, translators have done a great favor to women and men authors with a sexist mentality by presenting them as inclusive. On the other hand, however, they have not done any favor to women of the Third World. In fact, we have to face the androcentrism of those who think they are interpreting "our" faith experience. In this work, I will point out the sexist expressions in the original documents.

The area that I intend to examine is very specific, since I will limit myself to four final documents worked out in theological encounters sponsored by the Ecumenical Association of Third World Theologians (EATWOT). I should specify that I will not present a comparative study but rather a sequential approach in order to give a better presentation of the internal theoretical shifts between the documents as well as the intellectual molds which they share. I have selected two of the seven intercontinental Congresses sponsored by EATWOT:[5] São Paulo (Brazil 1980) and New Delhi (India 1981): the first because it focuses especially on the Latin American situation and the second because it focuses on questions of method in the theologies of liberation of the Third World.[6] The third document that I will consider is the result of the Latin American Meeting of women in theology. It took place in Buenos Aires (Argentina 1985).[7] The last and final document is the result of the Intercontinental Conference of Women Theologians of the Third World. It was held in Oaxtepec (Mexico 1986).[8]

THE ANALYTICAL INOPERATIVENESS OF WOMEN WITHIN THE ANDROCENTRIC FRAMEWORK: SÃO PAULO, BRAZIL, 1980

The final document of the Fourth International Ecumenical Congress of EATWOT, which took place in São Paulo, Brazil, in 1980, is divided into an introduction (#1-5) and three long chapters. The first chapter develops the understanding of the "irruption of the poor into history" as an analytical category (#6-26). The second chapter presents the "challenge to the ecclesial conscience" in terms of a theological interpretation (#27-52), and the third chapter shows the "demands and questions" for an ecclesiology from the Third World perspective (#53-95). The main theme of the meeting was the ecclesiology of the Popular Christian Communities or the basic ecclesial communities.[9] Several lines of thought coexist in this final document, and they are not necessarily reconcilable from the point of view of the studies of gender and race. "Social class" as a dominant analytical category is the articulating axis of the theoretical model used in the document.

A first line of thought that runs through the entire document is the pervasive use of androcentric categories such as *Christians [cristianos], brothers, sons of God, the Father, the men whom Jesus chose, men, the exploited classes,* and so on. This clearly expresses a tendency that conceals and submerges women's practices as well as the perception that we have of ourselves. The impact of such language on the contributions of women is noteworthy because, in the end, we are left in the darkness. We can see this process even better in the third part, in which the theological principles used to interpret the experience of faith in the struggles of the Christian communities are presented. The androcentric theological impact is overwhelming, beginning with the concept that God is a man who works with men (#29); he is a Father

(#31). It is assumed that Jesus Christ gathered a few men around him (#46). This is coherent with the statement that the church is the visible body of Christ among men (#32). It even ends up by saying that the mission of the church (our own mission) is to contribute to build up the "new man" in the new society (#89). The selectivity of this line of thought translates the existence of women as conceptually inoperative, analytically irrelevant and organically useless.[10]

In the document, a second problematic line of thought presents a fragmented vision of the processes of social change, as well as of the complexity of social relations. This creates an abstraction in epistemology that dissolves the multiplicity of political and ecclesial practices. By not offering theoretical tools that allow a critical interpretation of the lives and reality of the multiple *men and women* protagonists, the analysis turns out to be inoperative for those who seek transformation. As far as the São Paulo document is concerned, the oppressed classes and the humiliated races are the primordial sectors that are achieving the historical changes. Two paragraphs can serve to illustrate this observation:

> The most important historical process of our times has begun to be led by these very peoples, the truly "wretched of the earth." Their oppression finds its roots in the colonial system of exploitation of which they were victims for centuries. Their struggle to defend their lives, to preserve their racial and cultural identity . . . is as widespread as this domination" (#7).

> In the context of the Third World, the emerging popular classes generate social movements; in their struggles is forged a more lucid consciousness of society as a whole as well as of themselves (#8; paragraph #9 sums up the same idea).[11]

The theoretical model that the São Paulo document applies to social reality is the historical and dialectical model in its various traditions (basically European from the German school). This model has enabled the recognition of the structural contradictions created by the dependent, liberal, capitalistic system of the Third World. However, it only shows the contradictions that can be viewed from its own epistemological framework. Among the structures of domination, the document mentions the economic, cultural and political.[12] Here we find a brief statement about the overexploitation of women in the area of economy. However, because the document uses this limited theoretical model, it does not offer a satisfactory answer about how three crucial phenomena that were just below the surface in 1980 are inter-connected: the exacerbation of concentrative, unequal and excluding capitalism; the impact of the latter on the increase of social, racial and gender inequalities; the efforts of many people who strive

to modify this process, especially those carried out by feminist movements. As a matter of fact, countless feminist groups have continued
to expand and to become stronger, giving rise to a redefinition of social
forces, political action, and social analyses.[13] These movements had
already increased in number and impact in the struggles of the late
1960s and the early 1970s, although they had been present in Latin
America for several decades before that. The São Paulo document
covers the progress of these movements with a veil of silence.

What stands out, for example, are the deficiencies of this analytical
body to identify, or even to indicate, the profoundly sexist structure
of Latin American cultures and of the church. The connection of
dependent capitalism with the patriarchal structure inherent in our
societies is not acknowledged. There is no critique anywhere of the
symbolic constructions of gender that produce asymmetric social
relations in practically every area of one's existence, including intellectual life. The role that the sexual division of social work plays in
the exploitation of women is likewise bypassed. The implications of
these mechanisms for the lives of the great majority of oppressed
women, especially indigenous, black and mestiza women, are left in
the dark by this approach. This is why it can be said that this theoretical model is based upon premises developed out of an experience that
is foreign to women. This model also seeks to respond to questions
emerging from the experience of men. As it stands, we are dealing
with a sexist theoretical model.

A third line of thought found in the São Paulo document recognizes
the validity of the struggles of women insofar as they are inserted
"within the overall framework of the struggles of the poor" (#87),[14]
but not insofar as they represent women as a social group in their own
right. The same paragraph mentions that the church and theologians
have to recognize the struggles of women. It even suggests, in a
condescending way, that "women of the popular classes will always
deserve special attention from our church and a growing concern on
the part of our theology."[15] This third line shows an awareness of the
subordinate condition of women, but it still does not acknowledge the
precise capabilities of women's movements in the processes of social
change, nor how the condition of women affects the understanding
of society, of theology and of culture. In other words, women are not
acknowledged as social and ecclesial actors.

In spite of this, the document contains a paragraph that opens the
way for a reading of reality more in agreement with the heterogeneous
reality of social practices. Although this way does not contribute any
theoretical novelty and is not methodically pursued, at least it does
allow the document to suggest two things. On one hand, it suggests
the complexity of the social phenomenon at the crossroads of the
parameters of race, class and gender, and on the other hand, it shows
the articulation of the structures that cause asymmetric relations and

are not always perceived in the context of the androcentric analysis. This is the case of the convergence between capitalism, patriarchal societies and colonialism. In #16, it is stated that

> It is also important to stress the implacability of a whole series of mechanisms of a more subtle domination, often underesti- mated in the analyses, which produces forms of inequality and discrimination among blacks, indigenous people and women. It has to be noted that the different mechanisms are not opposed, nor even juxtaposed, one to the other, but on the contrary, they are articulated in one and the same comprehensive structure of domination.[16]

With this, and in an incipient manner, São Paulo accepts the poly- morphous nature of the dominant power and would hypothetically allow the recognition of the validity of feminist struggles in their theoretical and practical autonomy.

On the other hand, in #20, the document indicates the importance of the basic ecclesial communities for the renewal of the church. "The irruption of the poor is also occurring within the established church, producing a religious and ecclesial transformation."[17] As I have al- ready pointed out elsewhere, to a large extent, the emergence, the development and the consolidation of these communities is due to the work of women.[18] Yet, in the entire section which the document devotes to "Evangelization and the Basic Ecclesial Communities" (#39-45), not a single reference to the work of women can be found. The same thing happens when the document deals with the partici- pation of women in the church. While it is assumed that women are "implicitly" included as part of the poor people in what is known as "the historical irruption of the poor in society and in the church," the participation of women is not dealt with in its own right. What it consists of is not explained, and neither does it suggest how the clerical hierarchy of men will have to restructure itself in order to allow this participation.

Lastly, in spite of this connection in the lines of thought, the São Paulo document offers an interesting statement from the point of view of feminist theology. In paragraph #18, it states directly that "The discrimination that women suffer in the churches cannot be justified biblically, theologically or pastorally."[19] The sources of theological authority that support this affirmation are the New Testament, the Medellín Documents (Poverty) and the Puebla Documents (1140). The reasoning contains a strong tone of moral exhortation, but it does succeed in conveying the rejection of the official position of the church against the incorporation of women into the ministerial structure. The São Paulo document does not deconstruct the arguments on which the hierarchy bases the exclusion of women, but it does offer other fundamental principles in order to change that posture. Among them, it underscores the need for ecclesial structures to imitate the new way of conviviality inaugurated by Jesus (#84). This new style forces the church to welcome the ministries which the communities generate under the action of the Holy Spirit (#85). The church itself has to exercise the freedom in God that Jesus taught through his word, his life and his death (#86).

THE INFLUENCE OF WOMEN IN THE DISCOURSE: NEW DELHI, INDIA, 1981

The selection of the final document was based on several factors. First of all, in New Delhi, the objective was to find the unifying criteria and resources for the common theological task of the Third World. This entails an effort to overcome the rigidity of the theoretical model applied in São Paulo. In some parts of the final document, the significant influence of women is acknowledged. Because it was focused on questions of methodology, that congress provides a good opportunity to examine how the understanding pertaining to the experience of women is formulated.

The document is divided into an introduction (#1-8) and eight relatively short chapters: "Challenge of Reality to Theology" (#9-25), "Irruption of the Third World" (#26-31), "Inadequacies of Traditional Theology" (#32-37), "Elements of an Emerging Methodology" (#38-44), "Theology from the Oppressed" (#45-52), "Culture and Theology of Religions" (#53-60), "The God of Life and the Kingdom" (#61-71), and "Conclusions and Orientations" (#72-75).

In this general schema, only the first and seventh chapters present some elements to understand the makeup of the experience of women of the Third World. In keeping with the reductionist theoretical model used in São Paulo, the second, third and fourth chapters only mention the struggles of women in a fragmentary way, as if it were a perfunctory obligation, because otherwise the reception of the discourse would have been in jeopardy! The sixth and seventh chapters categorically eliminate any reference to the questions that concern women, with the exception of paragraph #68 of the seventh chapter. In that paragraph, there is an explicit mention of the struggles of women within EATWOT to achieve self-affirmation and recognition in the presence of the sexist obstinacy of the theologians of the Third World. Yet, when women did offer a ritual to the participants (women and men) which included a biblical text reread from their own awareness of gender, there were some theologians who "questioned the reinterpretation of the biblical message in non-sexist terms!"[20] Lastly, the eighth chapter establishes the foundations for the formation of the Commission of Women of EATWOT which was to be approved in 1983.

The selective, reductive, and excluding nature of the androcentric theoretical tools inscribed in the document is seen as in broad daylight in the sixth and seventh chapters. This aspect is all the more conspicuous because the sixth chapter examines the area of the relation between theology and culture, and the seventh chapter develops the understanding of God and the Reign of God. These two chapters do not even raise the question concerning the influence of the social construction of gender on the vision of culture, or on the formulation of theological knowledge. Neither do they present the question in reference to the influence of culture on concepts of gender, or of these concepts on sexual identity, and of both on the shape of social and personal relations. The implications of the social construction of gender in attitudes, in the intellectual frameworks, or in the understanding of God remain outside the analytical field in these chapters. Therefore, what the experience of women of the Third World in a religious and cultural reality highly "genderized" and "racialized" may mean, is left unanswered.

The sixth chapter starts with the statement that "Culture is the foundation of the creativity and way of life of a people. It is the basis and bond of their collective identity. It expresses their world view, their conception of the meaning of human existence and destiny, and their idea of God."[21] Nevertheless, by not addressing the fundamental questions that preoccupy women around the binomial nature/culture, and other equally essential questions deriving from it, the entire chapter falls on deaf ears because it does not have any social actors who express their cultural self-understanding. The chapter only deals with an abstract entity theorized as "people" that would be the normative subject of cultural constructions. Other social entities that interact in the reconstruction of cultural meanings—whose action reifies and fleshes out "the way of life of a people"—take on a certain analytical weight not insofar as they exercise the political intention to decide what concerns their own subjectivity, but instead only insofar as they are inserted into the "androfied" generic field of the people.

The second and third chapters follow a similar process. Especially in numbers 26, 29 and 32, the struggles of women seem conceptualized as peripheral factors of the change of society with regard to exploited classes and humiliated races.[22] The latter are understood as central categories for the analysis of social phenomena and identify those who are the protagonists of liberation movements.

The most fruitful approach to understanding some aspects of the experience of Third World women is presented in #49 of chapter 5 of the New Delhi document.[23] In my opinion, it is from here that one can best appreciate the impact of the struggles of women in relation to intellectual constructions marked by gender. There the first important line of thought points to the need to do a critique of the androcentric, racist and colonizing theologies: Women are especially discriminated against in the Third World. Theology in the First World and Third World has for too long been a male, white theology, and should be liberated from these constraints. The second line of thought recognizes the prejudicial consequences of the androcentric hermeneutics against women: The sexist interpretation of Scripture to legitimize the subordination and oppression of women must be recognized as sinful and seriously falsifying the biblical revelation. The third line proposes an evaluation of the exclusive positions that have characterized theology and the church vis-à-vis women. "Theology and the church should be sincere in expressing this act of divine creation, and not merely making more room for women in ecclesiastical disciplines and institutions that continue to be patriarchal at heart." From the point of view of feminist struggles, the fourth line of thought described in this paragraph forms the core around which all further thinking must turn. At last, here the intrinsic, epistemological value of the experience of women is recognized. "The common human experience of women in their liberation struggle constitutes a true source of theology." This statement had never been formulated before in the entire history of the church or in the theologies of the Third World. Finally, in the last part of this paragraph, a call is issued to Christian men to include the questions raised by women in their field of reflection. "Christians must seriously consider the grave injustice toward womankind in their action and include women's perspective in their theological reflection. Otherwise there can be no truly relevant theology, no genuine social transformation, no holistic human liberation."[24] These five lines do represent a theoretical improvement with regard to the São Paulo document. In addition, they express a new attitude in the self-understanding of women.

In order to appreciate the significance of this new attitude, we need to keep two aspects of it in mind. The first is that the experience of women shows that it is characterized by the will to be involved, to participate, to have a bearing in the configuration of social relations, and to transform the oppressive dynamics of the present order. This experience seeks to be present now in the theological and sociopolitical fields, where the decisions concerning matters radically affecting women as a social group are made. This new attitude involves understanding women as protagonists in society, in anthropological equivalence with other protagonists who also struggle for cultural, racial, and social parity. The New Delhi document reflects this insight, sometimes in an explicit way and sometimes in a fragmentary way. The second aspect has something to do with the context in which this new attitude appears. Such a context is described in detail in the first chapter. It is a matter of confronting and changing a multifaceted reality in which there is an interaction of mechanisms whose functioning oppresses women in a special way: the present international economic system, the neo-colonialism of the Northern nations, and the sexism that permeates the theology, the culture, and the societies of the Third World. These two aspects have become central components in the structure of our lives and of our consciences.

THE COLLECTIVE VERBALIZATION OF OUR EXPERIENCE: BUENOS AIRES, ARGENTINA, 1985

The final document of the Meeting of Latin American women in theology is entitled "Theology from the Perspective of Women. Final Statement: Latin American Conference." For the first time, in Buenos Aires, Argentina, this encounter brought together a group of twenty-eight women from various parts of the continent and from the Caribbean, with the objective of elucidating the specific features of the theological discourse elaborated by women. The encounter was organized by Elsa Tamez. Although it does not have numbers or chapters, the structure of the final document progressively formulates the concepts that serve to express the lives of women. I think it is important to know that in 1979 a theological encounter had already taken place in Mexico City for the purpose of examining the situation of women in the church and in theology.[25] In connection with this encounter, the importance of Buenos Aires is rooted in the fact that while the Mexico City encounter built up a theoretical ambit which included women and men—with a notable influence of the latter in terms of analytical tools—the Buenos Aires meeting was realized as an event that summoned women. Collectively these women expounded the governing categories of an intellectual work rooted in their own awareness of gender.

In this sense, the event and the document of Buenos Aires constitute both a concluding point and a starting point in the self-understanding of Latin American women. It is a concluding point because it provides a response to the question about the nature of the intellectual categories serving to interpret the experience of women on the basis of our own particular capacities. It is a starting point because here the intellectual frameworks utilized by women to apprehend personal and social life "were named." In the very act of "naming" and giving meaning to these frameworks, women exercise the will to decide what theoretical mediations to use in order to give an account of our lives in the multiplicity of our daily struggles. For example, what draws my attention is the insistence presented by the document concerning the new attitude of criticism and distancing that is assumed by women vis-à-vis the patriarchal schema. Here, the shared recognition about the validity of a pluriform language to express the practice and the knowledge of women does in fact break up the inertia of androcentric knowledge, insofar as the latter considers the existence of women as theoretically irrelevant. Among the most important lines of thought in this document, I would like to emphasize the following.[26]

A first line presents the initial formulation of a conceptual model as an alternative to androcentric theories. The identity of this model is based on the categories that build it up. At the same time, these categories are presented as open to future restructuring, and they are considered in their interactive character so that they correspond to the heterogeneity of the practices and knowledge of women. These categories strive to be: unifying, bringing together different human dimensions, communitarian and relational, contextual and concrete, militant, marked by a sense of humor, joy, and celebration, filled with a spirituality of hope, free and open, oriented toward refashioning women's history.[27]

A second important line of thought establishes the interaction of women's experience with Christian tradition, especially in its liberating aspect. A good example of this approach is found in the introduction of the document:

> God's happiness is like a woman, who, having lost a drachma, lights her lamp and goes about sweeping the whole house, carefully searching until she finds it, and then she calls all her friends and neighbors to share her joy at having found it (see Luke 15:8-10). The drachma symbolizes our self-encounter and self-discovery through our experience of God and through our theological work that we experience in our daily lives.[28]

As the document shows, the experience of women is no longer understood according to the categories of oppression on account of sexual configuration, or of self-devaluation, but rather is recognized on a path of personal and social reconstruction through common liberation. This change of attitude is directly attributed to the power of the Spirit of God at work in women's lives.[29]

A third line of thought presents the intrinsic inability of patriarchal theories to respond to the questions that preoccupy women. In the presence of these theories, the document of Buenos Aires recognizes the need to create new categories which would be meaningful for women's lives.

> We work in a constant process of breaking away, as though in an ongoing childbirth, in which we seek to release ourselves from old frameworks and from categories imposed by the patriarchal system, in order to give birth to something closer to life, something more densely packed with meaning for us. We have discovered that we can widen the horizon of our theological reflection in different directions, taking on different religious

expressions, and taking into account the problem of racial discrimination as well as social justice.[30]

Two central factors for the feminist perspective are presented in this paragraph: the awareness that exists among women concerning the influence of the social construction of gender on analytical frameworks and the recognition of the heterogeneity of practices and knowledge due to the interaction of social and racial factors in the struggles of women.

A fourth dimension clearly underlines the ethical element of a discourse rooted in the experience of women. The conceptual elaborations occur in view of the personal and social transformation as the document indicates, "struggling for our common transformation."[31] The transformation which is sought is not extrinsic to the creation of knowledge itself but, instead, forms an inherent part of intellectual life and of the implications of the latter for the modification of social relations for the benefit of women. This is what the paragraph seems to suggest:

> In our celebration in Buenos Aires, we inquired into what methods and what mediations we utilized in our theological activity. We were surprised to note that the characteristics that we have discovered amount to our own method, and the mediations embrace a whole range of possibilities that can take expression in many languages . . . What is expressed is our unifying and inclusive way of perceiving life.[32]

In this sense, it was recognized in Buenos Aires that theoretical mediations, along with those who create them, because they have a share in the mobility of real life, must be open to conceptual modifications. Openness is all the more necessary because the struggles of women imply an enormous creativity in strategies vis-à-vis the extensive patriarchal domination.

In continuity with the above, a fifth line of thought points to the need to consider the conceptual assumptions that accompany the explanatory theories about human life. In particular, there is a mention of the call to work out a synthesis between culture and practices of transformation.[33] In that area, the document does not establish what the fundamental point of reference might be to realize such a synthesis. From the context of the document, one might infer that the point of reference is the experience of women marked by the awareness of gender, in which case it would be proposing two things: a critique of androcentric theories in their sexist cultural construction and a reconstruction of cultural values convergent with the practices of transformation among women.

However, this point is not very clear, especially in the light of the sentence that presents as a task: "To pay attention to the theological experience and reflection that is taking place in base-level groups, especially by women."[34] Here the qualifying term "especially by women" indicates that the conceptual elaborations arrived at by the practices of women are still not perceived as the central point of reference for the construction of a significant discourse for women. The emphasis is placed on elaborations proposed by the generic category of "base-level groups." These terms are used in the same way as the conceptual abstraction "people" or "communities." This approach reduces the possibility of realizing a critical analysis of the influence of the social fact of gender on cultural constructions. At the same time, it also limits the perception of the impact which the transforming practices of women have on conceptual frameworks and on social relations. This fifth line helps explain the presence in the document of the sexist metaphor "new man" as the ideal to which we women must aspire![35]

Finally, among the contributions of this event and its document, we should note the energizing effect that it had on many women insofar as it did reaffirm women's own subjectivity. While androcentric conceptual formulations have led us to alienation and the rejection of our very selves, in Buenos Aires, the validity of the experience based on the corporal—physical and spiritual—structure of women was reaffirmed. The document unlocked the doors for an alternative intellectual construction of that experience made up of a variety of practices and expressed in a variety of languages: "There has been an enormous diversity of experiences, colors, and shadings. Within this diversity we have found common characteristics, some of which we had not foreseen."[36] The conscious acceptance of this experience has brought forth new elaborations which are now nourishing the commitment of women for our own reconstruction, and for that of the socio-ecclesial fabric with an egalitarian and liberating focus.

A THEOLOGY DONE WITH PASSION AND COMPASSION: OAXTEPEC, MEXICO, 1986

The document we are about to examine briefly is the outcome of the Intercontinental Conference of Women Theologians of the Third World which took place in the city of Oaxtepec, Mexico, in 1986. Twenty-six of us, women from Asia, Africa and Latin America, took part in this conference. It was organized by the Commission of Women of EATWOT, and the central theme was "Doing Theology from Third World's Women's Perspective."[37] The document consists of five parts. The first part serves as an introduction in which the steps leading up to this meeting are presented; the second part explains the process that was followed during the conference; the third shows in a general way the content of the reflections in the areas of the reality lived by women, our theological task, the Bible, the church, Christology and theological methodology; the fourth part offers a few recommendations for future work; the document concludes with an evangelical exhortation to confirm women's contribution in the field of theology.

In the final document of Oaxtepec, we can observe two perspectives which, in my opinion, run parallel throughout the discourse. The first perspective shows the understanding of women concerning our own experience as this experience is affected by the sociocultural constructions of gender. This view emphasizes the need to increase our dialogue and work with other women's groups involved in similar struggles against oppression, and from there, to establish bonds of solidarity with other sectors of society also fighting for justice. The second perspective expresses women's self-understanding not as a social group in its own right, but rather insofar as it constitutes a social entity within the analytical framework that prioritizes a unique subject of social changes. Here what women do and know becomes essential, inasmuch as women form part of a neutral social collectivity conceptually expressed as the "poor" and "oppressed." The configuration of the relations of gender and their interaction with other racial, social, sexual or cultural coordinates remains invisible, even within this neutral social collectivity. The presence of both perspectives in Oaxtepec has meant a challenge to women's creativity in the elaboration of a discourse that might reflect our own vision of justice and liberation. In this sense, I am going to indicate what I consider the greatest contributions of Oaxtepec.

A first important aspect is recognizing that oppression against women is a multifaceted reality.

> In all three continents, the oppression of women is affirmed as a hard and abiding reality of life, though this varies in form and degree from place to place . . . This oppression is felt in all sectors of life: economic, social, political, cultural, racial, sexual, religious, and even within the family itself.[38]

If we raise the question concerning the causes of this situation, the document does not offer a very clear answer. Nevertheless, some paragraphs enable us to identify a few analytical categories that could have had a greater critical impact on the discourse. For example, mention is made of the need to break with the present patriarchal order for the purpose of building up an equalitarian society, the struggles of women to eliminate colonialism and the strategies to confront injustices, impoverishment and marginalization.[39]

A second aspect that runs throughout the document is the affirmation of a new experience in women marked by an awareness of our own power to modify the relations of domination in the church and in society. The women's movements do vary, but they are vitalized by the vision of integral liberation as their common denominator. "Having become conscious of our human rights and of the injustices perpetrated against us in all sectors, as women we are teaming up and organizing various liberating movements and projects to help ourselves."[40] Like the document of Buenos Aires, the document of Oaxtepec points out the influence that the liberating interpretation of Christian faith has had on the experience of women. The document explicitly mentions that some women's movements have been motivated by this vision. "We are aware that our liberation is part and parcel of the liberation of all the poor and oppressed promised by the Gospel. Our efforts are rooted in Scriptures. Being created in God's image demands a total rupture with the prevailing patriarchal system in order to build an egalitarian society."[41]

A third aspect underscores the relational nature of women's struggles. In Oaxtepec, on one hand, it was affirmed that women's struggles are united to the efforts of other poor and oppressed groups struggling for their liberation; on the other, the concept of human integrity as a task which has to encompass all the dimensions of life and equally benefit women and men was incorporated.[42] However, even though relationality is a central category for feminist objectives, we should not lose sight of the influence of the second perspective that I explained earlier. In the Oaxtepec document, I perceive a certain fear of acknowledging the subjectivity of women's movements. In this respect, Oaxtepec moves in conceptual ambivalence in the sense that, at times, it affirms the theoretical and political autonomy of women's struggles and at other times insists too much on the fact that the discourse of women "includes" men and that we are working for their well-being as well.

This posture overlooks the fact that in the reality of life, women and men are not in situations of equality in any area of existence. As a result, what is urgent today is not to proclaim that we women are also working toward the well-being of men. At the present time, what is urgent is to support the theoretical and practical affirmation of women's human integrity, our well-being and self-determination, because women are an oppressed group in society. With a little bit of common sense, today no one would dare deny that women make up more than 50 percent of the Latin American population, that most of these women live in impoverished conditions, that as a social group, exploited men share in a relation of domination over women, and that it continues to be true that the great majority of Latin American women are still "the oppressed among the oppressed." We have to keep these factors in mind when we are trying to say who "the people" are and what are the objectives of our struggles.

A fourth aspect formulated in Oaxtepec refers to the interactive nature of the cognitive, ethical, and praxis dimensions in women's discourse. The conceptual elaborations rooted in the experience of women combine spiritual experience with action for justice, and so it is stated that: "Among the efforts being made toward liberation from oppression, theologizing emerges as a specific manner in which women struggle for their right to life."[43] Along these lines and under the influence of Ana María Tepedino's thinking, the document presents the epistemological implications of the corporal structure of women in the following way:

> The passionate and compassionate way in which women do theology is a rich contribution to theological science. The key to this theological process is the word LIFE . . . In doing theology, we in the Third World thus find ourselves committed and faithful to all the vital elements that compose human life. Thus without losing its scientific seriousness . . . our theologizing is deeply rooted in experience, in affection, in life . . . a theology based on feeling as well as on knowledge, on wisdom as well as on science, a theology made not only with the mind but also with the heart, the body, the womb. We consider this as a challenge and an imperative not only for doing theology from women's perspective, but also for all theology.[44]

Lastly, another one of the great contributions of Oaxtepec is what the document does not say but that we women all knew. Before and after this event, in the context of the Third World, it continues to be true that the experience of women is a far greater reality than what appears in writing. In terms of intellectual categories, the framework that gives an account of the experience of women is more readily found in the daily life of the communities and women's movements than it is found in systematic expositions. In my opinion, this is the origin of a methodological characteristic which gives dynamism to the feminist theological output of the Third World. This feature is the need to constantly confront conceptual advances with the processes that establish women as protagonists with social, political, and ecclesial impact. This confrontation becomes an integral part of the building up of feminist knowledge.

In conclusion, I would note that an encounter of Latin American women theologians took place in Río de Janeiro in December 1993. This encounter was organized by the Latin American Commission of Women of EATWOT. It was coordinated by Teresa Cavalcanti and Ana María Tepedino. There were between 35 to 38 of us women from several countries on the continent and from the Caribbean who participated. There, to be sure, we were not only able to note the vitalizing impact that the Latin American theology of liberation has exercised

on our lives, but also the great practical and intellectual steps forward
that we women perceive in our countless struggles. The encounter has
been like a lamp which does light up our path in terms of what other
women have done and what we strive to do in the present and in the
future in the midst of social and ecclesial tensions. Our work was
consolidated as a movement which requires theoretical and organic
autonomy so that, from here on, we may better clarify our objectives
and know in what areas we coincide with other movements seeking
change. The epistemological framework of Latin American women
theologians is clearly based on the experience lived by women in
terms of what we are as social, racial and sexual beings, voluntarily
committed to the objectives of justice and liberation. The results of
that meeting will give rise to future works that may similarly support
the struggles of women in our context.

In the meantime, I conclude with the words of Virginia Vargas, one
of the great theoreticians of Latin American feminism. She provides a
good summary of our process:

> The feminist proposal is oriented toward a "utopia" better de-
> fined now by what we do not want than by what we do know.
> Perhaps it cannot be in any other way since the very social
> practices that we are creating are those that are prefiguring the
> content of new forms of accomplishments, of new concepts . . .
> In the presence of this reality, it is not only necessary to revise
> our social practices and the [theoretical] assumptions that we
> weave around them. We must also raise the question of a dis-
> course which can crystallize concepts and which can force us to
> act according to a model (however libertarian and democratic it
> may be, it is still a model) without rescuing the contradictions
> of the process. We must also recognize that "fortunately" not
> everything is included in our proposal. Instead, its content is
> being profiled and nourished on the basis of our difficulties,
> doubts, pursuits, joys, frustrations, errors and our discussions,
> in short [our] vital social practices, which allows us to pave the
> way while we are building it.[45]

NOTES

1. *El Aporte de la Rebelida de las Mujeres* (Lima: Flora Tristan, 1989), p. 27.
2. The best example of the acritical application of this premise in the
definition of the concepts "anthropology" and "theological anthropology"
can reveal the androcentric makeup of the discourse in Felisa Elizondo,
"Antropología," in Casiano Floristán and Juan José Tamayo, eds., *Conceptos
Fundamentales del Cristianismo* (Madrid: Trotta, 1993), pp. 41-55.
3. Consult the interesting work on feminist theological anthropology by
Ivo ne Gebara, *As Incômodas Filhas de Eva Na Igreja da América Latina* (São
Paulo: Paulinas, 1990).

4. Gebara, p. 11.

5. These are: Dar-es-Salam (Tanzania), 1976, Accra (Ghana), 1977, Colombo (Sri Lanka), 1979, São Paulo (Brazil), 1980, New Delhi (India), 1981, Oaxtepec (Mexico), 1986, and Nairobi (Kenya), 1992.

6. The final document of São Paulo is found in Sergio Torres and John Eagleson, eds., *The Challenge of Basic Christian Communities* (Maryknoll, NY: Orbis Books, 1988), pp. 231-46. The final document of New Delhi is found in Virginia Fabella and Sergio Torres, eds., *Irruption of the Third World: Challenge to Theology* (Maryknoll, NY: Orbis Books, 1983), pp. 191-206. From this point on in the notes, I will indicate first the book which I am quoting and then the page where the quotation can be found.

7. The papers and the final document were published in E. Tamez, ed., *Through Her Eyes: Women's Theology from Latin America* (Maryknoll, NY: Orbis Books, 1989).

8. The final document and several papers by women theologians from Asia, Africa and Latin America were published in Virginia Fabella and Mercy Amba Oduyoye, eds., *With Passion and Compassion: Third World Women Doing Theology* (Maryknoll, NY: Orbis Books, 1988). The papers by Latin American women theologians and the final document were published in Spanish in María Pilar Aquino, ed., *Aportes Para una Teología desde la Mujer* (Madrid: Biblia y Fe, 1988).

9. See note 5, Final Document of São Paulo, in Sergio Torres and John Eagleson, eds., *The Challenge*, no. 2, p. 231.

10. To confirm this judgment, in the presentation it is stated that: One hundred and eighty persons of various Christian churches, including laity, bishops, pastors, priests, religious, and theologians participated in the Congress, ibid., no. 1, p. 231. The participation of only nine women is not mentioned.

11. Final Document of São Paulo, ibid., nos.7, 8 and 9, p. 232.

12. Ibid., nos. 13, 14, 15, p. 233.

13. Cf. Teresita de Barbieri and Orlandina de Oliveira, *"La presencia política de las mujeres: Nuevos sujetos sociales y nuevas formas de hacer política,"* Isis International, No. 11 (1989): 67-78.

14. Final Document of São Paulo, no. 87, p. 245.

15. Ibid.

16. Ibid., p. 234.

17. Ibid.

18. María Pilar Aquino, *Our Cry for Life: Feminist Theology from Latin America* (Maryknoll, NY: Orbis Books, 1993), pp. 42-61.

19. Final Document of São Paulo, p. 245.

20. Final Document of New Delhi, in Fabella and Torres, eds., no. 68, p. 204.

21. Ibid., no. 53, p. 201.

22. Ibid, pp. 195-97.

23. Ibid., p. 200.

24. The document in Spanish uses the androcentric term *los cristianos* (Christians [men]). There will undoubtedly be people who will note that when the document speaks of *los cristianos* (Christians [men]), it is also referring to women. However, such a remark would only show the existence of the androcentric principle in their reading.

25. Cf. papers and final document of the Mexico City encounter. See Ofelia Ortega, Elsa Tamez, María Pilar Aquino, et al., *Mujer Latinoamericana, Iglesia y Teología* (Mexico: Mujeres para el Diálogo, 1981).

26. See Document of Buenos Aires in *Through Her Eyes*, pp. 150-53.

27. Ibid., p. 151.

28. Ibid., p. 150.

29. Ibid., p. 151.

30. Ibid., p. 152.

31. Ibid.

32. Ibid.

33. Ibid.

34. Ibid.

35. This paragraph is overtly androcentric: "To seek, from this theological perspective, common paths with men, helping them to see the strength and tenderness that are part of the common task of bringing forth and nourishing the life of the [new man]—woman/man—and the new society." Ibid., pp. 152-53. In this case, the English translation used "new person" instead of the original in Spanish "new man."

36. Ibid., p. 151.

37. Final Document of Oaxtepec, in Fabella and Oduyoye, eds., *With Passion and Compassion*, pp. 184-90.

38. Ibid., p. 185.

39. Ibid.

40. Ibid.

41. Ibid., pp. 185-186.

42. Ibid., pp. 184, 189.

43. Ibid, no. 2.

44. Ibid., p. 188. See also Ana María Tepedino, "Feminist Theology as the Fruit of Passion and Compassion," in Fabella and Oduyoye, eds., *With Passion and Compassion*, pp. 167-68.

45. Virginia Vargas Varela, El Aporte de la Rebeldía de las Mujeres (Lima, Peru: Flora Tristán, 1989), pp. 144-45.

4

The Struggle to Name
Women's Experience

Ann O'Hara Graff

INTRODUCTION: NAMING WOMEN'S EXPERIENCE

With the publication of Mary Daly's *The Church and the Second Sex* in 1968, the work of constructing theology from the point of view of women was again underway in the United States.[1] The events of the Vatican Council, the civil rights movement, the peace movement, and the attention to feminist consciousness as articulated in Europe by Simone de Beauvoir and earlier by Virginia Woolf all lent impetus to the revival of the feminist movement in the late 1960s.[2]

The topic that immediately came to the center of the discussion among women students of theology was the identity of women's experience.[3] So women began the effort to grasp the omnipresent, immediate, yet elusive felt "throb," as Whitehead puts it, the sheer actuality that is experience enjoyed in the occasion "of being one among many, and of being one arising out of the composition of many."[4] Women wanted to know how to name their experience, how it had been named, and what it meant vis-à-vis the theologies that formed the tradition and that were currently being articulated. The early focus of this attention lay in the concomitant recognitions of the difference of women's experience from that of the implied universal "man" of the past and current theologies and of the very particularity of that "universal man" himself.

What was apparently unseen prior to these insights was that the abstract universal claim to describe "man" or human nature was not at all abstract. The descriptions of the human that functioned in earlier theologies were usually grounded in the particular experiences of those people who had access to the academy and were able to become published theologians. In the mid-twentieth century, and during many centuries prior to this, that group was largely, almost exclusively, white males who had either the wealth or the position within a major church that gave them access to the universities, to the avenues of publication, and to the pulpit. This privilege was supported by the social systems that enhanced the interests and opportunities of white males, especially those with class status or economic wealth, and discouraged or directly excluded others, notably women, the poorer classes, and nonwhites. Virginia Woolf's *A Room of One's Own* continues to be a classic narrative analysis of this situation.

Much of the feminist theological work of the 1970s through the middle 1980s was directed toward criticizing this particularity that once pretended to abstraction and universality. It was unmasked as a sometimes naive, often destructive participant in ideologies that partnered embedded systems of power and class, race, and gender interests. Let me specify this further with an example. The very recognition of the coincident issues of difference and particularity first appear simply as matters of common sense, at least to groups of people who are nondominant in a culture. Thus women will talk among themselves about men and their characteristic habits as opposed to themselves, blacks will talk similarly about whites, the poor about the rich. Seldom does particularity appear in the consciousness of the dominant group! There this issue is joined with reluctance. Because of its social position, this group takes its own consciousness as normative, even universal, and from this vantage everyone else appears as an "other," to use de Beauvoir's name. Thus the realization of difference brings the attendant recognition of social hierarchies, with their institutionalized patterns of domination and subordination in relation to political power, wealth, public voice and the like. It also indicates patterns of prejudice that inform ideologies that diminish, demean, and render invisible the "others." Moreover, these barely veil the contempt, grasping, and fear that riddle a people living in these social relations. To shift from sociological to theological language, sin, both personal and social, has become more clearly visible.[5]

Thus women have expended much energy to elucidate the dynamics of patriarchy and systemic sexism as well as their interconnections with other forms of systemic distortion, both ideological and practical, that mark western and other cultures worldwide. This has included attention to religious communities, contemporary and historical, their ritual life, sacred texts, mythology, creeds, ethics and theology. In terms of this task, feminist theology emerged as a hermeneutics of suspicion that has embraced a developing set of critical theories. This work has been directed toward naming ideological and institutional distortions and recovering women's contributions and experience where they have been buried from view. Here then, from the vantage of difference, the controverted issue of naming experience first arises, and I shall explore this in detail below.

However, as this critical work has been coupled increasingly with constructive moves, something new has begun to appear. It seems to me that the present attentiveness to particularity, as a located and detailed way to name our experience—whether from a feminist, womanist, *mujerista,* or other female perspective, or from that of the wider black communities, Native Americans, or from among the many voices now being raised across the cultures of the world—is causing major shifts both for living Christianity and for recreating its theologies.[6] This is continuous with the kind of insights provoked by historical consciousness, and to an extent renames our emerging cultural consciousness more carefully. In this essay I would like to remain within the realms of women's experience and use the related insights into difference and particularity as a doorway through which to examine this resource and ask how it begins to recreate theology. The clues I will arrange arise from what we have learned from the critical work with which feminists have been engaged.

LEARNING FROM THE CRITICAL WORK: HOW TO NAME WOMEN'S EXPERIENCE

Sex and Gender

Above I suggested, too simply perhaps, that ordinary common sense reveals difference and particularity. It is considerably more difficult to move from the insights of common sense to an academically careful naming of the experience those insights contain. The effort to substantiate a critical standpoint vis-à-vis the dominant institutions, practices and theologies of Christianty, as well as other institutions and ideologies, has taken us well beyond any uncritical appeal to what passes for simple common sense.

The efforts to sort out prejudice and stereotypes from authentic insights about the identity of women's experience led to the recognition of the "feminine" and the "masculine" as socially and culturally dependent gender constructs as distinct from biological sexual identity as male or female. This became quickly apparent when the contents of a gender construct, such as one that says women are nurturing, emotional, intuitive, and so forth, were not universalizable, and that men often shared these "feminine" characteristics. This also appeared to be reversible in that it is possible to find women who are rational, strong, brave and aggressive, as a typical Western model of the masculine suggests. Moreover, it was also clear that the very dynamics of gender constructs tend to support the arrangements of dominant powers and interests in a society. Thus irrational women cannot vote, while rational, preferably propertied, males can. It is insidious, but not undetectable.

The Contents of Gender Constructs: Social Location

This fundamental insight has become more complex and more accurate as we have recognized that gender constructs change both descriptively and normatively in relation to social location, especially in terms of class, race, or sexual orientation. Thus, we have understood that it means something different to be a white woman in the United States than it means to be a woman of color, or it means something different to be a wealthy woman than it means to belong to the working class. To take this one step further, there may be a gender construct imposed upon a group of women by one segment of society that is quite different from the one endorsed by her own social group, and these may be internalized differently.

Let me offer two examples. Certainly many white middle-class women of my own generation have been walking between two worlds. In one we live with the remnants of the Victorian cult of true womanhood, in which we are to be self-sacrificing wives and mothers, keeping the sanctity of hearth and home. Alternatively, we grapple with the emerging role of the self-fulfilled career woman, bright, competent and competitive, trying to shed the still condescending "baby" in the slogan about "how far we've come!" Thus one piece of the problem of naming women's experience is in relation to the way gender constructions have informed that experience.

From another perspective, in *I Know Why the Caged Bird Sings*,[7] Maya Angelou offers us an image of the strong black woman who was her grandmother. She went to the door to deal with the sheriff while her uncle hid under a crate in their store. Because the men were more vulnerable to white violence, the women often interacted with white officials. Racism had reversed the gender roles that might otherwise be in play. Yet Angelou's book indicates that black women also experienced forms of domination and even abuse by men in their own society, which are also experienced by white women. Thus the gender constructs she represents for black women are distinct from, but not wholly dissimilar to, those for white women.

Further reflection on the violence of racism and its effect on gender expectations for black women in the United States reveals that vis-à-vis the white world they had to wear two faces. On the one hand they often demonstrated great courage and perseverance as they sought to protect their families or redress injustice, while on the other hand, in the role of domestic help for white households, they cooked, cleaned, and nurtured other people's children, often within a role that demanded silence and self-effacement. What white society expected of a black woman, what black men expected of her, and what she expected of herself clearly could produce variant gender constructs that would uncomfortably shape a black woman's world.

The result of the convergence of these kinds of insights, which we find exemplified in the work of Adrienne Rich, bell hooks, Audre Lord, Susan Brooks Thistlethwaite, Virginia Fabella, among many others, is the recognition that social location is a major key to understanding the content of human experience, here especially women's experience. Both in practice and ideologically, one's experience is always qualified by this social location. I understand this location to include one's culture and subculture, its historical moment, one's class, race, ethnic group, sex, and sexual orientation. Within that mix are positive, supportive elements that give wholeness, meaning and value to human life. Also at work, however, are social powers of diminishment that include hierarchical patterns of domination and subordination that function to benefit some and demean others or that pull some toward the center of benefit in a social system while others are unjustly marginalized.

In theological terms, we live in social arrangements of grace and sin. Understanding these networks of relations in which we all participate has provided us with a tool to more adequately name ourselves. The insight into difference was the iceberg's tip that ineluctably has drawn us into the realization of the complexity of our particularity, with its rich, gracious array of human gifts and talents, and its damaged corpus, its death and resurrection faces, where the sinful infection of human violence gnaws and grace is in making whole and in transformation.

The Contents of Gender Constructs: Ideology and Language

This reflection on the complexity of gender constructs as descriptions or prescriptions for women's experience already opens up a problem with which we struggle constantly. This difficulty lies in the recognition of the gap between any thematization of experience and the experience itself. This is, of course, a widely accepted hermeneutical principle, but it is acute in this case because the variety of names women have to choose from to describe their own experience—in fact, the very language itself—may be inadequate, prejudicial, even systematically distorted. Because of this, critical work as a variety of hermeneutics of suspicion has been undertaken in several forms. The purpose of this is to make a more adequate naming of women's experiences possible and ultimately transform women's situations.

Among these efforts, there are those that can be grouped under the general rubric of ideology critiques, such as the work to name the Victorian ideal of "True Womanhood" and correlate it with the sociological data about the women who lived with it, as well as their narratives—diaries, letters, and the like.[8] Such correlation indicates the ways this shaped women's lives and the gaps between ideology and practice, including the human damage this caused.

From another vantage, there are studies of the myths that have defined our gender relations for centuries in western culture. These are the great narratives in which we have lived and which reappear with constancy amid their changing faces: mother earth, the overcoming of the mother by her son, the hero, his journey and his always supportive, faithful companion/wife, the romantic lovers in which a woman's life is resolved into her lover's fate. These myths and others have been engaged with the tools of philosophy, psychology and other disciplines, again to reveal the dynamics of these naming narratives themselves, and what they allow us to experience and what they consider impossible.[9] This work creates gaps both between what is named and what might otherwise have been named (perhaps even was named, but was lost) and what new names, new stories might be told. It also widens the gaps between the practical experience of women in particular social locations and these mythic names that informed their experience. As part of the great ideological systems that inform our culture, of which a particular instance, like the cult of true womanhood, is only a chapter, these myths have a profound religious depth. We have understood the narratives to speak of the ultimate meanings of ourselves and our world. They are often cast in the persons of the gods. Thus this archeological work, this cultural psychological analysis, is central to the problem of naming women's experience, as well as freeing women for new names.

While this rewriting of the mythic narratives is being done in literature,[10] it is also directed toward the Bible. Here no one has done more creative work than Elisabeth Schüssler Fiorenza.[11] Her painstaking analysis of the construction of the New Testament texts in relation to women in the particular historical, cultural and social locations in the first century has offered us a new way to read the texts themselves and hear the gospel anew for the community that was, and again is, called to be a discipleship of equals. She has opened up and reconfigured the mythic map.

On yet another surface of the problem of names, feminist suspicion has been directed at language itself. While language is uttered out of and in response to the sheer ongoingness of our experience, it is not neutral. It is bound up with the needs, interests, powers, desires, relations of the people who speak it. Thus in the United States, Mary Daly has been about the business of diving into the destructive language enveloping women and reclaiming women's gifts and powers, spinning afresh the linguistic skein itself to open new spaces in which women may wander and find new names.[12] Rebecca Chopp has also engaged this issue as she struggles to claim the perfectly open word that could be open to the experience of women who live in the margins, and so begin to name what has been unnameable.[13]

In sum, the problem of gender constructs and the narratives and language in which they are embedded sometimes leaves one wondering whether we can speak at all of women's experience, since the distortions are so great. However, the very distortions themselves, the way women have internalized them, and the ways women have struggled with them are part of the experiences we are seeking to grasp. While we cannot speak raw experience because of the limitedness and selectivity of language and its power to narrate our lives, we can more critically name the names, retrieve the names, reconfigure the names and study the gaps that we create among names and between names and practice when we speak.

Perhaps a not insignificant addendum should be made here. Women's experience also lives in nonverbal symbols, those we generate ourselves and those men have produced to describe us. We encounter these symbols in daily life as well as in art, ritual, music, architecture, and dance. While all of these are tied to the world of myth and language, it cannot be forgotten that symbols always exceed any single linguistic designation. Therefore they serve as another access way into the realities that women live. In them we can decode the multiple layers of meaning that are the home of any symbol. For example, we quickly see in the eucharistic bread the central tradition of women's lives, both in bread baking and meal preparation. We also see the male priest stand alone at the table and give this bread to others. We see the bread of community, of women's lives, and of the robbery and (perhaps accepted) victimization of women by patriarchy. Or again, we see a woman's foot. It may be nearly bent in half and bandaged; it may be vulnerable to the splintering of a fragile glass slipper; it may be showcased in stiletto black heels. We ask: Whose beauty is this and whose bondage? Whose delicacy and whose pain? In either example, the mute symbol blazes like a clarion call into the physical, affective, and cultural interstices of human life. It is tied to language, many languages, and to silence. It belongs to language, yet its own articulateness exceeds language. Such symbols provoke us to a thicker, richer naming of experience.

The Contents of Gender Constructs: The Quest for Human Wholeness

Having indicated the problematics of gender constructs, their social locations and their correlate embeddedness in the ideological narratives and languages, it is now possible to address some further issues. They are shaped by those already described but introduce a further concern, the quest for human wholeness. The first of these is the body.

The Body. It has become commonplace to recognize that western gender constructs have identified women with the body in a way that demeans both women and the body. Millennia ago, Greek culture placed the mind and its ability to be rational at the apex of the human soul. The emotions were subordinated to this rational capacity in a hierarchical order, separating the higher passions such as altruistic love or just anger from the lower appetites such as the desire for food or sex. Both because the body was seen as the matter which the soul animated and because it was most closely associated with the lower appetites, it was defined as subordinate to mind. Moreover, the men who ruled, philosophized, and educated in the Greek world identified themselves with mind and its rationality and identified women with the lower appetites and the body. Clearly, we are dealing with another ideological gender construct, and one that is still with us. As Henry Higgins bluntly sings in *My Fair Lady*, "Women are irrational, that's all there is to that."

Examples of the demeaning of women in relation to the body could be multipled throughout western history. Certainly its hellish nadir was the murder of thousands, perhaps millions, of innocent women as witches during a holocaust that lasted from 1500 to 1700, within a longer period of killing that reached from 1300-1800.[14] The charge against these women was that they had had intercourse with the devil. The study of witch burning has made plain the awful elision that was made between the female body and its sexual power and the demonic. The degree of fear and hatred vented toward women is shocking, and it has been with us from the myths of Eve and Pandora to the sinuous blond dressed in black velvet on the liquor commercials today.

While multiple forms of violence against women continue to derange our culture (a subject to which I shall return below), perhaps one of the most incisive indicators of the dismissal of women's bodies today can be found in Gloria Steinem's "hysterical" essay, "If Men Could Menstruate."[15] One need only invert the physical experience of the dominant group to suddenly shift the whole system of values. Thus, whether from the vantage of Greek philosophy, the terrors of the witch burnings or the casual disposal of women as hypochondriacs, feminist critical work has lifted up another powerful sexist ideology at work within our patriarchal cultural stream.

When this history of denial and destructiveness came to light, the value of the body, especially women's bodies, came to attention. The body is fundamental to who we are, and it is how we are in the world. It mediates all our perceptions, feelings and knowledge. This is not to say that the body is an unambiguous phenomenon, but rather to insist that it plays a profound role in human experience.[16] To deny the body is a delusion and finally silly; to demean it is to damage ourselves.

Since this troubling history has been lifted into view, it is important to note that our retracing of the identification of the body has become more complex. Carolyn Walker Bynum's study of medieval saints and their spirituality, which is bound up in the ways men and women treated their own bodies, indicates that the body, particularly woman's body, bears multiple levels of symbolism within medieval religious culture. While men are likely to remain within the gender dichotomies noted above, women themselves often turned their culturally prescribed weakness into strength, especially when their "weak" humanity comes to be identified with all humanity, including that of the Incarnate Christ.[17] Thus women have "reversed the reversals" and made holy what was demeaned.

With the reappropriation of the value of the body, white middle-class women have also engaged in an exploration of our relation to nature. This is a fruitful connection for some of us and for the relocation of human beings in nature, and has generated new spirituality and new theology that supports our wider ecological concerns. However, it is not a direction that has immediately involved black women in the United States. Again, difference and particularity in gender constructs may be the clue to this distinction. The Victorian skew to an already distorted western image of woman asked her to be nonrational, emotional, intuitive, and asexual (but a good mother). Although she was not bright enough to need higher education, she was the seat of education in the home and the keeper of the domestic, religious and artistic cultural values. In the United States, sexuality, even animality, was projected by whites onto blacks. Blacks were ideologically (not practically) divorced from any role in shaping culture. Thus it may be that black women are moving away from a raw connection to nature through the gender construal of their bodies, while white women are retrieving their bodies and their connection to nature.[18] Black women and white women share a concern for involvement in culture. Whites are working to broaden their access and attain credible public voices. Blacks are working to name and retrieve their own culture both in Africa and in the United States, to overcome being shut out of white public culture at all levels, and to transform that culture toward justice.

Also connected to women's physical life is our role as mothers. Adrienne Rich, among others,[19] has explored mothering as an experience white women have in this culture, and how it has been institutionalized as a social and familial role that has had some fairly strict boundaries. Black women have also been concerned with the different dynamics of their mothering.[20] While middle-class white women can reflect on the psychology of mothering and the learning it offers, black women continue to attend to physical and cultural survival. These concerns quickly take us from the body and its functions into society, particularly the sociology of the family. Here we re-enter the problem of gender constructs with their sex role identifications, especially within patriarchal, sexist, and racist societies. Again the particularity of social location provides a critical way into naming how women's experiences are configured and how they are different.

Similarly, one's sexual orientation is rooted in the understanding and disposition of the body, and regulated by social prescriptions. Lesbians have raised the matter of compulsory heterosexuality in our culture as part of the baggage of patriarchy and sexism. They also have explored women's styles of love and community building. As different from the heterosexual norm, lesbians again raise the problematics of distortions in the dominant cultural ideologies and practices, as well as the values and contents of the particularity of an alternative group's lifestyle and bonding patterns.[21]

A final issue connected with the body is whether our female sexuality generates experience that is truly distinctive and common for all women, across cultures. Such experience includes menstruation and giving birth. Although the meanings of these experiences may be intensely culturally defined, this biological commonality allows us to struggle with the problem of particularity from another angle. If women have some experiences that cross cultures, they already may be or may become able to be thematized in quite similar ways, and may provide a basis for some limited generalizations about women's experience. This might provide one constructive starting point, apart from shared forms of suffering due to systemic sexism.

Affect. Henry Higgins, and his multitude of friends, raise still another problem for us about human wholeness, and that is the role of affect. Again, because of the way women have been identified with emotions in western culture, as also secondary to male rationality, feminist critics have had to ask about the wholeness of the embodied human psyche and the role that affectivity plays in shaping experience for all human beings.

The comment that "desire is the reason for reason"[22] is telling. The body and affect are the context in which reason operates. Not only desire, but need, pain, suffering, passion are all reasons for reason. While the insight that some emotions or inclinations of the body can cause one to act inappropriately, without the perspective that reason might offer given some space, nevertheless, the generalization of that insight toward the disparagement or even denial of the context of affective and physical life as impacting our knowing goes too far and loses sight of the context and the purpose of reason itself. In hermeneutical language, we need to recognize the role of body and affect as fundamental informants of the horizon of every knower, not peripheral, dispensable or additional. The presence of affect in a person's response to an issue simply cannot be dismissed as a temporary lapse from reason, as we have been taught to treat such occurrences. The emotional tenor of a response signifies meanings, values, connections for that person; it is informative, not an opacity in the lens of a glass that must remain unsullied.[23]

Besides the critical work directed toward restoring the context of reason and reintegrating our vision of the human person, again correcting the ideology, feminists have also engaged the study of the emotional work women do in the lives of families, friendship networks and communities. Here again we encounter the problem of difference in practice in relation to gender, and the assignments of value when "feminine" human concerns are weighed against "masculine" corporate or political concerns (e.g., the quality of the human environment in the workplace vs. the sheer concern for efficiency leading to profit). In this area feminist sociologists and political scientists have begun to rethink economics, politics and class structures in relation to women's concerns for human well-being in family and society.[24]

Feminists have also taken up the work of psychology, both to criticize what has been offered thus far and to make their own constructive proposals. The plethora of new psychological work addresses the violation of women and healing processes, the dynamics of patriarchy in daily life and coming to value one's own wholeness in relation to it, work on grief, anger, love, sex, mothering, etc. In my view, the importance of this for theology is that it opens new horizons within which to think through the problem of human wholeness and wholemaking, to rename the sin and grace at work in Scripture, in tradition and in contemporary life, social and ecclesial.

For example, these dimensions of affectivity have pointed to the need to examine the asymetrical ways that Christian love, especially as *agape*, is practiced and understood along gender lines. The re-examination of this crucial tradition in the work of Beverley Wildung Harrison, Christine Gudorf, Sallie McFague, and others has been critical for new understandings of the meaning of the personal and social work of love as well as the role of self-sacrifice in Christian life.[25] Further, Anne Carr, Toinette Eugene, and Sallie McFague have also explored the problem of God as love within and beyond the metaphors of patriarchy, and have offered us new insight into God as Friend.[26]

Affect, then, criticized and being recovered, provides another angle of vision on women and, in fact, on the human person. The retrieval of body and affect are providing us with a renewed wholeness and integrity for our self-understanding as individuals and in community. This study is also suggesting new approaches to God.

Community. A third aspect of the quest for human wholeness is evident in the feminist concern for connection. Critical reflection on the hero, as well as on the individual, abstract "man" has again shifted our attention to the fact that we human beings belong to each other and to our earth. We are not finally separate, isolatable entities. We now see that the hero who journeyed apparently alone simply masked a huge supporting cast![27] We live, love, know, and are ourselves only socially. We make our humanity possible for one another, and we shape it with each other. We are also undeniably creatures of this earth, whose fate and future is utterly dependent on the well-being of the whole web into which we are woven. It is not romantic, but simply a matter of fact that our personal wholeness is bound up in the whole-ness of everyone else and earth itself.[28]

This concern for community and connection was taken up in psychology in the work of Carol Gilligan.[29] While Gilligan has sus-tained criticism, the early positive response to her work and the numerous efforts to continue to work with relationship as a key category for women's experience has remained. Both Beverley Wildung Harrison and Margaret Farley explore relationship as a key to understanding and evaluating ethical decisions.[30] Even more com-prehensive is Elizabeth Fox-Genovese's new study that pushes even a feminist notion of sisterhood toward the revelation of its own limitations as she propels us on to the realization of authentic com-munity.[31]

In the study of the church today, no term is more important than community. We are not merely individuals before God, but a people. The church needs constantly to strive to build real community; this is intrinsic to its mission. The many women I have worked with in the past ten years can only speak of church in terms of community, its health, nourishment and outreach among others. Their model for leadership is the team, or shared ministry; their internal model of the parish is of a common dance, a common interdependence and inter-change of gifts; their model for mission is walking with others, learning together.[32]

Thus women's experience at the heart of family, friendships and local community life insists on our social, ecological wholeness.

Violence against Women

The deeply troubling fact of violence against women has already been noted, but deserves separate attention. Feminist criticism has made us aware of many forms of violence rooted in patriarchy and sexism that have been and continue to be perpetrated by men against women. Moreover, it has been so internalized by women that we have become violators of ourselves and others. This violence is domestic and social. Feminists have called attention to rape, wife battering, incest, and child abuse. They also point out that women are the poorest and most numerous of the poor, as well as the least literate in this culture. Feminists are examining social, historical, economic, political, religious and psychological aspects of this violence.[33] Again, distinctions of class and race appear when white women recognize their own roles as both oppressed and oppressors.[34] Again, the twists of racial prejudice insure disproportionate numbers of minority women and children at the bottom of the social and economic scale, most vulnerable to violence in all its forms. Outside of this culture, similar violence against women persists in the patriarchal systems of other cultures.[35] In short, both the statistics and the systemic dimensions of this venomous Hydra in our midst are frightening. It is here that the charge to name and then to move from analysis and description to transformation appears most intense.

WOMEN'S EXPERIENCE AS A RESOURCE FOR THEOLOGY

The flood of diverse but related insights about women's experience and the problem of naming that experience threatens to take us everywhere and nowhere. I want to be clear that the research indicates there is no unified body of women's experience but rather that there are multiple forms and multiple dimensions of women's experience. However, this multiplicity, in my view, can be helpfully mapped out and identified in relation to the three key complexes I explored above: social location, language, and the quest for human wholeness.

The work of criticism has cleared enough space to be able to re-engage the interpretation of major theological symbols. This is already apparent in what we have observed above. It is less important here to try to rehearse the many constructive theological reinterpretations that are underway than to ask what the meanings and goals of these new uses of women's experience in theology are about. I would like to suggest that women's experience informs and recreates theology in three ways: in relation to revelation; in relation to practical and prophetic human transformation; in relation to the mystical encounter with God.

First, then, the exploration of women's experience itself is an exercise in the pursuit of truth and, as such, in seeking the revelation of God. It is deep in the Christian traditions that we trust that not only are we all, male and female, made in the image and likeness of God, but that the whole of creation is the handiwork of God, and so is revelatory. Thus warranted, it is the work of theologians to bring these faces of human experience, as we do others, into conversation with the Christian traditions that we have inherited.[36]

The goal of such sincere conversation between women's experiences and these traditions is the mutual illumination of each resource. That is, we work to offer deeper understanding of ourselves and God in order to know ourselves more wholly as well as to "clean the pasture spring," that God might well up bright before us, more available, more alluring. To be content with less than this is to risk contentment with an idolatry of the commonplaces of what we too easily accept, simply because it seems safe and familiar. To fail to bring women's experience into the theological task is no less than a refusal to seek the face of God and a refusal to pursue the truth. This is an exercise in allowing revelation to be further revealed. While the event and person of Jesus the Christ remain the primordial clue to the

Christian structure of meaning, value and truth, the work of theologians who render and renew our traditions is to continuously open up that mystery. Today the exploration of women's experience is a critical corrective and constructive element within this revelatory creative movement of tradition itself.

The first use of women's experience in theology already raises the second. Because of the conversation toward mutual illumination, the resource of women's experience will highlight the systemic distortions of Scripture and the multiple theological traditions that have done harm to women. This becomes plainly visible as the conversation also raises up the contrasting biblical and theological affirmations of the dignity and worth of all human beings and the concomitant ethics of inclusive love, respect and community building. These elements of tradition in turn call our attention to the quality of the transformation of social systems and personal and communal wholeness for which we strive. Major elements of tradition, especially the New Testament, quickly push us beyond any simple desire for mere access to the routes and roles of public status and power in patriarchy. The humble images of the common table, the one bread, the discipleship of equals, remind us that we dream about radical inclusiveness, mutuality and wholemaking on a truly utopian scale. This vision is not a leveling of us all into one but rather an entertainment, an enjoyment, a banquet of our diversity, our catholicity, nourishing one another with our many gifts.

Suddenly, with such a dream, we theologians have donned the coat of many colors, and everyone may say we are truly crazy. We feel the question: How can we truly expect the world to really change toward justice, inclusivenes, real political community? Here feminists join the ranks of liberation theologians.[37] Maybe we must become unrealistic for the only realism worth working for. Ours is a necessarily impractical practicality. We urge the interruption of history on the basis of human and earthly well-being, since what passes for realism today may be the death of us all. Because of the discoveries of women's experience, our theologies describe and prescribe new journeys toward wholeness, new discoveries of eucharist for earth's many peoples.

As we call one another to further action and reflection, our hope is in the God who hopes in us. Using the models of "communities of resistance"[38] or the experience of the strength and vision of American black women,[39] we have begun to name the mentors on our way and find a God who will walk and work with us to build the kin-dom in our midst.

Ultimately, bringing women's experience into the conversation that is theology is about walking into the dark, the unexplored worlds in which we have lived, but not fully, because they have not borne their proper names. Now, as we name our experience more adequately, we bring its truthfulness into the arena of interpretation. With it we walk into the dark again, where we will see God, Jesus the Christ, life, death, resurrection, sin, grace, holiness, humanity, earth and mystery in new light. As it is a prophet's journey, so also is it a mystic's way, because we must risk the many new faces of our God when we tell the truth of ourselves as best we can.

In doing this, the third manner in which women's experience resources our theology becomes visible. With it we take the risk of retrieved and new analogies. This is exciting but uncomfortable. Here we often meet even more resistance than we do to the prophetic call to justice and transformation. The work of liberation, however moved by grace, can appear to be more about ourselves. When we open new analogies, we touch the sacred nerve, the spine of hope and fear that leads from earth to heaven. Yet to be faithful to ourselves and to our God, we must allow our analogies to break open and encircle us, to lead us in the dance from, into and out of ourselves toward the riotous plenty that is God. We must risk the overmuch, trust the unfamiliar. For only here, in this precarious place, is love, and we will only know and taste it when we yield ourselves fully.

This risk and realization lie in the revelatory work that is analogy. Used not only in theology but in liturgy and prayer, in the new names we allow to spring forth in the meeting between our experience and the tradition, we open the deep veins in which courses the blood of our lives as they are met with God. We will find anew the ancient truth that we belong to God and God dwells in us. Yet this intimacy is sustained in the covenanted growth of understanding and love to which, as Christian theologians, we are pledged. Ours is part of the work of allowing the brilliant darkness of God to shine out in its own wonderful light. This is the human work of faithfulness that allows creative tradition to unfold, and our experience as women, in all our diversity, now belongs to this fragile and powerful process.

Theology is about truth, justice, hope, but finally and personally, it is about our Divine lover who chooses to love in us and in our midst. Our humble exploration of our experience is the music that continues to allow us to hear into the rich silence, the candle light that we hold in the great dark, as the God who alone is Holy dawns upon us.

NOTES

1. Mary Daly, *The Church and the Second Sex* (New York: Harper & Row, 1968). For a sense of women's contributions to religious life and thought in the nineteenth century, especially in the social reform and suffrage movement, see Rosemary Radford Ruether and Rosemary Skinner Keller, eds., *Women and Religion in America, Vol. 1: The Nineteenth Century: A Documentary History* (San Francisco, Harper & Row, 1981).

2. Simone de Beauvoir, *The Second Sex*, trans. H. M. Parshley (New York: Knopf, 1952); Virginia Woolf, *A Room of One's Own* (New York: Harcourt Brace Jovanovich, 1929).

3. Ellen Leonard clarifies the connection between women's search for their own experience and the increasing attention theologians have given to the foundational role of experience for theology since the modernists. See her "Experience as a Source for Theology," *Proceedings of the Catholic Theological Society of America* 43 (1988): 44-61.

4. Since the work of this essay is to grapple with the problem of naming women's experience, I begin here with the simplest formulation, borrowing from Alfred North Whitehead, *Process and Reality*, ed. David Ray Griffin and Donald W. Sherburne (New York: Free Press, 1978), pp. 145, 190.

5. The damage done by the subordination and disparagement of others because of difference cannot be overstated. While this paper focuses on difference as a major clue to the appearance of particularity, in all its richness, politically we have not yet accepted difference as interesting and enriching. On the contrary, it continues to generate fear and anger that divide. We need to learn that difference need not entail better or worse, and it need not be divisive. It can be enjoyed.

6. I am thinking here not only of the way feminist theologies have demonstrated that systematic attention to gender must be part of any fully responsible theological inquiry, historical or contemporary, but also of the way that cultural particularity raises questions about every aspect of Christian life and thought. This ranges from questions about the appropriateness of symbols and practices (rice for eucharist) to issues such as the fittingness of Native American traditions to serve as a foundational Old Testament as they appropriate the person and event of Jesus the Christ. See Steve Charleston, "The Old Testament of Native America," in Susan Brooks Thistlethwaite and Mary Potter Engel, eds. *Lift Every Voice: Constructing Christian Theologies from the Underside* (San Francisco: Harper & Row, 1990), pp. 49-61.

7. Maya Angelou, *I Know Why the Caged Bird Sings* (New York: Bantam, 1969). During the course of this essay, I will advert to the experience of black women. I cannot pretend to speak for them; rather, I can only offer what I have learned from them, as I understand it, to illustrate what I take to be critical issues within the problem of naming women's experience.

8. Colleen McDannell, "Catholic Domesticity, 1860-1960," in Karen Kennelly, ed., *American Catholic Women: A Historical Exploration* (New York: Macmillan, 1989), pp. 48-80.

9. In a popular vein, see Madonna Kolbenschlag, *Kiss Sleeping Beauty Goodbye* (San Francisco: Harper & Row, 1979), and idem, *Lost in the Land of Oz* (San Francisco: Harper & Row, 1988); for more sophisticated work, see Catherine Keller, *From A Broken Web: Separation, Sexism and Self* (Boston: Beacon, 1986).

10. See Marion Zimmer Bradley, *The Mists of Avalon* (New York: Ballantine, 1982) or Jean Auel, *The Clan of the Cave Bear* (New York: Bantam, 1980).

11. Elisabeth Schüssler Fiorenza, *In Memory of Her: A Feminist Theological Reconstruction of Christian Origins* (New York: Crossroad, 1983).

12. Mary Daly, *Pure Lust: Elemental Feminist Philosophy* (Boston: Beacon, 1984) and Mary Daly and Jane Caputi, *Webster's First New Intergalactic Wickedary of the English Language* (Boston: Beacon, 1987).

13. Rebecca Chopp, *The Power to Speak: Feminism, Language, God* (New York: Crossroad, 1989).

14. Elizabeth Clark and Herbert Richardson, eds., *Women and Religion: A Feminist Sourcebook of Christian Thought* (New York: Harper & Row, 1977), p. 116.

15. Gloria Steinem, *Outrageous Acts and Everyday Rebellions* (New York: Holt, Rinehart and Winston, 1983), pp. 337-40.

16. Susan A. Ross noted this in her perceptive article, "'Then Honor God in Your Body'(1 Cor. 6:20): Feminist and Sacramental Theology on the Body," *Horizons* 16 (Spring 1989): 7-27.

17. Caroline Walker Bynum, *Holy Feast, Holy Fast: The Religious Significance of Food to Medieval Women* (Berkeley: University of California Press, 1987), esp. pp. 260-302.

18. Susan Brooks Thistlethwaite, *Sex, Race and God: Christian Feminism in Black and White* (New York: Crossroad, 1989), esp. pp. 51-59.

19. Adrienne Rich, *Of Woman Born: Motherhood as Experience and Institution* (New York: Norton, 1976); Anne Carr and Elisabeth Schüssler Fiorenza, eds. *Motherhood: Experience, Institution, Theology, Concilium*, vol. 206 (Edinburgh: T & T Clark, 1989); Penelope Washbourn, *Becoming Woman: The Quest for Wholeness in Female Experience* (San Francisco: Harper & Row, 1977); Nancy Chodorow, *The Reproduction of Mothering* (Berkeley: University of California Press, 1978).

20. Thistlethwaite, *Sex, Race,* pp. 51-59; bell hooks, *Feminist Theory: From Margin to Center* (Boston: South End Press, 1984), esp. pp. 133-46; Alice Walker, *In Search of Our Mothers' Gardens* (New York: Harcourt Brace Jovanovich, 1983).

21. Mary E. Hunt, *Fierce Tenderness: A Feminist Theology of Friendship* (New York: Crossroad, 1991).

22. Elisabeth Young-Bruehl, "The Education of Women as Philosophers," in Michele R. Malson, et al., eds., *Feminist Theory in Practice and Process* (Chicago: The University of Chicago Press, 1986), p. 43.

23. Not only do psychologists operate with this assumption that feelings constitute information and clues to further information, philosophers and theologians have begun to insist on this as well. See Alison M. Jaggar, "Love and Knowledge: Emotion in Feminist Epistemology," in Jaggar and Susan R. Bordo, eds., *Gender/ Body/ Knowledge: Feminist Reconstructions of Being and Knowing* (New Brunswick, NJ: Rutgers University Press, 1989), pp. 145-71.

24. For example, Karen V. Hansen and Ilene J. Philipson, *Women, Class and the Feminist Imagination: A Socialist-Feminist Reader* (Philadelphia: Temple University Press, 1990).

25. Beverley Wildung Harrison, "The Power of Anger in the Work of Love," in Carol S. Robb, ed., *Making the Connections: Essays in Feminist Social Ethics* (Boston: Beacon, 1985), pp. 3-22; Christine E. Gudorf, "Parenting, Mutual Love, and Sacrifice," in Barbara Hilkert Andolsen, Christine E. Gudorf, and Mary D. Pellauer, eds., *Women's Consciousness, Women's Conscience: A Reader in Feminist Ethics* (San Francisco: Harper & Row, 1985), pp. 175-91; Sallie McFague, *Models of God: Theology for an Ecological, Nuclear Age* (Philadelphia: Fortress, 1987), pp. 125-55.

26. Anne E. Carr, *Transforming Grace: Christian Tradition and Women's Experience* (San Francisco: Harper & Row, 1988), pp. 134-57; Toinette Eugene,

"While Love Is Unfashionable: An Exploration of Black Spirituality and Sexuality," in *Women's Consciousness*, pp. 121-41; and McFague, *Models of God*, pp. 157-80.

27. Catherine Keller, *From a Broken Web: Sexism, Separation, and Self* (Boston: Beacon Press, 1986), esp. pp. 7-46.

28. McFague emphasizes these connections throughout *Models;* see also Carol P. Christ, "Rethinking Theology and Nature," in Carol P. Christ and Judith Plaskow, eds., *Weaving the Visions: New Patterns in Feminist Spirituality* (San Francisco: Harper & Row, 1989), pp. 314-25.

29. Carol Gilligan, *In a Different Voice: Psychological Theory and Women's Development* (Cambridge, MA: Harvard University Press, 1982); idem, Nona P. Lyons and Trudy J. Hanmer, eds., *Making Connections: The Relational Worlds of Adolescent Girls at Emma Willard School* (Cambridge, MA: Harvard University Press, 1990).

30. Harrison, *Making the Connections;* Margaret Farley, *Personal Commitments* (San Francisco: Harper & Row, 1986).

31. Elizabeth Fox-Genovese, *Feminism without Illusions: A Critique of Individualism* (Chapel Hill: The University of North Carolina Press, 1991).

32. This is also visible in the work of Fiorenza, cited above, as it is with Rosemary Radford Ruether in many works, notably in *Sexism and God-Talk* (Boston: Beacon, 1983) and *Woman-Church: Theology and Practice* (San Francisco: Harper & Row, 1985); it is also a major focus in the work of James and Evelyn Whitehead, *The Emerging Laity: Returning Leadership to the Community of Faith* (Garden City, NY: Doubleday, 1986).

33. For example see Andrea Dworkin, *Our Blood: Prophecies and Discourses on Sexual Politics* (New York: Harper & Row, 1976) or Alice Miller, *For Your Own Good: Hidden Cruelty in Child-rearing and the Roots of Violence,* trans. Hildegard and Hunter Hannum (New York: Farrar, Straus, Giroux, 1984).

34. For example, Adrienne Rich, "Disloyal to Civilization: Feminism, Racism, and Gynephobia," *On Lies, Secrets and Silence* (New York: Norton, 1979), pp. 275-310.

35. Mary Daly, *Gyn/ecology: The Metaethics of Radical Feminism* (Boston: Beacon, 1978). Elizabeth Johnson also cites the United Nations' statistics that show that women, as one-half of the world's population, do three-quarters of the work for one-tenth of the income and own one one-hundredth of the world's land. Women comprise two-thirds of the world's illiterate adults, and women and children are three-fourths of the starving. See *Consider Jesus* (New York: Crossroad, 1990), p. 102. Thistlethwaite reminds us repeatedly in her works how often women are battered, raped, molested—every three minutes, every five minutes, every ten minutes. See her *Sex, Race,* pp. 126-41 and idem, "Every Two Minutes: Battered Women and Feminist Interpretation," in *Weaving the Visions*, pp. 302-13.

36. Here I follow David Tracy's model of the theological enterprise. See *Blessed Rage for Order: The New Pluralism in Theology* (New York: Seabury, 1975) for an extended statement. I retain full responsibility for the variations on the theme.

37. This is quite similar to the method employed in liberation theology, of which some take feminist theology to be a type. For a concise summary of liberation method and its similarity to feminist theology, see Elizabeth Johnson, *Consider Jesus*, pp. 83-88.

38. Sharon D. Welch, *Communities of Resistance and Solidarity: A Feminist Theology of Liberation* (Maryknoll, NY: Orbis Books, 1985) and idem, *A Feminist Ethic of Risk* (Minneapolis: Fortress, 1989).

39. Jacquelyn Grant, "Subjectification as a Requirement for Christological Construction," in *Lift Every Voice*, pp. 201-14.

5

Elements of a *Mujerista* Anthropology

Ada María Isasi-Díaz

There are three Spanish phrases that I have come to recognize as critical to the self-understanding of Hispanic Women:[1] *la lucha* (the struggle), *permítanme hablar* (allow me to speak), *la comunidad/la familia* (the community/the family). These phrases are repeated with such frequency that they seem to express essential elements of who Latinas are, of how we see ourselves, understand ourselves, value ourselves, construct ourselves, describe ourselves. These phrases that are so common and at the same time so precious for Hispanic Women seem to be, therefore, a key to the elaboration of a *mujerista* anthropology. I will explore their meaning in this article, offering them—that is, the phrases and my explorations of their meanings—as elements that need to be considered when elaborating a *mujerista* anthropology, which must have as its source the lived-experience of Latinas and as its goal our liberation.

I am not claiming that these phrases constitute the only elements to be elaborated in a *mujerista* anthropology. Nor am I saying that the understandings they illumine are uniquely ours. But I am saying that they are central and specifically that they come out of our experience as Latinas living in the United States. Furthermore, I am saying that these phrases offer a valid starting point for an anthropological exploration of Latinas. A more complete anthropological elaboration from a *mujerista* perspective will, we may hope, critique and amplify this initial attempt.

LA LUCHA

The daily ordinary struggle of Hispanic Women to survive and to live fully has been the central element of *mujerista* theology from the very start because it is, I believe, the main experience in the lives of the majority of Latinas. Ever since I learned how hard and difficult life is for grass-root Hispanic Women, I have wondered how they manage to live in the midst of such arduous, demanding, rough and trying reality, in the midst of great suffering. One of my earliest insights, which becomes deeper and clearer with the passing of time, has to do with Hispanic Women's ability to deal with suffering without being determined by it. It is an indication that we are unwilling to allow ourselves to be defined by others or by the circumstances over which we have no control. Thus, I have come to see that the insistence on the value of suffering for Christians and its placement as a central element of the Christian message is questionable. I believe, applying a hermenuetics of suspicion, that it has become an ideological tool, a control mechanism used by dominant groups over the poor and the oppressed.

Allow me to make clear what I am saying, using the *via negativa.* I do not negate the reality of suffering in our lives, but I refuse to romanticize it, which I believe is what happens when one ascribes value to suffering in itself. I do not negate the connection between suffering and evil, nor do I dismiss or ignore either of them. I do not negate that Jesus suffered while he walked in "this valley of tears," but I cannot accept that his suffering was greater than all other human suffering or that the God whom Jesus called Father demanded, even required, Jesus to suffer in order to fulfill his mission on earth.

La lucha and not suffering is central to Hispanic Women's self-understanding. I have gotten the best clues for understanding how Latinas understand and deal with suffering by looking at Latinas' capacity to celebrate, at our ability to organize a *fiesta* in the midst of the most difficult circumstances and in spite of deep pain. The *fiestas* are, of course, not celebrations of suffering but of the struggle against suffering. The *fiestas* are, very often, a way of encouraging one another not to let the difficulties that are part of Hispanic Women's daily life overcome us. They are opportunities to distance ourselves from the rough and arduous reality of everyday life, at times mere escapism, but often a way of getting different perspectives on how to carry on *la lucha.* Listening to the conversations that go on at the *fiestas* and participating in them makes this evident. What one hears is talk about the harshness of life. Of course at times it is a matter of simply complaining. But often it is a matter of sharing with others in order to convince oneself of what one knows: that one is not alone; that what each Hispanic Woman is going through is not necessarily, or at least mainly, her fault but is due to oppressive structures. We also hope, by talking about it, to get the support of others, to get advice and help on how to deal with the situation. *Fiestas* are a very important way for Latinas not to allow only the suffering in our lives to determine how we perceive life, how we know, how we understand and deal with reality.

An old Latina song says *la vida buena, es la que se goza,* the good life is the one that one enjoys. This points to the fact that living is, among other things and maybe predominantly, a search for the good life. The struggle for survival, then, is not only a struggle not to die; it is a struggle to live, but not just barely. It is a struggle to live fully.[2] The struggle for survival is a search for pleasure among those who think of themselves as *familia/comunidad,* "a search for lasting joy, deep delight, gratuitous enjoyment, contagious good fortune."[3] The good life does not ignore suffering. It struggles to go beyond it, to transcend it. As a matter of fact, what our *fiestas* suggest is that Latinas need parties and celebrations to deal in a creative way with the suffering that surrounds us instead of allowing it to define us. The celebrations that we so easily pull together and enjoy so very much often are opportunities for Hispanic Women to "appreciate and accompany the affliction of others with solidarity and tenderness"[4] in *lo cotidiano*—the the everyday life—for us.

By *lo cotidiano* we mean

> The structured patterns of action, discourse, norms, and established social roles . . . considered "from below." A partial list includes particular forms of speech, the experience of class and gender distinctions, the impact of work and poverty on routines and expectations, relations within families and among friends and neighbors in a community, the experience of authority, and central expressions of faith such as prayer, religious celebrations, and conceptions of key religious figures like the saints, or Jesus and Mary.[5]

Lo cotidiano provides a needed framework for explaining *la lucha* as an important element of *mujerista* anthropology. A *mujerista* description of *lo cotidiano* would add to the perspective "from below" the consideration of "from within," and "of our own selves." In other words, *lo cotidiano* for us has to do with the way that we Latinas ourselves consider action, discourse, norms, established social roles, and our own selves.

It is precisely when Hispanic Women's perspective of reality—including ourselves—is the lens used that *la lucha*, not suffering, is seen as central to Latinas' humanity. Even in the moments of greatest suffering in our lives, if looked at from below and from within, the suffering is not what is most influential in determining how we act, talk, make decisions. Though Hispanic Women suffer racial/ethnic and sexist oppression and most of us also suffer poverty, we do not go about our *vida cotidiana*—our everyday life—thinking that we suffer but rather thinking how to struggle to survive, to live fully. We do not go around saying to ourselves or to others, "I am suffering." Instead we go around saying, "*así es la vida* (such is life)." Many think that this denotes a certain fatalism. But the "*así es la vida*" of Latinas goes hand in hand with our *lucha diaria*—the daily struggle which is the stuff out of which our lives are made.

It could be argued that *la lucha* and suffering are two sides of the same coin. But for *mujerista* anthropology there is a great difference between these two perspectives. Those who use suffering as their lens and see it as central to Hispanic Women's lives historically have idealized suffering in a way that results in a certain fatalism.[6] I believe Christianity has much to do with this focus. Christianity has tended to endorse and encourage a certain masochism that has influenced to a great extent the discourse about suffering and its role in the lives of Latinas. On the other hand, from the inside, from the perspective of Hispanic Women, it is the struggle against oppression and poverty and for liberation that is central to who we are.[7]

PERMÍTANME HABLAR

A *mujerista* anthropology is about Latinas as human beings, not in the abstract but within the context of our given reality. It takes into consideration what we understand our task in history to be. Each and every Hispanic Woman as a "human being is not primarily a definition but rather a history within space and time."[8] Latinas are makers of history. A *mujerista* anthropology insists on the need to denounce the way that Hispanic Women have been erased from the histories of our communities and our countries of origin and from the history of the U.S.A. This is what the phrase *permítanme hablar* indicates. We have never been absent from history, but we have been ignored by historical accounts. Therefore, our insistence on speaking, on making known our histories,

> is not a matter of reassuring nostalgia and pleasant reveries. It is a subversive memory, and it lends force and sustenance to our positions, refuses to compromise or equivocate, learns from failures, and knows (by experience) that it has the capability of overcoming every obstacle, even repression itself.[9]

Our insistence on speaking is not only a matter of making known our past; it is also a matter of participating in making present and future history, of being protagonists, of being agents of our own history. If when we speak we are not listened to, if Latinas continue to be spoken to, spoken about, or simply—supposedly—included into

what is said about Hispanics in general, our humanity will continue
to be diminished not only in the eyes of the dominant group but also,
unfortunately, in our own eyes as we internalize such objectification
of ourselves. As long as our voices are not heard, as long as the role
we play in history is not recognized and its specificity is not appreciated, we will not be able to become full moral agents, full persons in
our own right. This is why we insist that a *mujerista* anthropology has
to center on Hispanic Women as human beings in time and history; it
is an anthropology "from within" and "from below." It recognizes
that anthropology is not about an idealized type of humanity or an
abstract understanding of humanity, but that anthropology rises out
of a context. Since Latinas are an intrinsic part of that context, our
self-understanding cannot be ignored.

There are several difficulties in recognizing and affirming the
perspective of Hispanic Women about our humanity as a necessary
element of all anthropologies. First, when it comes to women, the
well-known split of the private and the public sphere continues to
exist. History is about the public sphere, and since women are given
a role and some authority—though little power—only in the private
sphere, women are mostly absent from written history, from what is
recognized as the official (the "true" version) of what has happened.
Much can be said about this false dichotomy, but we will limit our
comments here to two. First, what is called history deals mostly with
political and military events. Yet this history does not exist apart from
social history: history of the family, history of ideas, history of social
and religious movements, history of the churches and religions. Social
history is not mere secondary history.

Social history deals with that same *lo cotidiano* in which Latinas are
key players. It is important to point out that *lo cotidiano*, as defined
above, does not have to do only with what Hispanic Women do in our
homes, within our communities, in the activities that one classifies as
"Hispanic." *Lo cotidiano* also refers to what Latinas think about the
patterns of action, discourse, norms, and established social roles of
"institutional formations like church, state, or major economic groups
. . . [that] control real resources, both symbolic and material, which
they use to project messages and power over time, space, and social
boundaries."[10] In other words, Hispanic Women are very conscious
of how the world we live in is defined for us without taking us into
consideration. It is precisely this omission that a *mujerista* anthropology seeks to denounce and correct.

Another important consideration is this: the history of social movements is about movements that have been and are populated and
carried out by the common folk, with women playing a very important role in them.[11] In Hispanic communities, religion often plays a
key role in many of these social movements.[12] Though unrecognized
by many of the churches' institutions, Latinas are indeed most of the

leaders and workers in our communities. Therefore, though receiving very little credit, Hispanic Women play an important role within social movements and thus in a true understanding of history.

For example, without in any way diminishing the work and leadership provided by Cesar Chavez to the United Farm Workers, it is critical to study, know, and publicly acknowledge the role Dolores Huerta has played and continues to play in the struggle of the UFW as its vice-president. Another example is that of COPS, a Mexican-American community organization in San Antonio, Texas, that had several women presidents. The organization usually has depended on more women than men to carry out its programs and make effective demands upon the city, state, and industries on behalf of the Latina community.

Besides the desire and capacity of Latinas to have a protagonistic role in history, *permítanme hablar* indicates a second difficulty in asserting the role of Latinas' self-understanding and our view of reality as intrinsic to a *mujerista* anthropology. It has to do with the fact that women in general and Hispanic Women in particular are considered incapable of reflecting, of thinking, of conceptualizing. As we have always insisted, Hispanic Women are not only doers; we are thinkers also. We do engage each other and the society of the U.S.A—our reality—in a critical way. We analyze and we understand. Latinas reflect, and that is a way of making a real contribution to history, to the transformation of history. This is why as *mujeristas* we have always insisted that we must not separate action from reflection. We have always insisted that praxis is reflective action. Since the dominant culture and even our own Latino brothers often do not recognize Latinas' capacity to think, this is precisely why we have insisted on identifying grass-root Hispanic Women as organic intellectuals.[13]

We have been told that to highlight the phrase *permítanme hablar*— allow me to speak—would take power from Latinas, would seem to recognize that others have to give us permission to talk. This common expression might be construed that way if one were to start from the position that Hispanic Women have not spoken. But the fact is that we have repeatedly spoken throughout history, that we speak daily, constantly. In highlighting this phrase, I am insisting that people pay attention to us, to what we say about ourselves and the reality we and our communities live.

When Latinas use the phrase *permítanme hablar,* we are not merely asking to be taken into consideration.[14] When we use this phrase we are asking for a respectful silence from all those who have the power to set up definitions of what it is to be human, a respectful silence so others can indeed hear our cries denouncing oppression and injustice, so others can understand our vision of a just society. We know that if those with power, within as well as outside the Hispanic communities, do not hear us, they will continue to give no credence to the full humanity of Latinas. That is why we insist on the capacity of Hispanic Women to speak our own word. For Latinas to speak and to be heard is fundamental in the elaboration of a *mujerista* anthropology, for it makes it possible for us to attest to our humanity.

For many Hispanic Women who have seldom found anyone to listen to them—to hear them—their *permítanme hablar* is a way of insisting on recognition of our right to think, to defend our rights, to participate in setting what is normative of and for humanity. To demand that we be listened to is a way for us to assert our own identity, to demand that our understanding of our own humanity has to be taken into consideration in the understanding of all humanity. And, given all that we have said, our self-understanding is not divorced from our daily stuggle, from our *lucha* to live fully and to bring *lo cotidiano* into the full view of society at large.[15]

LA FAMILIA, LA COMUNIDAD

Recently several Latinas were sharing our reaction to the often heard comment that Hispanic families are "being destroyed," or "are falling apart." Though some of us agreed somewhat with these statements, all of us disagreed with this negative view of the status of Latina families. What we all did agree with is that, for us, *la familia* "is the central and most important institution in life."[16] Whether our family situation is positive or negative, still the ideology of family as central to our lives, to who we are, is primary. This is why it has to be an intrinsic element of a *mujerista* anthropology. But it is important that we understand what kind of *familia* are we talking about. We need to look at how *la familia* has changed, and we must evaluate those changes not by comparing them with the way family has been in our culture, but in view of the role it has today.

It is my contention that the often familiar comment about how poorly the Hispanic family is faring in today's society is a veiled but nonetheless direct accusation of the change in the role of Latinas in our families. I believe, however, that women continue to be the mainstay of our families and that what we are no longer willing to do—in part because more and more of us are gainfully employed outside the home—is to remain married or living with men who oppress us and, yes, even mistreat us. Careful observation of Hispanic Women who are single mothers is what led me initially to suspect that cries about the demise of Latina families are unfounded. What is really behind such cries is fear of the demise of the patriarchal family, not the destruction of Hispanic families as ethnic families.

First of all, we need to question seriously the conclusion that sees Latina families as they move from one generation to another and become acculturated as reaching a point where they stop being ethnic families and become "modern American families."[17] Neither modernization nor acculturation are the major reasons for the changes one can observe in our families, changes that are not anti-Hispanic. Instead it seems that the changes reflect the decreasing need for sex role differentiation because of technological innovations that make it unnecessary to "reward males with the myth of male superiority."[18] As women acquired more resources and skills through education and paid employment, "they achieved greater equality in conjugal decision making without sacrificing ethnicity in other realms of family life."[19] The changes have to do mainly with the way we Latinas look upon *machismo* and *hembrismo*. But there is very little credence given, even within our communities, to the reasons for these changes in behavioral attitudes because the dominant culture has successfully projected Latinas and Latinos as primary examples of male chauvinism and female inferiority.

Both *machismo* and *hembrismo* have become concepts that use Spanish nouns as their names. Though indeed both concepts are based on Hispanic ideologies and behaviors, nowadays they are pancultural and refer to "forms of individual deviancy . . . rarely normative in any culture."[20] What has happened to Latina communities is that the word *machismo* has been adopted in the U.S.A. as the accepted term— when speaking in English—to connote the idea of extreme male chauvinism. Though the word *hembrismo* is not used, what it depicts— traditional feminine roles characterized by weakness, passivity, and inertia—is considered by the dominant culture to be exemplified by Hispanic Women. In other words, Latinas are the best examples of such female characteristics.[21] Holding Latina Women and men as exemplars when it comes to behavioral and ideological deviance is a useful and efficient way for people of the dominant culture, both men and women, to consider themselves in a superior position to us.

This does not take away from the fact that as Latinas we have much struggling to do within our families. But in many ways, family has been Latinas' domain through the ages. It is in *la familia* that we are agents of our own history, that we can claim a historical role within space and time, that we make our mark—so to speak—by making viable and by influencing future generations. Though our realm has been a small one compared to the one commanded by Hispanic men, it certainly goes way beyond the small, nuclear family characteristic of the dominant culture. Our domain, *la familia,* is an amplified family that includes the nuclear family members, particularly the mother and children, plus the extended family—grandparents, cousins two and three times removed, aunts and uncles, in-laws—plus *comadres* and *compadres,* godparents brought into the family for a variety of reasons. Family for us is a vast network of relationships and resources in which Hispanic Women play a key role. I believe this is why Latinas want to preserve our families while ridding ourselves of oppressive elements and understandings about the family and about our role in it.

Instead of devaluing and rejecting our traditional roles in our families, what Latinas want is the opposite: we want the value of those roles to be recognized and their status to be enhanced.[22] Once this happens we believe Hispanic men might have an easier time in accepting their responsibilities as sons, brothers and fathers, as nurturers and transmitters of family values and ideology. This is of utmost importance if we are to change the terrifying picture of Hispanic children today, 38.4 percent of whom live in poverty.[23]

To understand better the kind of *familia* that is Hispanic Women's realm, we need to see how in Latina culture the community is an extension, a continuation of the family. As a matter of fact, the importance community has for us follows on the heels of the great significance of family in our culture. To understand the connection between family and community we need to look at *compadrazgo*, the middle point between family and community. *Compadrazgo* extends family, embraces neighbors, and through it Latinas extend our domain to include important members of the community. *Compadrazgo* refers to the system of relationships that are established between godparents and godchildren and between the godparents and the parents of godchildren. *Comadres* and *compadres*—co-mothers and co-fathers— are additional sets of parents who act as guardians or sponsors, caring for the godchildren and providing for them when needed. But the system of *compadrazgo* is extended beyond religious occasions such as baptism and confirmation to secular activities and enterprises. Dances have *madrinas* (godmothers) or *padrinos* (godfathers); so do businesses, sports teams, religious processions.[24]

The system of *compadrazgo* works because of the significance of "personalism" in our culture. Personalism is "an orientation toward people and persons over concepts and ideas."[25] Therefore, the connections among people are very important. Our amplified families function in many ways because of personal contacts. The more numerous the family, the more widespread the network of "intimate" connections. So the *compadrazgo* system creates an effective infrastructure of interdependence, with Latinas most of the time being at its center. Through *compadrazgo*, family ideology and family values of unity, welfare and honor reach into the community. It is this amplified family, in many ways a community, that guarantees protection and caretaking for its members as long as we remain faithful to it. It is not hard to see that, given the importance Hispanic Women have within our *familias*, rather than giving up or diminishing the role we have within them, we seek to enhance that role.

One very important area of Hispanic Women's self-understanding and self-worth that has not found a positive ambience in *la familia* is that of embodiment. On the contrary, most of the time, it is precisely because of the role we play in our families that we do not have control over our bodies, that our sexuality is restricted and negated, that our bodies are used against ourselves. *Familia/comunidad,* unfortunately, is not a safe place for women when it comes to considerations of Latinas' bodies. The aspects of sexuality that have to do with pleasure, communication, and affection are negated, and only procreation is valued. As a matter of fact, it is precisely because procreation is given such a high value that other aspects of sexuality are denied to us. Our procreative role and the functions connected with it—nurturing and responsibility for the children—most of the time work against us.

Latinas' bodies continue to be objectified. Hispanic men as well as other men and women of the dominant culture objectify Hispanic Women's bodies. Rape and all forms of irresponsible sex are perhaps the clearest examples of such objectification. Here I am not talking only about the begetting of children but also about the psychological and emotional trauma that sexuality outside of a committed relationship causes many of us.

Still another significant form of objectification of Latinas' bodies is exploitation of our physical labor. Many Hispanic Women endure sleep deprivation because of the double and triple work burden they bear. Luisa is up by five in the morning and never goes to bed before midnight. She is a single mother with two children. She keeps house, makes a living by working (a bus plus a subway ride away from home) and is trying to finish high school. María is a middle class woman who has to work outside the home. Her husband helps her with their child and the house. But, that is precisely it: he helps; it is her responsibility to bring up their son, to tend to the house even if she works many more hours than he does and earns more than double the amount of money he does.

Exploitation of the labor of Latinas is clear in the lack of available household conveniences that could ease the physical work we have to do to survive. And here I remember my own grandmother, who suffered from a very young age of a heart condition brought on by arthritis, caused in part by her exhausting work as a washerwoman. But then, as a single mother of two girls, and without much schooling, what else could she do to survive? Disregard for our bodies continues the custom among Hispanics for women to be served food last, for Latinas to consider it their obligation to give their food to the children and men and, if necessary, go hungry themselves. I have seen this happen many times, including yesterday, when I went to visit a friend in *el barrio,* East Harlem. This is not something that happens only among poor Latinas. For example, in my middle class family, my mother insists on serving my father, brothers, and brothers-in-law better and bigger portions of food. All of this, I believe, is grounded in the objectification of Latinas' bodies, in the exploitation of our bodies.

Again, what is most worrisome about this is that Hispanic Women have internalized—and continue to internalize—such negativity about our bodies. The negation of sexuality as a key element of our humanity, lack of understanding that our bodies are ourselves, is one of the main reasons, I believe, for the self-loathing of our teenagers, for the irresponsible way in which they "use" their bodies. We lack an understanding of the intrinsic-ness of our bodies to who we are, of the fact that we are at all times embodied beings, and that every human being is one single entity body-spirit. Unfortunately, *familia/comunidad* is a negative factor in this area by insisting on and supporting oppressive sexual relationships, with both Hispanic men and Hispanic Women being victims.

Yet *familia/comunidad* is women's domain because it is a distinct arena where we are historical protagonists. It is also what provides Latinas repeatedly with a sense of unity and cohesiveness, with a sense of self-identity and self-worth. *Familia/comunidad* relies on inter-dependence, and this allows some space for Hispanic Women to be counted, to be considered important and, therefore, to be dealt with in a respectful way, to be valued as a person and not just because of what we do. *Familia/comunidad* for Latinas/os does not subsume the person but rather emphasizes that the person is constituted by this entity and that the individual person and the community have a dialogic relationship through which the person reflects the *familia/comunidad* "out of which it was born, yet, as in a prism, that reflection is also a refraction. . . . In an authentic [family/]community, the identity of the 'we' does not extinguish the 'I'; the Spanish word for 'we' is *nosotros,* which literally means 'we others,' a community of *otros,* or others."[26] In *familia/comunidad* the "I" of Hispanic Women is heard and embraced without fear, for it does not in any way threaten the "we."

This is not in any way an attempt to romanticize Latina families and communities or downplay conflicts and the oppression we suffer even within what I claim to be "our domain." There is strife in our families and communities, and unity of interests often does not exist there. But the fact is that *familia/comunidad* is a cultural value. Often it is the first and last recourse for survival for Hispanics. *Familia/comunidad* is the grounding element for Latinas, for our self-understanding, and, therefore, must be a central element in a *mujerista* anthropology.

CONCLUSION

Since the goal of all *mujerista* enterprise is the liberation of Latinas, a *mujerista* anthropology seeks to illumine how we understand ourselves, how we perceive and construct ourselves as human beings with a history and within a time-frame of existence, how we live our women-selves, which is the only way we can live our human-selves. No narrative, no discourse can capture the richness of our own experience, of our searching for opportunities to be more than we are, of our amazement when we discover how roles have defined us and limited us while at the same time realizing the potential richness of such roles.

A *mujerista* anthropology is definitely framed by *la lucha*, not a struggle *against* anyone or anything but *for* recognition of the fullness of our humanity as women-selves, and on behalf of all persons.[27] To do this we have to repeat constantly, *permítanme hablar*, because as Latinas we are about begetting new realities for ourselves and for our *familias/comunidades*. We are about giving birth to a new understanding of humanity that starts by insisting on a protagonistic role for all persons and a society based on understandings of interdependence, while embracing differences that are at the heart of what it means for us to be *familia*.

NOTES

1. There is no agreement among Latinas/Hispanic Women as to what to call ourselves. In this article I will take turns using both terms.

2. Ada María Isasi-Díaz and Yolanda Tarango, *Hispanic Women: Prophetic Voice in the Church* (San Francisco: Harper and Row, 1988; reprint Minneapolis: Fortress Press, 1993), p. 4. See also Otto Maduro, *Mapas Para La Fiesta* (Buenos Aires: Centro Nueva Tierra para la Promoción Social y Pastoral, 1992), pp. 25-27.

3. Maduro, pp. 25-27.

4. Ibid.

5. Daniel H. Levine, *Popular Voices in Latin American Catholicism* (Princeton, NJ: Princeton University Press, 1992), p. 317.

6. It is undoubtedly true that as Latinas we have a *sentido trágico de la vida*—a tragic sense of life. But this tragic sense is much more tied to the emotionalism and hyperbolic sense of Latina character than to fatalism. This is particularly true of the strands of Latina culture that have a strong African influence. The strands of Latina culture that have more of an Amerindian influence might be considered to be somewhat fatalistic. But one has to understand the role that the magical or supernatural or surreal or psychic plays in Amerindian cultures—and by extension in Latina culture—before one talks about our fatalism.

7. See M. Shawn Copeland, "'Wading through Many Sorrows'—Toward a Theology of Suffering in Womanist Perspective," in Emile M. Townes, ed., *A Troubling in My Soul* (Maryknoll, NY: Orbis Books, 1993), pp. 109-29. To me it is significant that though Copeland sets out to elaborate "a theology of suffering," she finishes by pointing out that the focus for African American women is not suffering but resistance.

8. Ivone Gebara and Maria Clara Bingemer, *Mary: Mother of God, Mother of the Poor* (Maryknoll, NY: Orbis Books, 1989), p. 11.

9. Gustavo Gutiérrez, *The Power of the Poor in History* (Maryknoll, NY: Orbis Books, 1983), p. 80.

10. Levine, p. 317.

11. It is always important to remember that women are more than half the world population. With very few exceptions, such as Alaska and Australia, we are more than half of the population of all countries.

12. Gutiérrez insists that often the spiritual movements of the poor are social movements as well. See Gutiérrez, p. 94.

13. Isasi-Díaz and Tarango, pp. 7-9.

14. Nelly Ritchie, "SER MUJER—Parte integral de una eclesiología en marcha," in María Pilar Aquino, ed., *Aportes para una teología desde la mujer* (Madrid: Biblia y Fe, 1988), p. 107.

15. Cf. Carmen Lora Ames, "*Implicaciones teológicas en la experiencia de las organizaciones femeninas en el ámbito de la vida cotidiana*," paper presented at the Maryknoll School of Theology, January 1987 (photocopied); quoted in María Pilar Aquino, *Our Cry For Life* (Maryknoll, NY: Orbis Books, 1993), p. 92.

16. Roberto R. Alvarez, Jr., "The Family," in Nicolás Kanellos, ed., *The Hispanic American Almanac* (Washington, DC: Gale Research, Inc., 1993), p. 155.

17. Oscar Ramírez and Carlos H. Arce, "The Contemporary Chicano Family: An Empirically Based Review," in Agustine Baron, Jr., ed., *Explorations in Chicano Psychology* (New York: Praeger Publishers, 1981), p. 19.

18. Melba J. T. Vásquez and Anna M. González, "Sex Roles among Chicanos: Stereotypes, Challenges, and Changes," in Baron, *Explorations*, p. 63.

19. Ibid.

20. Ramírez and Arce, p. 63.

21. The term *hembrismo* was coined in 1955 by M. E. Bermúdez in her book on Mexican family life. Since *macho* means male and *hembra* means female, Bermúdez created the term *hembrismo* to parallel *machismo*. See Vásquez and González, pp. 51-52.

22. Ibid.

23. The breakdown of Hispanic children living in poverty is as follows: Mexican-American, 36.3 percent; Cuban, 31.0 percent; Puerto Rican, 56.7 percent; Central and South American, 35.2 percent. These figures were reported in *Hispanic Magazine* (August 1993), p. 12. They are taken from the U.S. Bureau of the Census.

24. In English one would talk about the sponsor of a dance or of a business rather than of a godfather or godmother. There is a Spanish word for sponsor—*patrocinador/a*—which is also used when the special sense of *compadrazgo* is not intended.

25. Guillermo Bernal, "Cuban Families," in Monica McGoldrick, John K. Pearce, and Joseph Giordano, eds., *Ethnicity and Family Therapy* (New York: The Guilford Press, 1982), p. 192.

26. "*Nosotros*: Toward a U.S. Hispanic Anthropology," *Listening—Journal of Religion and Culture* 27 (Winter 1992): 57.

27. Ritchie, pp. 105-7.

Part III

EXPLORATIONS IN EXPERIENCE

6

Extravagant Affections

Women's Sexuality and Theological Anthropology

Susan A. Ross

It is one of the marvels of a Catholic education that the impulse of a few words can bring whole narratives to light with an immediacy and a clarity that are utterly absorbing. "The poor you have always with you."... And until that moment, climbing the stairs in a rage to my ugly room, it was a passage I had not understood ... But now I understood. What Christ was saying, what he meant, was that the pleasures of that hair, that ointment, must be taken. Because the accidents of death would deprive us soon enough. We must not deprive ourselves, our loved ones, of the luxury of our extravagant affections. . . .
                                        —Mary Gordon, *Final Payments*

It is difficult to be on equally good terms with God and your body.
                                        —Etty Hillesum, *An Interrupted Life*

When it comes to sexuality, Christians have inherited a very mixed tradition. On the one hand, God has come to dwell with humanity, having a first home—as do we all—in a woman's womb, thereby gracing our entire existence. Within Catholicism, marriage bears sacramental status, an acknowledgment of the holiness of physical union. On the other hand, Etty Hillesum's observation is also painfully true. Our sexuality, we are told, is that dimension of our nature that we share with nonrational animals: it is powerful, sometimes dangerous, and always potentially sinful. How often has Paul's remark,

"Better to marry than to burn," been used to suggest that human sexuality is a necessary but unfortunate part of human being?

For women, this heritage is doubly mixed. In art and literature as well as theology, women have been portrayed as the very embodiment of sexuality and, consequently, of sin. As the fourteenth-century authors of the *Malleus Maleficarum* put it, "All witchcraft comes from carnal lust, which in women is insatiable."[1] Thomas Aquinas states that women lack "eminence of degree," the result of a lessened capacity for reason and grounds for denial of ordination.[2] For women, reflection on sexuality is at once both a reflection on our being as it has been socially and theologically constituted and a redefinition of sexuality on our own terms, only newly learned.

In this chapter, I will attempt to sketch out possibilities for a Christian theology of sexuality from a feminist perspective. Certain assumptions should be made clear from the beginning. First, the incarnational, sacramental dimension of the Christian tradition has the potential, as yet far from developed, for a theology that holds the body and sexuality of women as sacred. Isabel, the heroine of *Final Payments*, came to this realization almost too late. She finally saw that Jesus did not scorn earthly pleasures but urged that we delight in them while we can. Second, women and men both come to understand our sexuality within cultural and religious frameworks that privilege the experiences of men. As feminist thealogian Carol Christ put it, "In a very real sense, women have not experienced their own experience."[3] Women, therefore, must develop a new language for understanding sexuality that values it on its own terms, a language that places women as subjects of our sexuality, not simply as the objects of others' desires.[4]

Finally, there can be no adequate feminist theology of sexuality without an intrinsic ethical concern for the integrity and safety of women. That is, I write within a cultural context that is often hostile and dangerous for women. It is a context that commodifies and exploits women's sexuality and teaches most women that their bodies are inadequate. An adequate feminist theology of sexuality will both counter and condemn these currents while at the same time offer a more adequate vision of the beauty and delights of human sexuality for all people, women and men alike. In other words, an adequate feminist theology of sexuality is also a social ethics that values embodiment.

WOMEN'S SEXUALITY AND THE CHRISTIAN TRADITION

It is an axiom of feminism that we begin with our experience. But this is more easily said than done. Human experience is not an undivided unity, and it is interwoven within the multiple cultural frameworks that shape it. Especially in the last fifteen years, feminist theory has been challenged to be more attentive to the diversity of the experiences of women from many racial, class-based, and ethnic contexts.[5] Making any generalization about "women's experience" is fraught with the dangers of exclusion and oversimplification. Nevertheless, I will venture some generalizations, since I am convinced that the embodied experiences that women have had across cultures and time have some common characteristics and have also been the objects of some common perceptions that have helped to shape our present.[6] These generalizations always need, however, to be tested against the experiences of diverse women. Certain emphases will be more true for some groups of women than others.

In her informative and lucid article "Sexuality and the Family," theologian Christine E. Gudorf writes, "More than boys, girls are taught that their bodies are not their *selves,* but rather a commodity."[7] In contemporary American culture, where women's bodies are used to sell consumer products, it is difficult for women to attain a sense of subjectivity—of "ownership," if you will—in relation to their sexuality.[8] This is especially true for poor women, whose ownership of self, much less of possessions, cannot be taken for granted. In addition, as Lisa Sowle Cahill writes, our culture faces "a new dualism about sex."[9] The "sexual body" has become separated from morality, with the result that "our sexual lives [do] not really 'count' in defining whether we are good persons."[10] Cahill notes the universal sympathy extended to "Magic" Johnson upon his announcement that he had contracted HIV. The fact that he had had hundreds of sexual contacts did not detract from the concern expressed by the public and the press, and Cahill wonders what the reception would have been had a woman contracted HIV through similar circumstances.

The difficulty for women in gaining a sense of our own sexuality is further complicated by the Christian tradition's suspicion of female sexuality, as well as female subjectivity. In the Hebrew scriptures, the importance of women resided largely (but not entirely) in their potential for childbearing. A woman who had many children, especially many sons, was greatly blessed. The barren woman was a reproach, both to herself and to her husband. The woman whose sexuality was not under the control of her father or her husband was outside the realm of normative conduct: an adulteress or a prostitute. Rape was treated as a violation of the property of a man, and a woman who was not a virgin at marriage was liable to death by stoning (this was not true for men).[11]

While the Jewish tradition has always looked upon sexuality as a God-given gift of human life and has largely avoided the dualism of soul vs. body that has plagued Christianity through its Greek inheritance, sexuality in Judaism is nevertheless a powerful and potentially dangerous arena. Menstruation, childbirth, nocturnal emissions all require that the person be purified before public worship. Such ritual purity prescriptions affected women far more than men. And while some contemporary Jewish feminists such as the Orthodox Blu Greenberg argue for a retrieval and appreciation of practices such as *niddah*, the laws pertaining to menstruating women, it remains clear that the ability of women to define sexuality was at best highly circumscribed.[12]

In the New Testament, Jesus' attitude toward women is not, at least as the Gospels tell the story, determined by their sexuality. Contemporary feminists draw on Jesus' apparently egalitarian approach to women and their participation in his ministry.[13] But the early eschatological framework, in which neither sexuality nor the patriarchal family was of paramount concern, gave way to an attitude more in line with the culture, in which the roles of women were again subordinated to fathers and husbands. In addition, the dualism of soul and body in the Greek tradition profoundly influenced Christian thinking on the body and sexuality, and women in particular came under fire from some Christian thinkers—Tertullian being one of the most often mentioned—for responsibility in leading men to sin.[14]

But any consideration of sexuality in the Christian tradition must ultimately deal with the heritage of Augustine of Hippo (354-430). Augustine's reflections on Christian belief in the light of his own experience led him to interpret the nature of original sin as *concupiscence*: the inordinate drive to gratify one's own desires. Although found in all of human life, concupiscence was especially evident in human sexuality. Sexual expression could be redeemed only through its exercise in marriage, and then only for procreation. Indeed, Augustine argued that in paradise, procreation would have been untainted by desire and entirely rational.[15]

Augustine's writings on sexuality and marriage, because they have been profoundly influential in the Roman Catholic tradition, have led feminists to question the extent to which his understanding of *human nature* is, in effect, an understanding of *masculine nature*. That is to say, despite his own experience of partnership and parenthood with his unnamed companion, Augustine's interpretation of sexual desire and sinfulness seems to be so rooted in his own lived and embodied experience that its applicability to women's lives is not as clear as it is to men's.[16] For Augustine, one's sexuality is always linked with desire—and ultimately, desire for the self—and therefore must be subordinated to a higher good than pleasure: procreation. But women's experience, not only of sexual intercourse but also of the process of procreation, is very different from men's. Women can engage in intercourse without desire, although this is certainly not the optimal experience, and the process of procreation engages women's lives to a far greater extent than it does for men.[17] While I would not want to suggest that women's experience of sexuality could not be and is not also one of concupiscence, nevertheless Augustine's understanding of sin and sexuality reflects his own (necessarily male) experience and perspective and fails to account for the different perspective women's experience of sexuality would bring to its interpretation.

Thomas Aquinas's understanding of sexuality, derived as it is from an Aristotelian (i.e., a non-Platonic and empirical) framework, is somewhat more positive than Augustine's. While Augustine had thought that paradisiacal procreation would have been entirely rational (and thus very unlike our present physical experience), Aquinas argued that the pleasure that our first parents experienced in paradise was far greater than our own pleasures, since ours are muted by sin.[18] For Aquinas, rationality *enhances,* rather than diminishes, pleasure; therefore, pleasure in paradise would not have been overcome by concupiscence, as it is now. Nevertheless, sexuality belongs to our lower nature, where rationality pertains to our higher. And since men are more rational than women, naturally women are closer both to lower human nature and to sexuality. In fact, God's ultimate purpose in creating women was to assist men in procreation.[19]

The Protestant Reformers rejected the Roman Catholic valuation of celibacy as higher than marriage; indeed, they saw marriage as a *vocation* for both men and women. Martin Luther argued that it was against nature to be celibate; only a very few are able to live such a life.[20] Yet Luther, like Augustine and Aquinas before him, saw women's participation in sexuality as pertaining mainly to reproduction. For him as well, sex was impossible without sin. Later, the development of the "cult of domesticity" in the nineteenth century further removed women in dominant classes from subjectivity in regard to sexuality: white, middle- and upper-class women were the repositories of innocence and purity, especially with regard to sex, where lower-class women and women of color (as well as men) were seen to embody sexuality.[21]

This all-too-brief survey of Christian thought on women's sexuality reveals two related strands: women are either so immersed in bodily existence that they are unable to rise above it; *or* women are innocent of carnal desire and engage in sexual acts only to quell the lusts of their husbands.[22] In neither case are women the *subjects* of their sexuality.

While it is possible to argue—indeed, I would say it is necessary to do so—that treatments of sexuality throughout the Christian tradition are more diverse than they are generally acknowledged to be, they are still overwhelmingly from the perspectives of men and overwhelmingly negative towards, as well as ignorant of, women's sexuality. Women's sexuality is rarely a subject spoken of or written about *by women.* Rather, women are described as the objects of male sexual desire. When women are spoken of as having such desires, they are usually prostitutes, slaves, or witches. Criteria for sexual sins, and even for sexual pleasure, have been consistently drawn from male experience. This is true both in the secular literature and the religious traditions. Consider, for example, Sigmund Freud's conviction that in mature women, orgasm is normatively experienced in intercourse, not through clitoral stimulation.[23] Or consider Paul VI's encyclical *Humanae Vitae,* which condemns the use of "artificial" contraceptives in part because ". . . it is feared that the man, growing used to the employment of anti-conceptive practices, may finally lose respect for the woman . . . "[24] Only in more recent years, especially with the advent of the women's movement in the 1960s and 1970s, have women begun to explore the nature of female sexuality from our own perspective. What does it mean, then, to understand sexuality from a perspective that is both feminist and Christian?

FEMINIST PERSPECTIVES ON SEXUALITY

In 1973, a group of women who called themselves the Boston Women's Health Book Collective published a book called *Our Bodies, Ourselves.*[25] That volume, now in its third edition, provided basic information on women's physical and emotional lives, including doing vaginal self-examinations, learning how to masturbate and achieve orgasm, and getting a safe abortion. The emphasis through-out the book is that women need to "take charge" of their whole lives, especially including sexuality. Against the background of a medical establishment dominated by men, women have sought to redefine sexual pleasure, pregnancy and childbirth, and reproductive control from the perspective of women's own lived experience. Gudorf terms this "bodyright."[26]

Given contemporary American culture's emphasis on individual-ism, it is hardly surprising that *control* emerges from *Our Bodies, Ourselves* and other feminist books on sexuality as key for women's sexual self-determination. "The right to control our bodies" is the linchpin of the movement for women's reproductive rights, especially abortion. But not only in sexuality is control of such importance. Consider the emphasis in contemporary culture on the importance of being thin and the horror of obesity. Those who are overweight, our cultural "wisdom" holds, lack self-control, and eating disorders such as anorexia nervosa and bulimia are characterized by the person's having "total control" over how much she eats.[27]

But a larger context for considering the issue of "control" is raised by Delores Williams, who writes poignantly about the lack of control experienced by the biblical figure Hagar.[28] As the surrogate for an-other woman, Hagar was subject to rape, forced labor and forced pregnancy. Williams draws parallels between the situation of African-American women in this country who have continued to serve in surrogate roles for privileged white women with that of Hagar. "Control" is thus an essential dimension of a feminist understanding of sexuality, although it requires careful analysis. I will return to the issue of control later.

The rethinking of the term *erotic* has been a key theme in recent feminist writing, especially that of the late poet and activist Audre Lorde. Lorde defines the erotic as "the assertion of the lifeforce of women."[29] The erotic is that creative energy which comes from deep within our being, which we have been taught to fear, but which fuels joy, relationships, and mutuality.[30] The fear and loss of the erotic have resulted in its denigration into pornography. Many feminists have noted the need to articulate women's capacity for the erotic in language that affirms its joys as well as its pains.[31]

French feminism has also been concerned about the erotic. While a complex movement, French feminism is characterized by a concern to see women's experience, and in particular, sexuality, from a woman-centered perspective.[32] In general, French feminists have emphasized the quality of *jouissance* in women's sexuality, a term meaning enjoyment and delight that contrasts with male sexuality's emphasis on phallic power. While much of the language is more suggestive than formally descriptive, it is helpful in pointing out the limits of our dominant (French feminists would say phallocentric) language for female sexuality.[33]

Another source is in the growing area of feminist ethics. While her work has been controversial, Carol Gilligan and her colleagues have nevertheless raised many crucial questions in relation to women's sexuality.[34] Gilligan argues that the women she interviewed (e.g., in her abortion decision study) tended to be very concerned about relational issues in making moral decisions. While their concerns for issues of principle (e.g., rights, justice) were not absent, these more abstract issues were often interpreted in the context of relationships. What this suggests is that many women most often see their sexuality in the context of their whole lives and their relationships, with women as well as men.[35] Thus, an "act-centered" focus on sexual ethics— characteristic, as I would argue, of male sexuality and, not surprisingly, central to the Roman Catholic tradition in sexual ethics—can fail to do justice to women's experiences when it looks at sexuality in terms of particular sexual acts (intercourse, masturbation, etc.) and not in the context of the relationships in which these acts take place. Within relationships of mutuality, sexuality serves as an avenue for enhanced touch, tenderness, intimacy. Sexuality is thus far more than intercourse; it is that way of communicating and sharing one's entire existence, both body and spirit. This broadened conception of sexuality is much indebted to the work of lesbian and gay writers, some of whom have argued that homosexual relationships have greater potential for mutuality than heterosexual ones.[36]

That sexuality can never be entirely separated from reproduction is also important to note. While not all women are mothers, all mothers are women. The consequences of heterosexual activity fall more heavily on women. A man's participation in insemination may take only a few minutes, but pregnancy is not only for a far longer period of time, it also has long-ranging physical consequences. My point is not to identify sexuality with procreation, as the Roman Catholic magisterial tradition does, but to note that they cannot be completely separated.

In connection with reproduction, sexuality is inevitably connected with the physical world. Feminist perspectives on sexuality have noted how the treatment of women and the treatment of the earth have shared many unfortunate characteristics: women and the earth are means to greater ends (children, mineral resources), lack (full) rationality, are passionate and unpredictable, and need to be tamed or cultivated. Sherry Ortner's classic controversial article, "Is Female to Male as Nature is to Culture?" put this connection concisely.[37] A more adequate theology of sexuality will also have ramifications for the way in which human beings relate to the physical world.[38]

Finally, feminist perspectives on sexuality emphasize the role that women's bodies have played in consumer society. Women's bodies are used to seduce potential consumers into desire for more objects. Pornography portrays women in demeaning ways, and its status as protected "free speech" continues to provoke heated debate among feminists and First Amendment rights advocates.[39] Not least among these concerns, women are at risk of rape and domestic violence from both strangers and, more often, their own (overwhelmingly male) partners.[40] A woman is not free to enjoy her embodiment in public (on a beach or a street) without the assumption being made that she is "asking for it"—"it" being a sexual encounter. Women's physical safety is most at risk in the home, where partners abuse women (and their children) both physically and emotionally. The incidence of child sexual abuse is probably much more frequent than has been recorded.[41] Feminist perspectives on sexuality condemn such treatments of women as bodies to be used or abused and argue that our culture's understanding of women (and children) needs major transformation.

All of these issues—autonomy and control, the erotic joy and *jouissance* of female sexuality, the relational context, the connection with reproduction and the physical world, the rejection of pornography and violence—are crucial elements for an adequate understanding of women's sexuality. But while they are necessary, they are not sufficient for a theology that is also rooted in a critical interpretation of the Christian tradition. I turn now to such an interpretation, arguing that there are elements within the Christian tradition which could support an adequate feminist theology of sexuality. In connection with the more secular feminist perspectives outlined above, this theology is at times critical of the Christian tradition, and at times of the culture as well. There are also, inevitably, points of tension between secular and Christian feminism.

A FEMINIST *THEOLOGY* OF SEXUALITY

Christian feminist theology is possible because it is based in the conviction that the message of Jesus is one that brings salvation to all: women and men, poor and rich. In the words of Elizabeth Johnson,

> By Christian feminist theology, I mean a reflection on God and all things in the light of God that stands consciously in the company of all the world's women, explicitly prizing their genuine humanity while uncovering and criticizing its persistent violation in sexism, itself an omnipresent paradigm of unjust relationships. In terms of Christian doctrine, this perspective claims the fullness of the religious heritage for women precisely as human, in their own right and independent from personal identification with men.[42]

My own perspective draws on what I consider to be two essential (although not exhaustive) dimensions of the Christian tradition: the incarnation and the Christian community. Put in more traditional theological language, the first includes the christological affirmation that God has come among humanity in fully human form, that all creation is graced, that God is mysteriously present in all things. The second has to do with the way we live with others, as modeled by Jesus: that all are God's children, especially the least among us; that we are called to love and to live in justice, mutuality, and peace. In both of these dimensions, the radical potential for affirming the full humanity and the contributions of women as well as men has gone unfulfilled, with grave consequences for understanding human sexuality as well as all of human life.

In the history of Christian theology of the incarnation, it is unfortunate that the virginity of Mary and Jesus' virginal conception have been given the kind of emphasis they have. Mary's obedience and receptivity to God's message and her purity both before and after the birth of Jesus have suggested that women's role is to be the vessel of the will of God: "Let it be done unto me according to your word." What has not been remembered is Mary's active participation in the incarnation: the discomfort of pregnancy, the pain of labor, the energy and intelligence required in raising a child. Who could better say in relation to Jesus, "This is my body; this is my blood?"[43] The fact that virginity is less a statement about the body than about the power of God is largely ignored in the tradition.

If anything, the incarnation is about "beauty of body," to use Robert Penn Warren's felicitous phrase.[44] God has come to dwell among us, in our flesh and blood, in our desires and joys. All that is created, including our sexuality, is good and is to be delighted in. But Christians have tended to see the body, and certainly sexuality, as obstacles to be overcome on the way to eternal life. To be sexual in the service of future generations is permissible, but intercourse for mutual pleasure and joy, masturbation, homosexual love are inherently evil because they are not oriented to procreation.

The folly of this view becomes evident when we look at the perspective of women's physical experiences. While the potential for future life is present in every man's ejaculation, a woman ovulates but once a (usually monthly) cycle. The Roman Catholic teaching that permits "natural" forms of birth control neither takes into account the hormonal fluctuations that affect women's sexual desires nor that women's ovulatory cycles fluctuate widely, making reliable "natural" contraception extremely difficult. Or take the issue of masturbation— almost always discussed in terms of male experience. Unlike the penis, the clitoris has one function only: exquisite female sexual pleasure. It is not at all connected with procreation. To say that learning about and delighting in one's body through self-stimulation is inherently sinful suggests that physical pleasure for its own sake is evil. Is this the message of the incarnation? Episcopal feminist theologian Carter Heyward suggests that to think one must justify sexual pleasure is to misunderstand profoundly the erotic power of God. "We do not need to justify pleasure. Let us rather have to justify pain . . . "[45]

The second of the characteristics basic to the Christian tradition is that we are called to live in community—a community of justice. It is necessary to emphasize our communal nature and calling to put the sexual body in its proper context. Human beings do not live in isolation: we require human contact to survive, let alone thrive. And is it here that the renewed emphasis on the beauty and joy of our sexuality, found in flawed ways in the "sexual revolution" of the late twentieth century, needs to be balanced by our communal calling.

One of the most helpful contributions of feminist ethics has been its reminder that we do not emerge from the womb as full-blown "rational men." This is something that women are likely to remember better than men, since it is largely women who raise both women and men.[46] Human relationships are to some extent voluntary, as the mainstream ethical tradition holds, but our first relationships are not. We learn how to be in relationship from parents and siblings. This relational context is where we must locate the delight and joy—and also the frustration and pain—of our sexuality. In a Christian context, this relational nexus has further implications. It means that we are called to live in relationships of justice and mutuality and to have special care for the least among us—poor women and children. Christians are called to spread the good word of God's "extravagant affections" to all and through all. God's power comes alive in the dynamic of mutual relation.

A feminist Christian theology of sexuality is thus critical of elements both within the Christian tradition and within secular, including feminist, culture. In relation to Christianity, this theology critiques the male- and act-centered focus on sexuality that often fails to consider the relational context. This theology would thus judge sexual expression in heterosexual relationships both inside and outside of marriage and homosexual relationships in terms of the commitment and fidelity of the partners. This entails the very concrete dimensions of these relationships and their potential for future life. By the same token, this theology would look with concern upon secular culture's (and frequently also the feminist) emphasis upon rights, autonomy, and control because of the communal context in which all human beings live.

Let me make this more explicit in terms of particular issues in sexual ethics: abortion and reproductive technology. Abortion is surely one of the most neuralgic issues in both public and parochial debate. The Roman Catholic church's position is that all direct abortion is evil. But the church's position focuses on the particular act itself, outside of the context in which painful moral decisions must be made. Unlike the question of whether or not it is just to go to war (which always involves killing), where a pluralism of moral discourse has been the norm in the Christian tradition,[47] there is no pluralism in regard to abortion, and in fact little discussion at all of the contexts in which unplanned pregnancies take place. The church's position simply does not consider women's own experiences as a valid source of moral decision making.[48] Indeed, one wonders whether the church trusts women's capacity to make moral decisions. Not coincidentally, war is an issue that is almost always decided by men.

But this is not to suggest that secular feminism has all of the answers, either. The focus on "my body, my choice" emphasized so strongly by prochoice feminists is surely a necessary correction of long-standing laws and practices that regard women's bodies as male property. But is it really only "my" body? and only "my" choice? Are our bodies our own singular possessions, to be guarded as carefully as our homes, cars, computers? For Christian feminists, the fact that we are part of a moral community of mutual responsibility means that, to some extent, our bodies and choices are also the community's bodies and choices. But this mutual "ownership" cannot be maintained unless there is an intrinsic sense of the sacrality of all bodies and the integrity of each person's relationship to her own body. Sadly, we are far from this point. This does not mean, in my view, that some abortion decisions cannot be morally justified. But it is unfortunate

that the emphasis on autonomy and control so characteristic of contemporary American culture, and so unquestioned by at least some
feminist moral theorists, has become so central to the issue of reproductive "choice."[49] The language of mutuality and responsibility to
the other, so central in much feminist discussion of ethics, seems to
disappear in this discussion. A fully adequate sexual morality, from a
feminist Christian perspective, must be accountable to person and
community.

The feminist literature on women and sexuality rightly celebrates
its positive and graced dimensions; to speak of women's sin and
sexuality risks losing this needed emphasis. But it is important to
recognize the ambiguity of sexuality for women as well as men. While
Augustine's focus on uncontrollable desire may not be as historically
or psychologically relevant for women as well as men, *dishonesty*
might be an appropriate category for women's "sexual sin." In part
because women have lacked or been afraid to use a voice, women
have failed to communicate sexual needs and desires, have given
"double messages," have "faked" sexual responses. Much of this
dishonesty may result from being in a context where honest communication is difficult. But women's sexual dishonesty is not always the
result of victimization or lack of voice. Feminist theologians need to
exercise careful discernment of the potential for grace and for sin in
all human action. While sexuality may have unjustly borne the brunt
of sin, a feminist analysis ought not to exempt it from all potential for
sin.

In relation to the issue of "the right to choose," Lisa Sowle Cahill
has been critical of the use of reproductive technologies that suggest
that all of us have the "right" to have a child.[50] Along similar lines,
the moral issue of reproductive technology ought not to revolve solely
around the right of partners to make their own decisions, as the 1987
Vatican statement warns.[51] Other questions, such as who pays and,
in some cases, who bears and rears the child need to be answered in
the light of the Christian tradition's focus on mutuality and community.[52]

A feminist Christian theology recognizes that women are fully
human moral agents and therefore are responsible for their moral
decision making.[53] But what is an agent? Who is a person? In her book
Moral Boundaries, Joan C. Tronto discusses "changing assumptions
about humans" and notes that "humans are not fully autonomous,
but always must be understood in a condition of interdependence."[54]
That is, human autonomy is never absolute. The autonomy we have,
Tronto reminds us, is something that is achieved only through a long
period of dependence (largely upon women).[55] Moral decision making is done within this context of autonomy-interdependence, and in
the Roman Catholic tradition, women's autonomy is rarely considered seriously.[56] It is worth pondering that when Milwaukee Arch-

bishop Rembert Weakland sought simply to listen to the voices of women on the subject of abortion, he suffered attacks from both right-wing Catholics and the Vatican.[57]

In both secular consumer culture and church culture, the bodies of women have been problematic. Rarely if ever is a woman's body simply her body. Whether intended or not, a woman's body—especially a naked one—symbolizes sexuality. Consider the furor over Edwina Sandys' sculpture "Christa," which portrayed a naked crucified woman. While some argued that it was "theologically indefensible," others (including some feminists) argued that women's bodies are inevitably sex objects and that this sculpture perpetuated that perception.[58] Within the ecclesial context, women's embodiment has rendered women unfit for ordination and, in some cases, even for communion.[59] Women's bodies are considered "property," and the woman who ignores this does so at her own peril.

The violence that has been and continues to be perpetuated against women and children is tied to this understanding of women's (and children's) bodies as property. Secular culture supports this view by looking at all bodies as forms of property—both as abstracted from the moral life, as Cahill points out, and as instruments to be used determined by one's "personal choice." Church culture supports this view by overly identifying women with the bodily and by understanding men as "protectors," if not "owners," of women, as well as by its suspicion of sexual pleasure. As long as women are seen to comprise a different "psycho-symbolic" ontology than men,[60] women will be treated as less than fully human.

There is a connection between the refusal or failure to see women as fully human, as fully moral subjects, and violence toward women. As long as women cannot be seen by others as "the body of Christ," the message is that women are lesser than men and deserve to be treated as lesser than men. Christian social ethics, therefore, needs to be far more attentive than ever to the ways in which we care for an embodied community. The Roman Catholic natural law tradition, which has maintained a close tie between ethics and the body, has in my view failed to recognize that this tie takes place in a social context that does not view the body neutrally. This tie can only be maintained, at a far higher cost to women than men, within a theology that sees nature and the body "objectively" but is in fact a position defined from a male perspective. The Roman Catholic emphasis on objectivity is defective in that it has failed to take into account all of the data from human experience by systematically excluding the voices (and bodies) of women.

Sexuality is the avenue to deep and powerful feelings, to great joy. It can also be a deadly weapon. My intent in this chapter has been to suggest how feminist perspectives on sexuality can enhance joy, mutuality, and responsibility in human life. There is, of course, much more to be said on many issues. Further discussion is needed of the grace-filled dimensions of intentional procreation in a context of mutual love, of the capacity for sin in sexuality, of the need for changes in social policy. But in our present situation, aided by the critical perspectives of feminism as well as by the Catholic incarnational/sacramental reverence for the physical world, we can learn to cherish and delight in our extravagant affections, lavishing the love of God on ourselves and our communities.

NOTES

Epigraphs: Mary Gordon, *Final Payments* (New York: Random House, 1978), pp. 288-89; Etty Hillesum, *An Interrupted Life. The Diaries of Etty Hillesum 1941-43* (New York: Washington Square Press, 1981), p. 34.

I am grateful to William P. George and Cristina L. Traina for their careful and critical reading of earlier drafts of this essay and for their many helpful suggestions.

1. Quoted in Elizabeth Clark and Herbert Richardson, eds., *Women and Religion: A Feminist Sourcebook of Christian Thought* (New York: Harper and Row, 1977); see also Mary Daly, *Gyn/Ecology: The Metaethics of Radical Feminism* (Boston: Beacon Press, 1977).

2. Thomas Aquinas, *Summa Theologiae,* III (Supp.), Q. 39, a. 1

3. Carol Christ, "Spiritual Quest and Women's Experience," *Womanspirit Rising: A Feminist Reader in Religion* (San Francisco: Harper and Row, 1979), p. 228.

4. I am deliberately using the loaded language of "subjectivity" in this essay, well aware of the postmodern perils to which I open myself. In my view, it is essential, especially in dealing with sexuality, to argue for women's agency and selfhood.

5. See Elizabeth V. Spelman, *Inessential Woman: Problems of Exclusion in Feminist Thought* (Boston: Beacon Press, 1988); and Cherrie Moraga and Gloria Anzaldua, eds., *This Bridge Called My Back: Writings by Radical Women of Color* (New York: Kitchen Table, 1983).

6. See Jane Roland Martin, "Methodological Essentialism, False Difference, and Other Dangerous Traps," *Signs* 19 (Spring 1994): 630-57.

7. Christine E. Gudorf, "Sexuality and the Family," *Second Opinion* 10 (March 1989): 32.

8. For two feminist philosophical observations on this point, see Susan Bordo, *Unbearable Weight: Feminism, Western Culture, and the Body* (Berkeley: University of California Press, 1993); and Iris Marion Young, *Throwing Like a Girl and Other Essays in Feminist Philosophy and Social Theory* (Bloomington, IN: Indiana University Press, 1990), especially "Women Recovering Our Clothes."

9. Lisa Sowle Cahill, *Women and Sexuality* (1992 Madaleva Lecture in Spirituality) (New York: Paulist Press, 1992), p. 3.

10. Ibid.

11. On rape and property: Deut. 22:28-29; on virginity at marriage, Deut. 22: 20-21.

12. See Blu Greenberg, *On Women and Judaism: A View from Tradition* (Philadelphia: Jewish Publication Society of America, 1981).

13. See Leonard Swidler, "Jesus Was a Feminist," *Catholic World* (January 1971): 177-83, for one of the earliest articles. Swidler's position has been criticized for the implicit anti-Judaism suggested in the essay. Amid the vast literature on women and the New Testament, see Elisabeth Schüssler Fiorenza, *In Memory of Her: A Feminist Theological Reconstruction of Christian Origins* (New York: Crossroad, 1983).

14. See Tertullian, "On the Dress of Women," I, 1, 2, quoted in Elizabeth Clark, ed., *Women in the Early Church* (Wilmington, DE: Michael Glazier, 1983), p. 39.

15. Augustine, *City of God,* Book XIV, Ch. 26.

16. See, for example, John Mahoney, *The Making of Moral Theology: A Study of the Roman Catholic Tradition* (Oxford: Clarendon Paperbacks, 1987), p. 66: "Lacking, of course, from Augustine's introspective make-up was any positive appreciation of women, and he seems to have considered them as little more than sex objects." See also Felisa Elizondo, "Violence Against Women: Strategies of Resistance and Sources of Healing in Christianity," in Elisabeth Schüssler Fiorenza and Mary Shawn Copeland, eds., *Violence Against Women, Concilium* 1994/1 (London and Maryknoll, NY: SCM Press and Orbis Books, 1994), p. 101, where she discusses Augustine's admiration of his mother's unquestioning acceptance of his father's infidelity.

17. See Sidney Callahan, "Abortion and the Feminist Agenda: A Case for Pro-Life Feminism," in Patricia Beattie Jung and Thomas A. Shannon, eds., *Abortion and Catholicism: The American Debate* (New York: Crossroad, 1988), pp. 128-40, for a discussion of women's experience of sexuality as well as a discussion of abortion.

18. Thomas Aquinas, *Summa Theologiae,* I, q. 98, a. 2, repl. obj. 3.

19. Ibid., q. 92, a. 1.

20. Martin Luther, "The Estate of Marriage," and "Lectures on Genesis," quoted in Clark and Richardson, pp. 131-48.

21. See Nancy F. Cott, *The Bonds of Womanhood: "Women's Sphere" in New England, 1780-1835* (New Haven, CN: Yale University Press, 1977).

22. For a study of literature that sees women in both of these characterizations, see my "The Bride of Christ and the Body Politic: Body and Gender in Pre-Vatican II Marriage Theology," *Journal of Religion* 71 (July 1991): 345-61.

23. See Sigmund Freud, "Some Psychical Consequences of the Anatomical Distinction Between the Two Sexes," in *Standard Edition,* Vol. XIX, pp. 248-258; also "Female Sexuality," ibid., Vol. XXI, pp. 225-43, trans. James Strachey (London: Hogarth Press, 1961).

24. *Humanae vitae,* par. 17. I agree with Pope Paul VI that it is entirely possible that the use of contraceptives *may* contribute to a loss of respect for women, but so do many other things. What Pope Paul VI does not consider is the effect on a *woman's* sexuality if she does not have to worry about a pregnancy. A fear of pregnancy is seen by Pope John Paul II as "selfish, irrational, and unnatural" (John Paul II, *Love and Responsibility,* trans. H. T. Willetts [New York: Farrar, Straus, and Giroux, 1981], p. 280). I am indebted to Cristina Traina for pointing this out. See her "Oh, Susanna: John Paul II's Theology of the Body Confronts the Catholic Moral Theological Tradition," Midwest AAR Meeting, April 10, 1994.

25. Boston Women's Health Book Collective, *Our Bodies, Ourselves* (New York: Simon and Schuster, 1973).

26. Christine E. Gudorf, "Embodying Morality," *Conscience* XIV/4 (Winter 1993/94), pp. 16-21: "every person has a right to control her or his own body," (16).

27. See Bordo, *Unbearable Weight* (n. 8 above), for extensive discussion of this.

28. Delores S. Williams, *Sisters in the Wilderness: The Challenge of Womanist God-Talk* (Maryknoll, NY: Orbis Books, 1993), esp. pp. 60ff.

29. Audre Lorde, "The Uses of the Erotic: The Erotic as Power," in *Sister Outsider: Essays and Speeches* (Trumansburg, NY: Crossing Press, 1984), pp. 53-59.

30. See also Carter Heyward, *Touching Our Strength: The Erotic as Power and the Love of God* (San Francisco: HarperCollins, 1989) and Rita Nakashima Brock, *Journeys by Heart: A Christology of Erotic Power* (New York: Crossroad, 1989).

31. One such attempt is Mary D. Pellauer, "The Moral Significance of Female Orgasm: Toward Sexual Ethics That Celebrates Women's Sexuality," *Journal of Feminist Studies in Religion* 9, Nos. 1-2 (Spring-Fall 1993), pp. 161-82.

32. See Arleen Dallery, "The Politics of Writing (the) Body: *Écriture Féminine*," in Alison M. Jaggar and Susan R. Bordo, eds., *Gender/Body/Knowledge: Feminist Reconstructions of Being and Knowing* (New Brunswick, NJ: Rutgers University Press, 1989), pp. 52-67.

33. During the time I wrote this chapter, I saw a film (*Sirens*) that seemed to express what Irigaray and others mean by the *jouissance* that characterizes women's sexuality.

34. Carol Gilligan, *In a Different Voice: Psychological Theory and Women's Development* (Cambridge, MA: Harvard University Press, 1982).

35. Mary E. Hunt, *Fierce Tenderness: A Feminist Theology of Friendship* (New York: Crossroad, 1991).

36. See Carter Heyward, "Sexuality, Love, and Justice," in Judith Plaskow and Carol P. Christ, eds., *Weaving the Visions: New Patterns in Feminist Spirituality* (San Francisco: Harper and Row, 1989), pp. 293-301.

37. Sherry Ortner, "Is Female to Male as Nature Is to Culture?," in Michelle Zimbalist Rosaldo and Louise Lamphere, eds., *Woman, Culture and Society* (Stanford: Stanford University Press, 1974), pp. 67-87.

38. See Carol J. Adams, ed., *Ecofeminism and the Sacred* (New York: Crossroad, 1993).

39. Most recently, see Catharine MacKinnon, *Only Words* (Cambridge, MA: Harvard University Press, 1993).

40. For a thorough (and chilling) summation of this situation, see Elisabeth Schüssler Fiorenza, "Introduction," Schüssler Fiorenza and Copeland, pp. vii-xxiv.

41. See Joanne Carlson Brown and Carol R. Bohn, eds., *Christianity, Patriarchy, and Abuse: A Feminist Critique* (New York: Pilgrim Press, 1989).

42. Elizabeth A. Johnson, *She Who Is: The Mystery of God in Feminist Theological Discourse* (New York: Crossroad, 1992), p. 8.

43. Frances Croake Frank, unpublished poem.

44. Robert Penn Warren, "Auto-da-Fe," *The New Yorker* (December 31, 1979), p. 28.

45. Heyward, p. 47.

46. Both Virginia Held, *Feminist Morality: Transforming Culture, Society and Politics* (Chicago: University of Chicago Press, 1993) and Joan Tronto, *Moral Boundaries: A Political Argument for an Ethics of Care* (New York: Routledge, 1993) make this point central to their arguments. Sara Ruddick, *Maternal Thinking: Toward a Politics of Peace* (Boston: Beacon, 1989), was one of the first to make this a central point.

47. I am indebted to William George for his reflections on this point. See his "War and Other Issues," lecture given at St. Joseph College, Renssalaer, IN, March 1994.

48. See Christine E. Gudorf, "To Make a Seamless Garment, Use a Single Piece of Cloth: The Abortion Debate," in Beverly W. Harrison and Robert L. Stivers, eds., *The Public Vocation of Christian Ethics* (New York: The Pilgrim Press, 1986), pp. 271-86.

49. See Sidney Callahan, "Abortion," n. 17 above.

50. See Cahill, pp. 76-79.

51. Congregation for the Doctrine of the Faith, *Instruction on Respect for Human Life in Its Origin and on the Dignity of Procreation: Replies to Certain Questions of the Day*, Feb. 22, 1987.

52. See Delores Williams, *Sisters*, pp. 60ff.

53. Beverly Wildung Harrison, *Our Right to Choose: Toward a New Ethic of Abortion* (Boston: Beacon, 1983).

54. Tronto, *Moral Boundaries*, p. 162.

55. Ibid., p. 163.

56. It is worthwhile considering the enormous amount of literature in Roman Catholic moral theology that dealt with questions such as ectopic pregnancies, etc., that failed ever to mention the mother's own voice.

57. An honorary degree was to have been bestowed upon Weakland, but under pressure from the Vatican, this was withdrawn.

58. See *The New York Times*, April 28, 1984, I:27; also see Susan B. Thistlethwaite, *Sex, Race and God: Christian Feminism in Black and White* (New York: Crossroad, 1989), p. 93. Thistlethwaite comments here that her original reaction to the sculpture was negative, but that she later revised her view.

59. In some Orthodox churches, my students tell me that menstruating women are not to receive the Eucharist.

60. See Rosemary Radford Ruether, "Women's Difference and Equal Rights in the Church," in *The Special Nature of Women?*, Concilium 1991/6, ed. Anne Carr and Elisabeth Schüssler Fiorenza (London and Philadelphia: SCM Press and Trinity Press, 1991), p. 13.

7

Strategies for Life

Learning from Feminist Psychology

Ann O'Hara Graff

Understanding who we are requires cultural, social, historical, psychological, and theological analysis—and no doubt more. The sheer complexity of human experience requires multiple forms of exploration. This essay offers one account of the value of recent feminist psychological work, contextualized by awareness of cultural and social location, for the theological project of understanding ourselves. This project is a way to participate in human healing and whole-making, because theology informs the religious dynamism toward this vision and practice.

It is good to recognize that while feminist research and practice in the psychological arena is relatively new, there is already too much excellent material to draw from in so brief an exploration as this one. Therefore, I have chosen to work first with material from the Stone Center for Developmental Services and Studies at Wellesley College, especially associated with the name of Jean Baker Miller and her collegues, who have been developing a theory of self-in-relation.[1] Their studies have been going on in a collaborative conversation since 1982. The theoretical work is continually generated in relation to practice, and has become nuanced and multidimensional. This group has also been in conversation with Carol Gilligan and her teams of collegues at Harvard. I will draw on their longitudinal studies with culturally homogeneous and culturally diverse adolescent girls in the United States, which have traced the journey from girlhood to womanhood.[2] This work qualifies the self-in-relation theory as it reports the effects of growing up in patriarchy.

Moreover, because we human beings are always located in social and cultural systems—and within those, family systems—I have also chosen to attend to some recent work in these areas. Some of the associates of the Stone Center have engaged the concerns of race and class, and two of my students, Franca Onyibor from Nigeria and Dabula Mpako from South Africa, have explored psychotherapy among people in colonized cultures. In family therapy, there are new contributions from the Women's Institute for Life Studies in Houston, Texas, founded by Thelma Jean Goodrich, Cheryl Rampage, Barbara Ellman, and Kris Halstead.[3] Finally, I will explore the issue of trauma and its impact on the self-in-relation. These sources will be my major conversation partners for theological reflection on being human in the embrace of God.

THE SELF-IN-RELATION

I will begin with the Stone Center's model of women as selves-in-relation. While this model draws particularly on the experiences of white middle-class women, it is currently being explored by and with women of color, notably blacks and Latinas. Moreover, it may also indicate a pattern pertinent to the experience of many men. Janet Surrey suggests that fundamental to this model is the notion that "the self is organized and developed in the context of important relationships."[4] This is both primary to the self and a continuous way of growing. As distinct from models that emphasize autonomy and separation, this model underscores that relationship remains an important goal of the self throughout life. Thus the model expects growth to entail a "deepening capacity for relationship and relational competence" and that other qualities of the self such as autonomy or creativity develop within this relational context.[5] The use of the term *self-in-relation* is an attempt to name identity in the fluid context of ongoing growth in and through relational development.

It may be helpful to pause over the definition of relationship. Surrey states:

> By relationship I mean an experience of emotional and cognitive *intersubjectivity:* the ongoing, intrinsic inner awareness and responsiveness to the continuous existence of the other or others and the expectation of mutuality in this regard.[6]

> The self creates herself both by internalizing and interacting with the significant people in her life. Creation of self and relationship are simultaneous. This is not loss of self in the other; rather it entails the ability to identify and care beyond the limits of a separated self, while maintaining clarity about self and other in the connection.[7]

Key to this model of understanding the self-in-relation is the notion of mutuality, especially as exemplified by empathy. Empathy is a complex affective and cognitive behavior we teach to and learn from one another so that we are able to feel with another while remaining clear about the distinct experiences of the self and the other involved.[8] Healthy daughters and mothers interact from the child's infancy forward in such a way that feeling is mirrored and shared, fostering connection. As the child develops, her capacity for mutual empathy grows in the context of an emotional matrix of connections. This can eventually lead to a mutual empowerment of self and other in the context of support, challenge, conflict resolution, and ongoing care. Thus the child's relational capacity can grow and deepen throughout her lifespan, as can that of the mother and other significant persons in the child's life.[9]

In brief, the model suggests that the self is organized and develops as self-in-relation, and that these essential relations are nutured through empathic mutuality. Thus we are selves who extend ourselves toward others as genuinely different and valuable, and who are open to the other, receptive to, without merging with the other.[10] I have outlined this first because it can function as a fundamental referent for healthy development among the emerging insights of contemporary feminist psychology. From this vantage, the layered complications may be more easily engaged.

QUALIFICATIONS OF THE SELF-IN-RELATION MODEL

The psychologists who participate in the conversation at the Stone Center are grappling with some of the ways in which the quality of this relationality is impacted and made more complex. Others doing feminist psychology also afford insight into this process. As indicated at the outset, there are several studies I will include in what follows: the process of girls' development as self-silencing and disconnection as indicated by the research of Carol Gilligan and her collegues; the fact of cultural diversity, and particularly the problems posed to empathy in a racist and classist culture; the dynamics of gender and power in family systems; the incursion of trauma, especially through violence and abuse in women's lives. The first of these offers insight into the enormous accommodation to patriarchy at the heart of girls' development into women. The second names the fissures that divide and set us against one another as oppressor and oppressed. The third finds these at work in the intimacy of our families. The last is the extension of the systemic violence of the first three into brutal personal abuse.

Thus the harmonious development of empathic selves-in-relation outlined by Surrey provides a narrative model that may tell some, and the best, of the truth of our connected lives. However, what follows will begin to account for the distortion, defilement, and destruction of relation that theologians rightly call sin. Yet this is not to undo the insight into the primordial dance of relations in which we weave and interweave ourselves. The research indicates that building relations is like a fugue in women's lives. It proceeds despite the distortions of patriarchy, the complexities of difference, the losses due to violence and diminishment. And in each delineation of harm, there is also a charting of paths toward healing, not only for women, but for all of us in relation to one anther, whatever sex, class, race, or nation.

THE CHALLENGE OF RESEARCH ON GIRLS' DEVELOPMENT

Carol Gilligan and teams of women and some men working through Harvard, among them Nona Lyons, Trudy Hanmer, Annie Rogers, Normi Noel, Lyn Mikel Brown, and Deborah Tolman, have been studying the development of girls from childhood through adolescence toward womanhood. This research has entailed two major longitudinal studies with girls from ages 7 through 17 at the Emma Willard School and the Laurel School, as well as sustained research in a variety of schools in the Boston area, including ethnically diverse public schools.

At the core of their findings is the phenomenon of girls giving up clear relationship with themselves and others based on what they know of feelings and interactions in favor of "relationships" maintained by being nice and silencing what they know and feel. Their work documents the steady loss of connection to self and other through a process of self-silencing, shaped by our patriarchal culture, which gradually causes a diminution of authentic voice in order to accommodate oneself to the needs and feelings of others, especially men.[11] The self-silencing is so complete that many women do not even remember that it occurred and no longer know what they feel clearly or why they do not or cannot speak what they feel or what they see around them. A fine-tuned relational acuity, so clear in girls in middle childhood, erodes through adolescence until it is worn away into being the perfect young woman.

Interestingly, this pattern is persistently present in white girls/women and Latinas (Gilligan notes the onset of this change is slightly further into adolescence and more precipitous), but it is less the case for blacks, who may incur problems with institutional systems rather than lose their own voices.[12] Gilligan and Brown speculate that this may be because some girls who live on the margin, constantly aware of difference, maintain an acute ear for false relationship and resist staunchly. They may also continue the struggle for both gender and racial identity painfully aware that they live in two worlds.[13]

At its core, the Harvard researchers demonstrate that adolescence poses a crisis in the development of many girls in which their authentic relational experience of self and others is fundamentally distorted. If health is found in the ability to stay in authentic relationships, then the demand of patriarchy that girls and women accommodate themselves to the care and feelings of others precipitates a severe relational loss that can result in psychological problems such as the high incidence of depression in women.[14] Moreover, this study indicates that healing work requires both the restoration of authentic relationship for women and the prevention of the loss of connection to self and other, especially for girls coming into adolescence. For all of us it means countering the seduction, indeed the violation, of the image of the perfect woman.[15]

Thus the research on the movement from girlhood to womanhood appears to entail a kind of loss that suggests there are monstrous pitfalls in growing as selves-in-relation. Acculturation to patriarchy presses upon girls the loss of authentic relation and the nuturing of "nice" relationships. The relational dynamic proceeds, but is severely undermined. Thus the deepening attunement to relation and growing relational capacity Surrey describes may be deflected or may detour through a wilderness only to be rediscovered and re-engaged as one matures. Yet the fact that the psychologists at the Stone Center are able to describe healing and health persistently as the practice of authentic relation (including in therapy), which Gilligan and her teams also affirm, indicates that the losses of adolescence, however profound, are not absolute. Our very turning and returning to seek real relationship to ourselves, others, and the world evinces this.

SELVES-IN-DIVERSITY

Jean Baker Miller has noted that women carry relation and the need for it in patriarchal society. But we carry it to our great cost, and then not without participation in the schemes of class and race that continue to do harm. The costs and harms are complicated. They intersect in this culture where embodiment and wealth are met and encoded in the institutionalized practices of patriarchy, racism, classism, ageism, homophobia, and the like. Thus what could be the enjoyment of diversity among us, through which we could learn from one another or simply play with one another, has become a source of suffering. If diversity might make relationships more interesting and complex, it now creates complicated barriers of conscious and unconscious pain. Exploring this pain yields insight into generations of harm done, especially by whites to blacks, Native Americans, and other people of color in this country. It uncovers the massive denial of white America about this ongoing history. It opens up to grief, anger, rage, and violence in whites and people of color living in this history. It emerges in feelings of superiority or inferiority that distort our sense of self, crippling our humanness. It demands redress and healing, and the price is high.

This is edged more deeply by intersecting this American narrative with the equally American prejudices that inform our class identities. These are shaped solely by wealth. Wealth provides status reinforced by powerful practices that keep some people in secured positions of relative luxury while others, who are blamed for their poverty, have been systemically restricted within that position. Social attitudes, even while laced with resentment, confirm that to have wealth is somehow to be a superior person, while to be poor is to be dirty, lazy, weak, and inferior. The attitudes are harsh; they are part of denying that we are bound up in systems larger than ourselves, for which we are nevertheless responsible.

While none of this is new, it needs to be repeated because it deeply affects relation on two levels. First, it makes even engaging in conversation, let alone forming bonds of trust or friendship, extraordinarily difficult.[16] While this functions privately and personally, it also puts at risk all of our efforts at institutionalized conversation, notably our educational processes and therapy. At the Harvard Medical School Conference of April 29-30, 1994, Robin Cook-Nobles, a black woman, and Cynthia Garcia Coll, a Latina, asked a mainly white audience of nearly 1,000 women, for the most part therapists and social workers, could we hold the anger and the pain of women of color? Perhaps some white women might also want to ask, can you acknowledge our grief that such suffering has and continues to exist? Authentic relation must acknowledge this pain and deal with the history, present practices, and consequences of racism and classism in this culture.

While this alone is difficult, it points up the deeper interaction between external social practices of sexism, racism, classism, homophobia, ageism and the like, and the psychological impact of these on people in a culture that engages these practices. Social and cultural practice cannot be separated from the shaping of human beings. The self-in-relation theory, named again by Cook-Nobles and Coll as self-in-diversity, indicates the impact of difference. But it can also thematize the effects of harm, analogous to the Gilligan research, in persons who internalize the demeaning, diminishing messages of racial and class inferiority. Thus a "colonized personality" is the result of social and cultural assault on the self, yielding grave damage, crippling a person's authentic relation to self, others, and his or her own heritage and culture.[17]

If we grow our very selves in and through and with relations to others, then we must recognize that we form ourselves in relation to the persons and institutions that carry the illnesses and "isms," the practices of diminishment we personally and socially embody. Such relations are as effective as those that carry and generate the strengths and creativity we live in our histories and cultures. Thus relation is not only qualified by social location, and thus diversity, but we experience growth and deepening connection—or diminishment and disconnection from self, others, and world—in the web of these located, embodied, human relations.

The formation of healthy identity in people who belong to groups oppressed and disvalued by the dominant culture links resistance to multiple forms of social rejection together with the formation of strong, positive, same-race relationships. It requires important disconnections and connections that function in behalf of a confident sense of a self who can develop the capacities to relate appropriately with persons of the same race/class/culture or with those of another.[18]

OBSERVATIONS ON THE FAMILY

We all also live in the intimate systems of our families. As Surrey, Jordan, Miller, et al., indicate, we grow as selves-in-relation first within our families. As the Harvard teams who have uncovered the silencing of women indicate, we learn to accommodate to patriarchy from those closest to us, which again entails our families. Family therapists attentive to the concerns of women are now making clear that while the movement to do the work of therapeutic healing not simply with individuals but with those in the intimate system of relation to which they belong is appropriate, it cannot be enough unless we factor in the dynamics of patriarchy in family systems.[19]

This relatively new area of family systems psychology has often treated the family as if the spouses were in equal relation to each other.[20] Feminists quickly recognize that in many marriages the social practice of gender relations dictates that men have far more real power in the marriage relation than women do. Most often the husband controls the family economically, although the wife may carry far more labor both outside and inside the home. His personal and sexual needs take priority over hers. Yet she is usually deemed responsible for the entire welfare of the marriage, and she is more severely sanctioned if something goes awry.

The typical roles of men and women are, of course, undergirded by social, legal, religious and cultural prescriptions. What Thelma Jean Goodrich, Cheryl Rampage, Kris Halstead and Barbara Ellman make clear is that gender roles and their attendant dissimilar power relations are embedded in the family. Here women's accommodation and male entitlement, to use language from the Stone Center,[21] are institutionalized in the core relationships in which we live.

The Huston family therapists go on to suggest treatment that responds to and disrupts the strategies that keep these systems intact. They also discuss how therapists can rename the dynamics of gender relations in the family and change the imbalance of power. What concerns me here is naming the fact that our most intimate life practice, living in a family, is the chief location for our socialization and maintenance in damaging gender roles that intrinsically rely on an unequal distribution of power. This power can be used against women, and is used this way. The ideology of the gender constructs that women internalize, as so aptly described in the Gilligan/Harvard research, clearly embedded in the processes of education, is learned, re-enforced and stabilized by the politics of intimate power in the family, which practices the norms and sanctions of the wider culture. Violence is merely the extension of this form of interested power.

TRAUMA

A third major qualifier of our experience of growing ourselves in relation to others is that of trauma. Feminist psychologists, notably Judith Herman, Mary Harvey, Jean Baker Miller, Irene Stiver, and Judith Jordan of the Stone Center, are steadily moving away from naming present symptoms as pathological, and toward under-standing the histories of violence and abuse, intensified by the per-missions of patriarchy, which deeply damage the lives of many people, especially women and children. The traumas of childhood physical and sexual abuse, of rape and battering at any age, and of verbal lashing, belittling, and ridicule cause crises about how to stay connected to the self and to others when disconnection is forced or necessitated as a strategy for survival. Both the Gilligan teams and the women connected to the Stone Center have identified resistance (Gilligan) and strategies of disconnection (Stone Center) as critical efforts to protect authentic relation to self and others when circum-stances assault such relation.

The effects of trauma wreak havoc in a child or woman's relational world and can radically divorce her from parts of her very self. While psychology has had labels for some of these effects (e.g., borderline personality, splitting, depression), what is at issue here is the damage to the relation to self, others, and world, and the questions about how to heal into authentic relations with oneself, others, and the larger world.

Judith Herman and Mary Harvey particularly have done extensive research on victims of trauma. While Herman's studies indicate that most victims of violence suffer similar forms of damage to relational networks of care, protection and meaning, she poignantly charac-terizes the situation of the abused child in a way that emphasizes this relational destruction.

In this climate of profoundly disrupted relationships the child faces a formidable developmental task. She must find a way to

form primary attachments to caretakers who are either dangerous or, from her perspective, negligent. She must find a way to
develop a sense of basic trust and safety with caretakers who are
untrustworthy and unsafe. She must develop a sense of self in
relation to others who are helpless, uncaring, or cruel. She must
develop a capacity for bodily self-regulation in an environment
in which her body is at the disposal of other's needs, as well as
a capacity for self-soothing in an environment without solace.
She must develop the capacity for initiative in an environment
which demands that she bring her will into complete conformity
with that of her abuser. And ultimately, she must develop a
capacity for intimacy out of an environment where all intimate
relationships are corrupt, and an identity out of an environment
which defines her as a whore and a slave.

   The abused child's existential task is equally formidable.
Though she perceives herself as abandoned to a power without
mercy, she must find a way to preserve hope and meaning. The
alternative is utter despair, something no child can bear. To
preserve her faith in her parents she must reject the first and
most obvious conclusion that something is terribly wrong with
them . . . All of the abused child's psychological adaptations
serve the fundmental purpose of preserving her primary attach-
ment to her parents in the face of daily evidence of their malice,
helplessness, or indifference.[22]

What Herman grapples with is the enormity of the disruption and
corruption of relations an abused child must cope with and still
engage the tasks of survival and construction of a self. This violated
child self-in-relation undertakes major defensive tasks of dissociation,
numbness, amnesia, splitting or fragmentation of the self, *precisely in
order to maintain relations* with parents/caretakers whom she desper-
ately needs and who also are doing her grave harm. The so-called
"dysfunctional" patterns of behavior that adult victim-survivors may
indeed experience as dysfunctional functioned positively to manage
survival and connection in impossible and destructive relations in
which the child had no options but to remain.

   The process of healing that Herman and her Stone Center colleagues have affirmed entails the establishment of safety, the engagement in the process of remembering and mourning, and eventually
an ability to reconnect with self and others in ordinary life.[23]

   A variety of safety issues are the necessary first effort of every
therapeutic engagement with victims of violence. Bodily and environmental safety are the primary needs of a victimized person, and they
are essential to any further therapeutic work dealing with the trauma.
Only when these are secured can therapy proceed, cautiously, and at
the client's own pace, into the terror of her experience.

This work is intended to gradually uncover the memories of experience and feeling so as to name and integrate what happened. Remembering (Mary Daly's re-membering), in all its dimensions and complexity, becomes a pathway toward healing. Remembering allows the possibility of bringing the terrible experiences into relation with others/another by telling the story. It allows for the self to know and name what happened more truthfully. It allows the critical process of grieving to take place. It allows the appropriate expression of rage. As these fundamental steps occur, compassion for oneself is possible, feeling opens through deadness and numbness, awareness of ordinary reality deepens. Moreover, dysfunctional defensive strategies may be discarded in favor of more appropriate, safe, mature connections and boundaries with others. Memory and mourning lead out of the terrors and tombs of the past into a reconnected and more hopeful future.

In the work of Herman and Harvey, as well as those who accompany them in this work, the Stone Center's model of self-in-relation takes on the impact of dramatic harm. For a primordially relational self who must fluidly be self-in-dynamic-relation to others, trauma is visible in relational damage. This is damage to the self and in the self, as a result of damage in the relational networks that involve that self. The model recognizes the symptoms of trauma as strategic disconnections for the sake of connection. Healing is about engaging in authentic relational connection in order to foster healthy reconnection to self, others, the world. Thus however awry the relational nexus, it remains the case that we function as selves-in-relation and need healing, or perhaps can only be healed, with that relational reality fully attended to.

THINKING THEOLOGICALLY

This all-too-brief overview of the self-in-relation model of women's human self-construction and some of the ways in which this living self is undercut and damaged precisely in relations, and (with the Harvard teams) for the sake of relationships, offers a rich source for theological reflection. There is a way in which it sketches the Garden of Eden, the losses of original sin, and the hope of redemption as healing and transformation for us all. The model may be interpreted in relation to a critical reading of the multivalent Christian mythos. I will offer some approaches to such a reading in what follows.

As with Eden, and accompanying biblical myths of creation, covenant, and God, the model is not about a primordial first moment but a primal, creative pattern in which we might grow ourselves into wholeness that is holiness. It is what is always possible and, in part, what we experience and are best nourished by. This fluid creation of self-in-relation offers a dynamic content to the theological symbol in

Genesis 1:27 of human beings created in the image and likeness of God.[24] As the Trinity is the event of the distinct persons who are God in full, continuous relation with one another—God as selves-in-relation—so we human beings are creating ourselves continually out of our ongoing relations, each of us structuring those relations uniquely to be our own dynamic self.[25] Catherine Keller, in her brilliant book *From a Broken Web,* formulated this with striking clarity, within the framework of process thought, in her depiction of the unique self emerging from the dynamic web of its relations.[26] Moreover, as we weave ourselves in relations, God is the very context, ground and possibility of those relations. We continually create ourselves, including this fundamental relatedness that is both our transcendental ground and the inmost thread, the core capacity, of our very being. This offers another way of thematizing our relation to God in whom we live and move and have our being, God in whom we dwell and who also dwells within us. On the basis of the analogical character of the *imago Dei,* this invites us to imagine God as included in our being/becoming and dynamically inclusive as Godself. As we grow in relation, including God primordially in our relatedness, so God as relational may be really related to us, gathering us into the life of the Divine Persons who are the Trinitarian community.[27]

Following this suggestion, our own growth in the deepening capacity for relation may also mirror God, who, as Charles Hartshorne suggests, may be the capacity for infinite relations.[28] Human beings are continually creating selves-in-communities, and God as Trinity appears as reasons in community, while both humanity and God, differently, but really, dwell in intercommunion.

Taking the thread of Surrey's exposition of the model, not only relational capacity, but relational competence may characterize the maturing self-in-relation. For human beings, such competence entails flexibility in the variety of relationships life offers, respectful of limits yet able to be appropriately present and intimate with others. This includes the ability to be faithful to the covenants of marriage and to vulnerable children who need responsible, trustworthy, kind parents. It also means attending to other commitments of varying importance.

Surely such competence, flexibility, respect and faithfulness, coupled with as much love and creativity as we can muster, constitute wholeness that is holiness in human beings. This wholeness/holiness models the competence of the biblical God, whose love is expressed in presence and the covenants of faithfulness in which God chooses to bind Godself with us.

While the self-in-relation model can offer an interpretative basis for theological understanding of both the human and the Divine, the psychology explored here further provides a language of loss and healing. Theologically it is a language of limit and transcendence. It is also a language of sin and grace, a language that might be cast in terms of redemption, or liberation, or transformation, or even escha-tology. It is at the same time a language of memory and hope, a language about a new creation. I will reflect on each of these in turn.

As a description of human experience, the self-in-relation model, and the qualifiers I have briefly explored, indicate the process of human growing into ourselves as one immediately limited by our particularity: this body, this family, this place, this time, these circum-stances. Yet as we grow in relation to what is given and to our ever-widening range of possibilities—including our ability to imag-ine and incorporate the new, the different—we are persistently able to transcend our starting points and so change ourselves and our interrelated world. Perhaps most remarkable is our ability to embrace the Wholly Other who in turn embraces us and chooses to dwell in us, the God who discloses Godself again and again in incarnation. In this meeting we encounter the sheer liveliness,[29] the love, the good-ness from which the cosmos and ourselves spring forth. Here is the practical, mystical center, the ground and guide of who and what we are. Thus limit engages transcendence doubly, both in our capacities to reach beyond our present self and in ongoing relation to our ground and horizon, God.

Beyond the sheer fact of limit, however, there is sin in what is, at the same time, a world of grace. The women collaborators at Harvard, in Huston, and at the Stone Center, differently but clearly reveal the effective practices of systemic sin and the distortion and damage done to human persons and systems (families, communities, institutions), and the earth itself,[30] because of its vitiation. The central form this takes is in the loss of authentic, creative relation to self and others.

Naming that as the fundamental loss, the practices of harm become visible, including their damaging ideologies, which are given physi-cal, emotional, and spiritual force in the oppressive ways people maintain and manipulate power in our ordinary lives. The extension of the systemic sinful damaging that is patriarchy, or racism, or other similar harms, toward the individual commission of violent acts is but a step, yet these actions are also the substance, the instance of the systematic sin. Whether the crime is rape or women violating other women, the core is the same: the systemic infection that vitiates relation to self and other is at work. Examples could be multiplied.

To specify this theological language, the systemic effectiveness of violence and oppression is original sin; the particular actions of individuals to do harm is personal sin. Clearly, the two interact. The myth of Eden suggests harmony in all relations is possible,[31] but in the world as we experience it, there is evil at work that is greater than ourselves, and in which we participate. Yet the responding Christian myth of cross and resurrection suggests that however profound the damage of evil, hope, creativity, life and love are greater. This is the mystery of sin and grace worked out in our personal and social lives.

However, there is more to learn of sin and grace in this. Sin acquires new names when seen in the guise of socially learned self-silencing and the accompanying loss of authentic relation to self and others. Or again, in it appear the reasons for the complicated struggle toward self-esteem and positive identity experienced by people of color in a racist society. Or again, it is visible in the inequities and abuse of patriarchal marriage. Grievously, it is at work in the horrors of abuse.

Mary Potter Engel and Mary Pellauer, in paired articles on sin and grace in *Lift Every Voice*,[32] indicate that abuse sin is the most blatant as the violation of covenant between parent or trusted other and the child. Here relational violence is at its worst, when the powerful, needed parent, in whom a vulnerable child must trust, violates her/him. Herman's categories that name the multiple dimensions of trauma, such as terror, captivity, isolation, and enslavement, also lend their names to sin.[33]

The processes of recovery of voice, of healing into authentic relations to self and other, of healing wounds of race and class oppression, of transforming patriarchal marriage and family relations, or of re-membering and healing from trauma and abuse, are all works of grace. The very research that offers these insights into self-under-standing is grace. Here knowing anew leads to renewal in our being and becoming. In each study, however powerful, we see the work of holy life and love, the powers of compassion and creativity, the practice of hope where damage and death have wounded.

This gracious human work might also rightly be called works of liberation, setting free the voice, the self, the hurt and captive person and communities to live well beyond the damage once inflicted. In many cases this is not only a setting free for the self to live authentically in right relations, a freedom for covenant and community in the broadest sense, but also some of these specific works of psychological healing are redemptive. For the woman who has lost herself in patriarchal relations or suffered abuse as a child, the fact of her survival and the possible work of therapy may be her redemption. In this work, while the scars of the past remain, that suffering and its attendant real losses are not the final word. Real change in who we are and how we live—as we live in different relationships and differently in relation—is truly possible. Therapeutic practices of healing in relationship can change and transform because they can help a person find safety, integrate terrible memories, bear grief and rage. These practices can support a person into a new way of life and a changed relational world. These are concrete acts of redemption, and their result is the liberation, indeed the transformation, of a person toward a more vital and authentic relational wholeness and growth.

One dynamic of psychology is that both client and therapist labor between memory and hope. Christians also live between memory and hope. For Christians the dangerous memory of suffering (to use

Metz's famous phrase), especially, but not only that of Jesus, is coupled with the hope for a future marked by radically egalitarian relationships borne in a community of followers of Christ who practice his vision of living genuine love and care for one another. This practice is supported by the memory of suffering as a "Never again!" that interrupts any easy alliance with the present and empowers its work for a different future.[34] A Christian practice of hope is exercised toward building a world of authentic relations, a world of covenant fulfilled in the attentive work of care that right relations to self, others, community, institutions and earth require. It is also a vision of utopia. Nevertheless, it provides an always prophetic framework for finding creative ways of living in the present, whatever our situation. The therapeutic works of re-membering the self-in-relation through a recovery of memory, of voice, of courage, and a support for self-esteem, authentic connections and hope, is a work of re-membering and transforming ourselves in community with one another. As a work of love in behalf of human beings, it is a holy work, and it can be a genuine practice of the gospel. Insofar as psychologists and others who engage the work of healing work in hope, both incremental and political-societal, this work is eschatological—it is an activity that resists sin in the present and energetically labors in behalf of a new world.

In sum, I hope that this brief essay has been able to sketch some of the key contributions in recent feminist psychology and indicate how they might provide a rich resource for theological anthropology—understanding ourselves in relation to ourselves and one another, and in and through these—in the embrace of God.

NOTES

1. This center has over 60 papers in their series, *Work in Progress,* 1982 to date. For recent key papers, see Judith V. Jordan et al., *Women's Growth in Connection* (New York: The Guilford Press, 1991).

2. Carol Gilligan, *In a Different Voice: Psychological Theory and Women's Development* (Cambridge, MA: Harvard University Press, 1982); idem, Janie Victoria Ward and Jill McLean Taylor, eds., *Mapping the Moral Domain: A Contribution of Women's Thinking to Psychological Theory and Education* (Cambridge, MA: Harvard University Press, 1988); idem, Nona P. Lyons and Trudy J. Hanmer, eds., *Making Connections: The Relational Worlds of Adolescent Girls at Emma Willard School* (Cambridge, MA: Harvard University Press, 1990); idem, Anne G. Rogers and Deborah L. Tolman, eds., *Women, Girls & Psychotherapy: Reframing Resistance* (Binghamton, NY: Harrington Park Press, 1991); idem, and Lynn Mikel Brown, *Meeting at the Crossroads: Women's Psychology and Girls' Development* (Cambridge, MA: Harvard University Press, 1992).

3. These women have coauthored *Feminist Family Therapy: A Casebook* (New York: W. W. Norton & Company, 1988). See also Goodrich, ed., *Women and Power: Perspectives for Family Therapy* (New York: W. W. Norton & Company, 1991).

4. "The Self-in-Relation: A Theory of Women's Development," in Jordan, et al., *Women's Growth*, p. 52.

5. Ibid., p. 53.

6. Ibid., p. 61.

7. Ibid., and Judith V. Jordan, "The Meaning of Mutuality," *Women's Growth*, pp. 81-96. See also Jordan's comment in Miller et al., "Some Misconceptions and Reconceptions of a Relational Approach," *Wellesley College, The Stone Center: Work in Progress* 49 (1991): 4.

8. Surrey, pp. 53-59; Jordan, "Empathy and Self-Boundaries," in Jordan, et al., *Women's Growth*, pp. 67-80.

9. Ibid., pp. 54-59, 63-66.

10. Jordan, "The Meaning of Mutuality," *Growth*, p. 82.

11. The initial insights about this surface in Lyons and Hanmer, eds., *Making Connections*, and it is carefully documented and developed in Brown, *Meeting at the Crossroads*.

12. Gilligan, *Reframing Resistance*, pp. 13-14; Tracy Robinson and Janie Victoria Ward, "'A Belief in Self Far Greater Than Anyone's Disbelief': Cultivating Resistance Among African American Female Adolescents," *Reframing*, p. 96.

13. Brown, *Meeting at the Crossroads*, pp. 226-27. See also Janie Victoria Ward, "Racial Identity Formation and Transformation," in Lyons and Hanmer, eds., *Making Connections*, pp. 215-32. This article indicates the strong role of the black family in analyzing racism in the encounters their children experience. This can be a critical resource for resistance. Further inquiry into Latina experience is being pursued by Cynthia Garcia Coll at the Stone Center.

14. Rogers and Tolman, eds., *Reframing*, esp. p. 23; Brown, *Crossroads*, esp. pp. 216-32.

15. See especially Annie Rogers, "A Feminist Poetics of Psychotherapy," in Rogers and Tolman, eds., *Reframing*, pp. 33-53; Brown and Gilligan, *Crossroads*, pp. 230-32.

16. See, for example, the letters of Carter Heyward and Katie Geneva Cannon in *God's Fierce Whimsy: Christian Feminism and Theological Education* (New York: The Pilgrim Press, 1985), pp. 35-59.

17. Debula Anthony Mpako, "Decolonizing the African Psyche: A Pastoral Counselor's Reflection" (M. A. thesis, Loyola University Chicago, 1994); Franca Onyibor, "Empower African Women: Toward a Generative Approach to Pastoral Counseling" (M. A. thesis, Loyola University Chicago, 1994).

18. Beverly Daniel Tatum, "Racial Identity, Development, and Relation Theory: The Case of Black Women in White Communities," *Work in Progress* 63 (Cambridge, MA: The Stone Center, 1993); Robinson and Ward, "A Belief in Self," and Ward, "Racial Identity Formation and Transformation," in Lyons and Hanmer, eds., *Making Connections*, pp. 215-32.

19. Goodrich, et al.

20. Here note the presumptive family is two parents, male and female, with children. The contemporary variations of the family unit call for further accounting.

21. See Deborah L. Tolman, "Adolescent Girls, Women and Sexuality: Discerning Dilemmas of Desire," in Rogers and Tolman, eds., *Reframing*, pp. 55-57.

22. Judith Lewis Herman, M.D., *Trauma and Recovery* (New York: Basic Books, 1992), pp. 103-104.

23. Herman, pp. 155-213. Also Judith Jordan, "Challenges to Connection: Traumatizing Society," and Jean Baker Miller and Irene Stiver, "The Therapy Connection: From Relational Theory to Practice," papers delivered at the conference, "Learning from Women," Harvard Medical School, Boston, April 29-30, 1994.

24. See the article by Mary Catherine Hilkert in this same volume for another way of developing this insight in terms of human relationality.

25. For a critical and constructive view of God as fully relational, see Elizabeth Johnson, *She Who Is: The Mystery of God in Feminist Discourse* (New York: Crossroad, 1992), esp. pp. 124-273.

26. Catherine Keller, *From a Broken Web: Separation, Sexism and Self* (Boston: Beacon Press, 1986), esp. pp. 115-215.

27. See Johnson for another formulation of this pattern of thought.

28. Charles Hartshorne, *The Divine Relativity: A Social Conception of God* (New Haven, CT: Yale University Press, 1948).

29. This is Elizabeth Johnson's term. See esp. pp. 236-43.

30. See Anne Clifford's article in this volume for ecological development of the relational theme.

31. Note, however, that Eden clearly embraces patriarchy and that systematic subordination and oppression are rejected here.

32. Engel, "Evil, Sin, and Violation of the Vulnerable," and Pellauer with Susan Thistlethwaite, "Conversation on Grace and Healing: Perspectives from the Movement to End Violence Against Women," in Thistlethwaite and Engel, eds., *Lift Every Voice: Constructing Christian Theologies from the Underside* (San Francisco: Harper & Row Publishers, 1990), pp. 152-64 and 169-85. Further reflection in this area is also available in Rita Nakashima Brock, *Journeys by Heart: A Christology of Erotic Powers* (New York: Crossroads, 1991), and in Joanne Carlson Brown and Carole R. Bohn, eds., *Christianity, Patriarchy, and Abuse: A Feminist Critique* (Cleveland: The Pilgrim Press, 1989).

33. For further reflection in these areas, see the article by Sallie McReynolds on sin in this volume.

34. Here I am bringing together the ubiquitous "Never again!" of Elie Wiesel as well as a key theme in Johan Baptist Metz, *Faith in History and Society: Toward a Practical Fundamental Theology* (New York: The Seabury Press, 1980).

8

For Women in Pain

A Feminist Theology of Suffering

Patricia L. Wismer

It is one thing to sit in the isolation of my study and weave together some wise-sounding words about suffering; it is quite another to address them directly to real-life women in pain. Suddenly, the ideas about which I had felt so confident seem like straw. Yet this is precisely the task of any theological reflection on suffering that claims to be both Christian and feminist. An adequate Christian theology of suffering must have this experiential relevance because the man whom Christians call the Christ developed and shared his thoughts, healing words, and actions with real-life women and men caught in the midst of suffering. Feminist theology, for its part, grows out of and speaks to the experiences of real-life women, women who come in all the shades and hues of humanity, women of all nationalities, ethnic groups, and social classes, women of all ages and physical capabilities, women who are feeling every emotion ranging from ecstacy to despair.

And so, in an attempt to be faithful to my task, I address and dedicate these reflections to a group of eight women. In focusing on women, my intention is not to exclude men, but merely to concentrate on some specific ways that suffering affects women. Many of these reflections may also be relevant to men's experiences. I invite men to make these connections and comparisons for themselves.

Each of these eight women has touched my life in some personal way. These women represent only a tiny fraction of women who have had, for one reason or another, suffering thrust upon them. Some of these women are simply enduring their suffering; some have responded by actively passing their suffering on to others; some are struggling to transform their suffering by growing through it or by working to create justice out of their oppression; one of these women is now dead. All of them will be our conversation partners in this attempt to develop a feminist theology of suffering. Their experiences will help us begin our reflection and be used as a reality-control throughout. If a theological position or its implication would function to increase their suffering, this counts heavily against it. Who, then, are these women in pain?

> Emily is the "good Christian" mother of a large family. Abused by her father when she was a child, she passes on her sexual, physical, and emotional abuse to her own children. She cannot understand why her grown children, now beginning to recover the long repressed, painful secret of the family and to move towards healing themselves, are angry.

> Amanda is an artist, the wife of a successful lawyer and the mother of two sons and an 18-month-old daughter—until one day the husband backed the car out of the driveway and ran over the daughter, killing her instantly.

> Kathleen is an alcoholic. In her mid-fifties, her second husband, also an alcoholic, commits suicide. Six months later she discovers she has cancer. Two years after this, unable to bear the pain and physical degeneration any longer, she takes pills to facilitate her death.

> Joanne is an elderly woman sitting in an expensive, well-run nursing home. She is comfortable, but her mental functioning is that of a small child, and her memory is gone. She cannot remember, for example, the abortion her then-fiancé, a physician, decided unilaterally to perform on her to keep her from "showing" at their wedding; she cannot remember the long-time affair her husband had with his office nurse; she cannot remember the abuse her husband committed on her children and grandchildren.

> Mary's very promising career as a ballet dancer was cut short by the flare up of a congenital skeletal abnormality. For years afterwards she wrestled with the suspicion, confirmed every-where she looked, even inside the Church, that she was "a mistake" that God made. Now Mary walks only slowly and painfully with crutches, but in her ministry with others who are also physically challenged, she is learning "to dance shoulder to shoulder with those who suffer."

An anonymous woman in Guatemala City stands at a traffic light begging. She holds up her infant daughter who is missing the lower part of one arm. The social worker who is driving me around the city rolls up her window angrily and says: "They do that to their own children, to get more money."

Lenore was raped by two young teenage boys when she was 8. She never told anyone else about the event until she was in her seventies. For the first fifteen years or so she felt too guilty. She knew she should confess her sin, but she felt too embarrassed. After that, there just didn't seem to be any point in talking about it. Lenore still cannot quite understand why she responds to everything that happens as if it were a catastrophe.

Elaine is a lesbian struggling to free herself from her own internalized heterosexism and to change the external heterosexism so deeply ingrained in Christianity and U.S. society. She and her lesbian spouse were married last fall in an official Protestant ceremony, yet she still sometimes feels uncomfortable when they walk down the street arm in arm.

Given the variety of causes of the suffering described here—social sin, moral evil, disease, accident, severe psychological damage—we might well ask what links these experiences together as suffering. Physician Eric Cassell provides a definition of suffering that points to a common thread. Suffering, he says, is "the state of severe distress associated with events that threaten the intactness of the person."[1] What renders an experience suffering, then, is the effect it has not just on one part of our being, but on our total centered self. Because this total self is composed of several interrelated aspects, I find it helpful to consider four main dimensions of suffering: physical pain, emotional trauma, social isolation, and spiritual crisis. The main locus of the suffering may vary in different instances. The four dimensions will play off one another in diverse combinations, but if the distress is indeed severe, there will usually be at least three dimensions represented in any given instance. This is the case with all eight of the women whose stories we have heard.

None of these women has been well-served by the traditional Christian theology of suffering. In fact, in each instance the traditional Christian response has actually contributed to her suffering, often adding a spiritual dimension where there would not otherwise have been one. Because of this, it is necessary to begin our reflections with a critique of some traditional Christian responses (both implicit and explicit) to suffering. This critique will serve as a reminder of all the pitfalls we must avoid in our reflection if we are not to make the last state of women in pain worse than the first. Given how thoroughly these destructive approaches have interpenetrated Christian theology, extending even to some of its central doctrines, this will be no easy task.

Following the critique, I will make some methodological suggestions for a feminist theology of suffering. The approach proposed here will be to work within the tension created by two opposing perspectives on suffering, both of which are well represented in feminist theology. These positions might be briefly described as the "suffering: never again" and the "suffering: part of the web of life" perspectives.

The final section of this paper will present some implications for central areas of theological anthropology that grow out of this feminist reflection on suffering. Five main topics will be treated: embodiment, relationality, virtues, sin, and grace.

Poets often have a genius for saying in few words what ordinary mortals (and that includes especially academics) can only faintly approximate after speaking volumes. In this instance, Adrienne Rich conveys in a couplet from her poem "Splittings" the essence of the approach to suffering I am advocating here.

> I believe I am choosing something new
> Not to suffer uselessly   yet still to feel.[2]

This message is what I would have each of the eight women in pain say to herself and to her world. This is why we must critique the traditional Christian responses in order to clear the way for this new mode. This is what the proposed feminist approach must allow to be said. And, finally, this is what a feminist theological anthropology must speak to all those who have ears to hear.

CRITIQUE OF TRADITIONAL CHRISTIAN RESPONSES TO SUFFERING

I divide these traditional Christian responses into two main groups: implicit and explicit. The implicit responses, which center in the doctrines of God and Christ, are in some ways the most problematic. Because of their foundational character, they lie close to the very heart of Christianity. The explicit responses that grow organically out of the implicit ones are closer to people's real-life experiences. They appear often in the form of pastoral advice to people caught in the grip of suffering. Tragically, the ways of responding they portray lead to destruction rather than to healthy, creative coping. Let us examine first the two implicit responses, beginning with the doctrine of God.

The theodicy problem has long been recognized as a perennial dilemma in Christian theology. How can we reconcile the existence of an omnipotent and all-good God with the existence of evil, especially evil in its most radical forms? This is not the place to rehearse once again the responses that have been made to this dilemma throughout Christian history. We can only say that none of them completely answers the question and that even taken all together, they still fail to satisfy. An omnipotent God who sends, allows, or permits suffering for whatever reason theologians can dream up (as a spur to growth, as a punishment for sin, as a test of our faith, as a means of redeeming others, as a way of increasing the fullness of life, etc.) still looks remarkably like a sadist if we take off our theological spectacles and see what is actually before our eyes.

This critique is not peculiar to feminist theology but has been voiced many times before. Most of these voices, however, stop their critique at this point. They would apparently be satisfied with an omnipotent God if he (male pronoun intended) could simply get his act together and reduce the suffering to more manageable proportions. Feminist theology, however, goes further. The existence of even such a benevolent autocrat cannot resolve the underlying problem whose ultimate source is the domination-submission relation between God and the world. This domination-submission relation creates two main problems. The first can be rather broadly stated in the following epigram: "as God goes, so goes the world." If God is the highest and holiest form of all life, then the (self-perceived) highest and holiest form of human life strives to emulate the divine mode of being. Therefore, the dominant will rule over everyone else.

The second problem comes down to this: what is given today can be taken away tomorrow. Women and other oppressed groups throughout history have repeated to the death the immortal words of Job: "The Lord gave; the Lord has taken away; blessed be the name of the Lord" (Job 1:21b). So, for feminists, the solution to the problem of God and suffering cannot emerge as long as God has any kind of power-over. The solution can only come through a different understanding of power, power exercised as empowerment, as power-with.

Another increasingly popular response to the theodicy problem comes from the opposite direction, in the idea of a Suffering God. In this view, God shares with humans precisely their lack of power, their weakness, their humiliation. Many feminists, myself among them, have adopted this notion of God as an extremely helpful counter to the Almighty Father God. The Suffering God does indeed provide comfort, companionship and perhaps hope to us in our afflictions, as well as actualizing in some credible way the meaning of God's goodness and love. Some feminists, however, are raising a further challenge to many versions of Suffering God theology. Exactly how, they ask, does God's suffering with us actually help eliminate, or at least mitigate, our suffering? The usual answer to this question leads into the areas of Christology, soteriology, and the doctrine of the atonement, which together constitute the second implicit response to suffering that needs to be explored here.

If Jesus' life-work and his significance are reduced to the cross, as often happens in popular piety (e.g., "God the Father sent his Son to suffer and die for our sins"), it is hard to avoid the conclusion that God the Father is not only a sadist but also a divine child abuser. But the problem extends far beyond popular piety. In their provocative article "For God So Loved the World?" Joanne Carlson Brown and Rebecca Parker present a radical critique not only of the three classical theories of the atonement, but also of many contemporary versions. It is impossible to do justice here to their detailed analysis of the problem with Christian soteriology. Their conclusion, however, is a simple one: "No one was saved by the death of Jesus."[3] The Resurrection too must be radically reinterpreted to avoid the appearance of a "happy ever after" ending coming in to reward the faithful sufferer.[4] Any less-than-radical reinterpretation is simply one more example of the justification of suffering that abounds in Christian theology and has been used so often to keep women locked in their pain, waiting for deliverance that never comes.

Brown and Parker conclude their study with the judgment that "Christianity is an abusive theology that glorifies suffering."[5] However, they leave open the question whether that is an essential component of its nature or whether Christianity's abusiveness can itself be redeemed. My own hope is that, since the cross as a historical event and a symbol is more primary and more multidimensional than any theory of the atonement, a theology of the cross can be worked out that does not, even implicitly, glorify suffering. I can imagine Christianity without the atonement; I cannot, however, imagine Christianity without its central symbol, the cross. The preceding discussion of the doctrines of God and Christ indicates that even aspects of Christian theology far removed from the blood, sweat, and tears of real-life people can create or reinforce destructive pastoral approaches to suffering. It is now time to consider five of these explicit responses.

Masochism is perhaps the most prevalent of all the destructive approaches perpetuated by Christianity. It is certainly the one to which women are most susceptible, because their socialization as well as their religious training supports it. Masochism is grounded in both the omnipotent, sadistic God and the faithfully suffering Christ discussed above. Masochism counsels turning the other cheek, patiently enduring whatever suffering comes one's way rather than taking action to eliminate the cause of suffering. All of our eight women in pain struggled, in one way or another, with masochism. The ones who eventually rejected it moved on to healing, at least a healing of psyche and spirit, if not also of body, e.g., Mary (the dancer) and Elaine (the

---

* Since we are dealing with so many women, I will refer to them both by name and a brief description. The description is not intended as a label, but rather as a brief way of recalling each woman's story.

lesbian). * The ones who remained in its clutches as "good Christian
women" found other ways to express their anger and despair, often
by directly causing or indirectly contributing to the suffering of
others, e.g., Emily (the abusive mother) and Joanne (the senile grandmother).

A related response involves the counseling of what I call cheap
forgiveness of the person who causes the suffering. Taught to follow
Jesus' teaching ("seventy times seven") and example from the cross
("Father, forgive them . . ."), women often move too quickly to
forgiveness before they even begin to experience their own anger. This
attempt to short-circuit the natural process of anger, however, is
doomed to failure. As psychologists remind us, no true forgiveness is
possible until one's anger is expressed; any attempt to short-circuit
the process produces only denial and repression. Emily (the abused
child/abusive mother), Joanne (the senile woman with the abusive
husband) and Lenore (the rape survivor) all fell into this destructive
pattern.

A third response is apathy. Apathy means, literally, "notsuffering."
It is the attempt (ultimately doomed to failure given the realities of
human existence) to escape from suffering. On the surface, apathy
appears to be more the result of our secular society's dream of "the
good life" and "the beautiful people" than of Christianity's influence.
Seeing the goodness, beauty, and success portrayed all around us in
advertisements, movies, magazines, television shows, etc., we feel we
must pretend that this is our reality too. In order to keep up the
illusion, we turn to alcohol, drugs, food, sex, compulsive consuming—anything to keep us away from our own experience of pain.
Kathleen (the woman with cancer) did this with her alcohol and, to
some extent perhaps, with her pills as she ended her life. Like cheap
forgiveness, apathy produces denial and repression of one's own
pain. Apathy also leads to "icy indifference" to the suffering of others.
And, because love inevitably leads to suffering, the apathetic person
eventually begins to avoid love in order to avoid the concomitant
suffering.[6] Kathleen's two daughters, although they understood their
mother's desire to end her suffering, felt that she was oblivious to the
effect her decision had on them.

Christian-inspired apathy takes other forms that are, perhaps, not
so obvious at first glance. Christians do not usually arrive at apathy
from an overindulgence of the body and the senses but from the other
direction, from depriving the body not only of delights but even of
necessities. By going through suffering, Christians have tried to learn
detachment and hence rise above and escape suffering. Acceptable
Christian forms of escape include compulsive work, compulsive
cleanliness, constant worry over the children, etc. These forms of
addiction are certainly cheaper and more socially acceptable than the

more secular forms, but they are equally destructive to the "user" and the persons close to her.

The miracle mentality, a fourth traditional Christian response to suffering, is fostered today particularly in more fundamentalist churches. But it lies hidden somewhere in the unconscious of every Christian who has ever listened intently to sermons on the miracle stories in the gospels or wondered at "the faith that moves mountains." The destructiveness of the miracle mentality is twofold. In the first place, because so few people who pray and hope for miracles ever get healed, the overwhelming majority of them are left with not only the physical problem they had in the first place but also a truckload of guilt because their faith wasn't strong enough. Mary (the former ballet dancer) went through this added spiritual suffering when the miracle she, encouraged by her "Christian friends," had prayed for did not happen.

The second problem is succinctly stated by Don Wanderhope, the protagonist in Peter DeVries' powerful novel on suffering, *The Blood of the Lamb*. Wanderhope says to a woman he loves who is dying of tuberculosis:

> Asking Him to cure you . . . implies a personal being who arbitrarily does us this dirt. The prayer then is a plea to have a heart. To knock it off. I find the thought repulsive. I prefer thinking we're the victims of chance to dignifying any such force with the name of Providence.[7]

What DeVries is suggesting here is that the Siamese twin of the miracle-worker God is the sadistic God.

In rejecting the miracle mentality, I am neither denying that many healings happen that we cannot yet explain nor implying that reality is bounded by the limits of our rational-scientific worldview.[8] My only point here is to call attention to the theological, spiritual and psychological problems that develop when it is expected that God will perform miracles.

The fifth explicit Christian response to suffering is actually a class of responses, all sharing a similar characteristic. All prescribe easy answers to suffering. Examples include: God is sending you this as a test. You will become a much stronger person through all this. God took your daughter, mother, sister, etc., because He loved her so much. And, my all-time (least) favorite: "God never sends you more than you can handle." One well-meaning churchgoer tried this last one on Kathleen just after she discovered she had cancer. Kathleen's carefully considered theological response is the best I have ever heard—brief and to the point: "Bullshit." The stated purpose of all these easy answers is to support the person in her suffering, to give her some meaning to grasp onto in her suffering, to reassure her that it won't last forever, etc. Their real effect, however, is quite different. They trivialize the sufferer's suffering and serve to protect the would-be consoler from being "contaminated" by that suffering.

The preceding discussion of the implicit and explicit traditional Christian responses to suffering should serve to underline the severity of the problem facing us. No pastoral facelift, no localized surgery on the margins of Christian doctrine will suffice. The problem is pervasive and radical. Any effective solution must be so, as well. Our incentive, however, is clear: to ease the suffering of real-life women in pain. With this in mind, let us attempt to work out a method for a feminist theology of suffering.

FORMULATING A FEMINIST THEOLOGICAL APPROACH
TO SUFFERING

Feminists seem to speak with two strikingly different voices on suffering. The first voice, which I characterized earlier as "suffering: never again," is passionate, sparked by a healthy and righteous indignation at the suffering that women have endured at the hands of patriarchy and that has been exacerbated by the layers of justification provided by Christianity. The kind of suffering at the center of this analysis is that caused by human agents—either individually or through unjust social structures.

The article discussed above by Brown and Parker is a good example of this first voice. Their goal is to expose and criticize any rationalization, any argument, any implication that encourages, trivializes, justifies, or legitimizes the suffering of women. The concept of "redemptive suffering" that undergirds Christian soteriology lies at the center of their critique, but at points they move beyond their Christological focus and make general statements on a more pastoral level. For example, they state that "Suffering is never redemptive, and suffering cannot be redeemed."[9] Any appeal to sacrifice self for the sake of another is rejected, even if, as in the case of Martin Luther King, Jr.'s nonviolent resistance movement, the suffering is chosen voluntarily and is for the sake of transformation to a more just society.[10] Since the ideal of self-sacrifice has been used time after time to keep women in their suffering, Brown and Parker repudiate it. Suffering will often occur in life, they realize, but it makes a big difference *how* one goes to meet it.

> It is not acceptance of suffering that gives life: it is *commitment to life* that gives life. The question, moreover, is not, Am I willing to suffer? but Do I desire fully to live? (emphasis added)[11]

Thus, for them, suffering should never be chosen directly, even for the sake of others. The only acceptable motivation for taking on suffering is when it is rendered absolutely necessary by one's choice for life.

The second voice, characterized earlier as "suffering: part of the web of life," does advocate a kind of acceptance of suffering. The tone here is gentler, somewhat sorrowful, but in a strange way, almost welcoming. In part, this is because the kind of suffering focused upon is that caused by natural processes rather than moral agency. To illustrate this second voice further, I want to provide two examples.

In her article "Rethinking Theology and Nature," Carol Christ describes her theological vision of the cosmos, the web of life, as follows.

> For me the divine/Goddess/God/Earth/Life/It symbolizes the whole of which we are a part. . . . We come from earth and to earth we shall return. Life feeds on life. We live because others die, and we will die so that others may live. The divinity that shapes our ends is life, death, and change, understood both literally and as metaphor for our daily lives. We will never understand it all. We do not choose the conditions of our lives. Death may come at any time. Death is never early or late. With regard to life and death there is no ultimate justice, nor ultimate injustice, for there is no promise that life will be other than it is . . . There will be no end to change, to death, to suffering. But life is as comic as it is tragic. Watching the sun set, the stars come out, eating, drinking, dancing, loving, and understanding are no less real than suffering, loss, and death. Knowledge that we are but a small part of life and death and transformation is the essential religious insight. The essential religious response is to rejoice and to weep, to sing and to dance, to tell stories and create rituals in praise of an existence far more complicated, more intricate, more enduring than we are.[12]

Here life and suffering/death are not opposed, but interrelated. Being committed to life includes accepting death. Here one can drift quietly into death, whereas the first voice challenges one always to "rage, rage against the dying of the light."

Another example of the second voice comes from an experience recounted by Nelle Morton, an experience she had of the Goddess. This experience is complex: a three-part vision, during which the Goddess, her mother, and a huge spider all appeared in her living room. The aspect of interest here is the interaction with her mother. In the vision, Morton's mother apologizes for the negative attitudes she had bequeathed to Nelle about her body, particularly regarding menstruation. At the time of this vision, Morton is suffering from a rare and very serious blood disease, sapping both her strength and her spirits. Her mother offers the following advice.

Forget all this visualizing of whole red blood cells that you will never have. Remember the hematologist who described your cells as shown under a microscope—"wild and bizarre." Be thankful for your "wild and bizarre" blood cells. They are keeping you alive. They are now normal for you.[13]

For Morton, this message about accepting her disease and the suffering it involved proved to be life-giving.

I am able now to receive the "bizarre and wild cells" as a special gift. In that sense the Goddess gave me back my life and called me to live fully with what I have, adjusting my activities to what energy I can summon and use creatively. Since then I have resumed my writing. I participate in social and political issues as I am able. It is as if the Goddess restored that part of myself that was wasted with fear from the false images in my unconscious.[14]

Both the "never again" and the "web of life" positions provide needed emphases for a feminist theology of suffering. The "never again" position challenges us never to minimize suffering or settle for suffering that could be eliminated, especially when it is rooted in injustice. It provides the passion and the anger to fuel the critique of that injustice and the struggle for liberation. However, it doesn't help us discover any meaning in suffering that cannot be eliminated. Nor does it help us learn how to accept such suffering or how to live and grow through it. Those points, however, are precisely the strength of the "web of life" position, especially when such suffering is rooted in natural causes. But if the "web of life" position constituted our total framework, we might be tempted to give in too soon rather than exploring all possibilities for healing.

What I am suggesting is that feminist theology should approach suffering within a framework created by the tension of affirming both those positions. A feminist theology of suffering, then, should state both that suffering can never be justified *and* that suffering must be accepted as part of life. It should state both that suffering can never be redeemed *and* that meaning can be found in suffering. In this way, a simplistic treatment of suffering is automatically avoided. The diverse forms of suffering and the different responses each requires must both be recognized. Further, even when dealing with only one type of suffering, the tension of working with and between both positions will produce a fuller and more adequate response than either taken alone.

As a preliminary indication of how this dual framework might actually work, I want to propose four questions that I think are essential in beginning any reflection on suffering. The first two questions were suggested by Dorothee Soelle in her book *Suffering*.[15] The last two questions are my own. These questions are stated here in the first person, but they are applicable (as a change of pronouns would readily indicate) not only to the sufferer but to any companion who would walk with her, as well as to anyone reflecting on suffering in general.

The first question—What are the causes of my suffering and how can they be eliminated?—affirms the centrality of the critique proposed by the "never again" position. Unless we begin here, we will inevitably fall into masochism.

The second question—How can I find meaning in suffering and grow through it?—builds on the acceptance of suffering that the "web of life" position embraces. Unless we move to this question, we will never be able to integrate unavoidable suffering into our lives.

The third question—When and how should I take on suffering I could avoid?—recognizes both the problematic character and the necessity (for the sake of love and justice) of becoming involved in situations that will increase our suffering. The "never again" position proposes that one should only do it out of a commitment to life, never out of a self-sacrificial, masochistic attitude. The "web of life" position agrees, but reminds us that accepting rather than denying suffering can sometimes produce a fuller life than was possible before. Even though there is always a "cost" to suffering, it is a human, natural cost that one can never escape.

The fourth question is actually a combination of two questions: Why am I suffering? and Who suffers with me? The first part, in my view, must be asked but cannot be answered. We must voice the question because it arises within the experience of suffering. We must resist closing the question because we cannot know the ultimate reason for our suffering. Every proposed answer that I have ever read or heard either trivializes the suffering or makes God into some kind of a sadist. Instead of pretending to answer the unanswerable, I propose that we follow the advice of German poet Rainer Maria Rilke and simply "live the question." We need, Rilke says, to:

> . . . be patient towards all that is unsolved . . . and try to love the questions themselves like locked rooms . . . not seek the answers; that cannot be given because you would not be able to live them. And the point is, to live everything. Live the questions now. Perhaps you will then gradually, without noticing it, live along some distant day into the answer.[16]

In this instance, I doubt that we will be able (even in eternity) to live into the answer. I do, however, believe that if we live the question, it may gradually be transformed into the second part of the fourth question: Who suffers with me? This latter question can be answered, and the answer reveals support and meaning that are essential in healing our suffering. Although each sufferer must answer the question for herself, a full answer includes some significant human others who walk with her, God/Goddess, and, indeed, the entire web of life. This full answer, it should be noted, integrates elements from both feminist voices on suffering.

Building on the critique of traditional Christian responses to suffering and on the methodological proposal just outlined, we can now discuss some implications of this material for developing a feminist theological anthropology that will help rather than hinder the healing processes of women in pain. These final remarks will be more in the order of exploratory suggestions than a developed systematic position. Five topics will be considered: embodiment, relationality, virtues, sin, and grace.

THEOLOGICAL ANTHROPOLOGY FOR WOMEN IN PAIN

Embodiment has been a central concern of feminist theology since its inception. The literature is varied and voluminous, and I cannot hope to summarize it here. My intention is only to mention two points that bear directly on the theology of suffering. The first point is the most basic one: that we *are* our bodies. It is more accurate to use expressions such as "our bodies/ourselves" or "my body-self" than to say "I have a body." Further, my body-self includes my feelings. Bodies, especially female bodies, and the feelings they include, have been much maligned in traditional Christian theology. Bodies and feelings are also the source of two of the dimensions of suffering. For all eight of the women in pain we discussed earlier, bodies and feelings formed the major roots of their suffering. All of this means that having an accurate picture of the basic goodness and worth of our bodies/ourselves is essential to a theological anthropology for women in pain.

Two qualifications may, perhaps, be needed here. Emphasizing bodies and feelings is not, of course, to say that minds and spirits are inconsequential to such a theological anthropology. No one raised in Western culture is likely to forget about them. The point is that bodies and feelings, dismissed or disparaged for so long, need to be welcomed back into our theological reflection. The point is to develop a holistic understanding of the human person, which cannot occur until all parts of the person are understood and integrated. Secondly, emphasizing the basic goodness of bodies and feelings is not to deny the ambiguity that is also part of our bodily experience. This should be obvious, given that our subject is suffering. The goodness is present but is not untouched by tragedy. If we mourn the tragedy, we must also celebrate the goodness.

A second element in our treatment of embodiment follows from this dual recognition of our bodies' goodness and ambiguity: that God is related to our bodies much more closely than traditional Christian theology would ever admit. Carter Heyward provides a powerful poetic description of this link that I want to quote at some length.

> The grass-roots theology springing up in Latin American countries today, rising out of the struggle of the poor for food and survival, instructs us that the body is to be taken with ultimate seriousness. There is nothing higher, nothing more holy. It is wrong, to contrast God with the body . . . Our hands are God's hands in the world. Our hearts are God's heart in the world. God pulsating. God beating. God yearning and open and growing in history. Our suffering and our tears are God's pain and trauma in history. Our laughter and our pleasure are God's own joy in history. Our work and our commitments are God's activity in this world. Our sexualities, our expressions of sexuality, our lovemaking in this world, is God's own expressiveness, God's own lovemaking, in history. When a human being reaches out to comfort, to touch, to bridge the gap separating each of us from everyone else, God comes to life in that act of reaching, of touching, of bridging. The act is love and God is love. And when we love, we god. And I use the word god here intentionally as a verb. If we are as fully human as we are able to be, and Jesus suggested we *are* able to be, then we are godders, we god—human beings/created bodies bringing God to life again, and again. Serving God in the act of serving humanity. Loving God in the act of loving humanity and one another.[17]

Note in this passage not only the delight of God in our sexuality when expressed in a loving context (which might help Elaine overcome her internalized heterosexism) but also the additional implications this would have for those suffering from some kind of abuse to their bodies (e.g, Emily, Joanne, Lenore, and the anonymous Guatemalan woman) as well as for those who pass on such abuse (some of whom are the same persons).

Relationality is a second foundational principle for feminist anthropology. In this view, the self is ontologically constituted not just by its physical dimensions but also by its relationships. This means that individualism is decisively superseded by the larger perspective of self-and-other(s). This shows up in many different ways in feminist theology. I will mention only one, taken from Beverly Harrison and Carter Heyward's excellent article entitled "Pleasure and Pain: Avoiding the Confusions of Christian Tradition in Feminist Theory."

We must also relinquish the association of "autonomy" and "identity" and not speak . . . of "the autonomy of identity." We are even doubtful of the value of the notion of "identity" in feminist theory. It is better, we submit, to think in terms of "self-integrity" and "other-integrity," such that we may simultaneously possess our own power, be empowered by others, and empower others.[18]

Such a profound emphasis on relationality requires a paradigm shift from the Western liberal view of the person. Such a paradigm is not, however, something new under the sun. It is actually a much older form of wisdom that many non-Western societies have managed to retain. John Mbiti gives an example of this kind of thinking from an African proverb. "I am because we are. We are because I am." Or, in short, "I am we," a statement that makes little sense to Western ears. Mercy Amba Oduyoye, a theologian from Ghana, illustrates this same perspective in a poem she quotes entitled "Dream Girl Dream":

What's the future going to be?

Dream girl dream.
What we may become, that's what matters.

Dream woman dream
Woman's dream. Africa's dream.

Dream of the least of the world,
Permissible dreams.

Dream, for the other is you turned inside out.

Make the other strong and you will be strong,
We shall all be strong together.
Dream girl dream.

Be a woman, and Africa will be strong.[19]

Such a deep sense of relationality, if it could be developed in people—which I realize is not small "if"—would significantly reduce the amount of humanly perpetrated suffering. So far, our society has been markedly unsuccessful in curtailing violence even within the family (as Emily and Joanne witness), much less on a global level (as illustrated by the fact that the link between the Guatemalan woman's poverty and U.S. wealth perturbs very few U.S. citizens). Even now, however, this view of relationality can provide a helpful framework for those who do wish to get involved in solidarity with people who are oppressed. In particular, it helps us address the thorny question of how to avoid masochism and self-sacrifice when participating in someone else's struggle for liberation or healing. If "I am we," I suffer in any case. I cannot be committed to my life without also being committed to our life, whoever that "our" may be.

Virtues are a third aspect of theological anthropology that require revision if they are not to do further damage to women in pain. Such revision is vitally necessary because so many of the (so-called) virtues advocated by traditional Christianity are toxic to women. The most basic of these sorely needed feminist virtues, I believe, is the ability to feel one's own feelings, including one's pain. Beverly Wildung Harrison argues persuasively the ethical importance of feeling one's feelings, whatever they are.

> If we are not perceptive in discerning our feelings, or if we do not know what we feel, we cannot be effective moral agents. This is why psychotherapy has to be understood as a very basic form of moral education. In the absence of feeling there is no rational ability to evaluate what is happening. Failure to live deeply in "our bodies, ourselves" destroys the possibility of moral relations between us. . . . Feelings deserve our respect for what they are. There are no "right" and "wrong" feelings. Moral quality is a property of acts, not feelings, and our feelings arise in action. The moral question is not "what do I feel?" but rather "what do I do with what I feel?"[20]

Psychologists such as Alice Miller, who have studied child abuse, underline the importance of feeling rather than denying or repressing our feelings. As long as one's own pain is repressed, one cannot acknowledge anyone else's pain. This, Miller argues, is the key to why abused children become abusers, indeed to why anyone perpetrates a willful act of violence on another person.[21] Feeling one's pain is also, not coincidentally, the first step in the healing process from any kind of suffering. All this suggests that Adrienne Rich's paradoxical sounding statement, "not to suffer uselessly yet still to feel," is based not on poetic fantasy, but in sound psychological knowledge.

Because anger (one of the "seven deadly sins") has been so misunderstood in Christian theology, it is important to focus for a moment on the special challenge it provides and the special gifts it offers as a feminist virtue. Once again, Harrison's analysis is very instructive. Anger, she says, "is a mode of connectedness to others" and "a vivid form of caring"; it is always "a sign of some resistance in ourselves to the moral quality of the social relations in which we are immersed."[22] I would add two comments here: (1) that the person harmed by those social relations can be another or ourselves; and (2) that we have a right to feel our anger at another person or even at God, even if that other is not "guilty" or "to blame" for the harm.

These additions are necessary to account for difficulties that arise in certain instances of suffering. Consider, for example, Amanda, whose husband accidentally caused the death of their daughter. Among the multiple feelings Amanda is bombarded by is anger: anger at God for letting such a tragedy happen; anger at her husband for "causing" it. Amanda doesn't really believe that either God or her husband are "to blame" for the tragedy, but her anger has to be expressed, and it needs some focus for that to occur. The psalms of lament provide a very useful justification, model and outlet for expressing anger at God. The anger at her husband is, perhaps, even harder to express. The price of not expressing and working it through, however, is denial and repression.

"Where anger is hidden or goes unattended, masking itself, there the power of love, the power to act, to deepen relation, atrophies and dies."[23] Divorce statistics among couples who have one child die through no fault, negligence, or accident on the part of either spouse are extremely high; if one spouse is implicated in some way, they are even higher. If anger is promoted as a virtue, as an essential aspect in the work of love, then women like Amanda will move forward more easily in their grieving process.

A fourth aspect of theological anthropology that requires revision in light of the experience of women in pain is sin, particularly original sin or the underlying state of sinfulness of the human person. The traditional view of original sin—stemming from Eve and Adam's act of disobeying God, passed down through procreation, and rendering each child born guilty, shame-filled, and in need of redemption—is well-known. The implications of all this for sexuality, women, and the "suffering as punishment" argument are also well known. Less known, perhaps, are the ways in which this theology contributes—not intentionally but actually, nonetheless—to child abuse. Alice Miller describes how psychological theories of "the wicked child" not only provide an environment in which child abuse can flourish but also actively support some of its "milder" forms.[24] Although Miller doesn't directly draw a parallel with the doctrine of original sin, the similarity is obvious to anyone familiar with Christian theology. Lest anyone think that young children themselves can't draw connections between general religious teachings and their own experience, I want to quote the words of one woman recalling her own abuse.

> He started abusing me when I was five years old. This was when I was beginning my religious training which taught me that women were vessels of sin. It was my sin of incest that made him [i.e., Jesus] hang on the cross.[25]

Other important aspects of the critique of the Christian doctrine of sin from the perspective of women have already been done by Valerie Saiving and Judith Plaskow. Highlighting the gender bias in the traditional doctrine, they argue that the basic sin of women should be viewed as self-loss, self-denial, self-destruction or, stating it in language we have been using here, masochism. Susan Thistlethwaite adds an important footnote to this analysis: that race (and the different socialization that accompanies that dimension of our experience) plays an important role as well. We cannot, she argues, simply assume that the basic sin for black women will be the same as that for white women. In fact, a reading of black women's literature reveals that it is something quite different.[26] What all of these feminist analyses share is the perception that sin is historically and socially produced, rather than innate in fallen humanity.

In *Journeys By Heart*, Rita Nakashima Brock proposes another reinterpretation of sin that grows out of her consideration of child abuse. She understands our basic human sinfulness as damage, brokenness, or brokenheartedness stemming from our radically relational nature. She describes the origin of this damage as follows:

> At the earliest part of our lives we are dependent on the loving power of others to nurture us. Their failure to do so has serious consequences. We are broken by the world of our relationships before we are able to defend ourselves. It is not a damage we willfully choose.[27]

Therefore, she concludes, "sin is not something to be punished, but something to be healed."[28] Her discussion of the healing process leads to our fifth aspect of theological anthropology that needs revision for the sake of women in pain. Grace (also called "Heart" and "original grace") is, for Brock, the source of this healing power. It is rooted in the fundamental relational character of human beings. "This ontological relational existence, the heart of our being, is our life source, our original grace."[29] "Heart" is Brock's metaphorical way of describing our "true self," with its capacity for intimacy and its integration of body, spirit, reason, and passion.[30] As we saw earlier, this ontological relational character is also, paradoxically, the ground of our damage, of our sinfulness. Heart is fragile and vulnerable, especially in young children, but it is also incredibly resilient. Our heart, even damaged and brokenhearted as it is, can still lead us to "relationships that will empower our self-healing."[31] Only by following our hearts and reaching out to those others who reach out to us can we heal our damage, gain self-acceptance, and fulfill our basic human desire to give and receive love.

As this brief sketch illustrates, Brock's understanding of grace is radically immanent. Grace is not the special gift of some divine being "up" or even "out there." Rather, grace is the erotic power (another term Brock uses to describe this dimension of connectedness) always present and available within and between humans. Although Brock develops and articulates this understanding of grace specifically in the context of recovery from child abuse, it has implications far beyond that particular form of suffering.

Consider, for example, the experiences of Mary (the dancer) and Elaine (the lesbian). Mary found healing in her relationships with Bob and Sue, two people with debilitating and eventually fatal diseases. Together they learned to laugh, cry, rage at and be at peace with their struggles to perform the "simplest" daily activities (like eating, bathing, picking up an object dropped on the floor). In that community, "where two or three were gathered together," Mary, Bob and Sue were healed. Even though Bob and Sue have died, that community survives in Mary's "heart."

For Elaine, significant healing came not only through her love for her spouse but also through her larger community, the two hundred or so people (gay and lesbian, straight, lay and clergy, including the local bishop of her denomination) who attended the wedding ceremony. That public recognition (including the use of the term *marriage* to describe their union) was an essential dimension in the healing of wounds created by living within a heterosexist and homophobic church and society. Since relationships (interpersonal and social) caused the original damage, only relationships (at both those levels) could provide healing.

CONCLUSION

Now that we have come to the end of this reflection on and for women in pain, it might be helpful to consider once again Adrienne Rich's statement:

> I believe I am choosing something new
> Not to suffer uselessly   yet still to feel.

That choice *is* something new—especially for Christian women who have been counseled (*ad nauseam* and sometimes *ad mortem*) in the ethic of self-sacrifice. "Give until it hurts, and then give some more." Men hear this advice and apply it to their wallets. Women hear it and apply it to their lives. But human lives are not like wallets. An empty wallet will still be there, unchanged, ready to hold more money when it again becomes available. But a human psyche, unable to handle an overload of pain, eventually shuts down. Then one stops feeling. But without feeling, no healing is possible.

This psychic reality creates a major dilemma for women in pain. A way out must be found, a way to say no to unnecessary suffering. A way to make the necessary suffering "useful." A way to feel the pain that accompanies that necessary suffering. A way to heal.

The task of a feminist theology of suffering, then, is to do the massive work of critique and reconstruction at all levels of Christian theology so women may eventually be empowered to make that new choice envisioned by Rich. This paper is one step in that process, offered—which is not to say "offered up"—for women in pain.

NOTES

1. Eric Cassel, "The Nature of Suffering and the Goals of Medicine," *The New England Journal of Medicine* 306 (March 18, 1982): 640.

2. Adrienne Rich, "Splittings," *The Dream of a Common Language: Poems 1974-77* (New York: W. W. Norton, 1978), p. 10.

3. Joanne Carlson Brown and Rebecca Parker, "For God So Loved the World?" in Joanne Carlson Brown and Carole R. Bohn, eds., *Christianity, Patriarchy and Abuse: A Feminist Critique* (New York: The Pilgrim Press, 1989), p. 27.

4. Ibid., p. 28.

5. Ibid., p. 26.

6. Dorothee Soelle, *The Strength of the Weak: Toward a Christian Feminist Identity,* trans. Robert and Rita Kimber (Philadelphia: Westminster, 1984), pp. 25-26.

7. Peter DeVries, *The Blood of the Lamb* (New York: Penguin Books, 1961), p. 104.

8. For helpful discussions of these issues from two very different perspectives, see Rita Nakashima Brock, *Journeys by Heart: A Christology of Erotic Power* (New York: Crossroad, 1989), ch. 4, and Bernie Siegal, M.D., *Love, Medicine and Miracles: Lessons Learned about Self-Healing from a Surgeon's Experience with Exceptional Cancer Patients* (New York: Harper and Row, 1986).

9. Brown and Parker, p. 27.

10. Ibid., pp. 19-21.

11. Ibid., p. 18.

12. Carol P. Christ, "Rethinking Theology and Nature," in Judith Plaskow and Carol P. Christ, eds., *Weaving the Visions: New Patterns in Feminist Spirituality* (San Francisco: Harper and Row, 1989), p. 321.

13. Nelle Morton, *The Journey Is Home* (Boston: Beacon Press, 1985), p. 163.

14. Ibid.

15. Soelle, p. 5.

16. Rainer Maria Rilke, *Letters to a Young Poet* (New York: W. W. Norton, 1934), p. 33.

17. Carter Heyward, *Our Passion for Justice: Images of Power, Sexuality, and Liberation* (New York: The Pilgrim Press, 1984), p. 140.

18. Beverly W. Harrison and Carter Heyward, "Pain and Pleasure: Avoiding the Confusions of Christian Tradition in Feminist Theory," in Brown and Bohn, eds., *Christianity, Patriarchy and Abuse*, p. 165.

19. Mercy Amba Oduyoye, "Be a Woman, and Africa Will Be Strong," in Letty Russell, et al., eds., *Inheriting Our Mothers' Gardens: Feminist Theology in Third World Perspective* (Philadelphia: Westminster, 1988), p. 35.

20. Beverly Wildung Harrison, "The Power of Anger in the Work of Love," in Judith Plaskow and Carol P. Christ, eds., *Weaving the Visions: New Patterns in Feminist Spirituality* (San Francisco: Harper and Row, 1989), p. 219.

21. See, for example, Alice Miller, *Banished Knowledge: Facing Childhood Injuries,* trans. Leila Bennewitz (New York: Doubleday, 1990).

22. Harrison, p. 220.

23. Ibid.

24. Miller, *Banished Knowledge,* ch. 3.

25. Quoted in Sheila A. Redmond, "Christian 'Virtues' and Recovery from Child Sexual Abuse," in Brown and Bohn, *Christianity, Patriarchy and Abuse,* p. 77.

26. See Susan Thistlethwaite, *Sex, Race, and God: Christian Feminism in Black and White* (New York: Crossroad, 1989), ch. 5.

27. Brock, *Journeys by Heart,* p. 16.

28. Ibid., p. 7.

29. Ibid.

30. Ibid., p. xiv.

31. Ibid., p. 16.

Part IV

EXPERIENCE AND SPECIFIC
THEOLOGICAL ISSUES

9

Sin

When Women Are the Context

Sally Ann McReynolds and Ann O'Hara Graff

This essay is an introduction to the stream of feminist conversation around the subject of sin. To our deepening pain, but perhaps also toward our common healing, women theologians have steadily uncovered both the neglect of women's experience in regard to sin, and the extent to which women have been defiled through overidentification with sin in the symbols of the Christian tradition. To open the theological conversation about sin through the lens of women's experience is both to explore uncharted territory and to begin the work of exorcism, naming the demons that have worked their (often hidden) evil on us all. In so limited a space, this essay cannot begin to be comprehensive; however, it can offer a sense of the questions raised and the issues under discussion.

THE PATH THAT BEGINS WITH VALERIE SAIVING

In 1960 Valerie Saiving published "The Human Situation: A Feminine View."[1] In this ground-breaking article for feminist theology, Saiving asserts, "I am a student of theology. I am also a woman."[2] She notes that she has slowly become convinced that the temptation to confound a limited perspective with universal truth may be at work in the writing of theology. She proposes, therefore, to examine two

This article emerged out of the joint effort of the authors. The major research was pursued by McReynolds, while the writing prcess was undertaken by both and put into final form by Graff.

key theologies representative of her period, those of Anders Nygren and Reinhold Niebuhr.

The theme she identifies is their representation of the human situation. Each characterizes our situation as typified by anxiety that arises from the sense of separateness we experience in terms of each other. In this predicament the theologians name sin as self-assertion while love is recognized as selflessness.[3] In this form of existential theology, sin is visible in the human attempt to overcome anxiety by magnifying one's own power, knowledge, or righteousness.[4] It is an effort to make oneself the whole, rather than remaining a part of that whole. It is unjustified concern for one's own power and prestige. It is an aggrandizement of self that treats others as objects or append-ages. Moreover, it is not an occasional act but pervades the entirety of human action.[5] In short, this position is a mid-twentieth century version of the sin of pride, a key description of sin in the Christian tradition.

Given this condition, love is its opposite. Love is the norm for human existence, and it is defined as completely self-giving, seeking only the good of the other, without any self-interest. Love makes no judgments about the other, forgives unconditionally, and as Paul said eloquently, bears all, believes all, hopes all, endures all. It is personal, but wholly receptive to the other.[6] In contemporary parlance, it seems to be without boundaries.

Following this delineation of this theological description of our human situation and its relation to reciprocal identifications of sin and love, Saiving goes on to ask about the distinct experiences that shape men and women. To sketch this she uses the work of anthropologists Ruth Benedict and Margaret Mead, as well as a number of other representatives of that discipline, and those of psychoanalysis and sociology. She wants to argue not whether there should be differences in gendered identity but that cultures treat men and women differ-ently in relation to our sex and its biological consequences. Thus, in contemporary terms, cultures form our gendered identity and prac-tice. (Here a reader can clearly see that while sex is a biological given, gender identity is socially constructed.) Moreover, Saiving notes that while there is a wide variety of culture constructs of male and female identity, she finds some broad coherence in the treatment of women, given our biological role as mothers.

Ultimately, Saiving contrasts the role of women as mothers in modern society to that of modern men.[7] She concludes that while mothers rejoice in their maternal role and know the tremendous importance of personal, I-Thou love relationships and the experience of self-transcending love in this context, that cannot be an unrelieved ideal. While surrender of body, of time, of viewpoint, of one's own feelings is all necessary to meet the needs of children, to give without regard to self unceasingly can be deadly.[8] Woman's wholeness requires the balance of withdrawal into self and periods of enrichment that meet her individual needs. This qualifies the ideal of selfless love as announced in male theologies constructed to counter the will-to-power; it reconfigures the drive to the personal in these theologies driven by the anxieties of male separated selves.[9]

Sin, then, in this context is not pride or drive to power and prestige over against others, or the whole. Rather, for Saiving, sin is better described as

> triviality, distractibility, and diffuseness; lack of an organizing center or focus; dependence on others for one's own self-defini-tion; tolerance at the expense of standards of excellence; inability to respect the boundaries of privacy; sentimentality, gossipy sociability, and mistrust of reason—in short, underdevelopment of the self.[10]

Saiving's work was a first effort at what is now named feminist theology. It was a new, insightful essay that pointed to the way women's experience in culturally bound situations gives rise to quite different interpretations of elements of Christian life—in this case, love and sin—due to a different lived experience of the human situation. We have laid out this essay in detail because feminist work on sin since its writing has continued to take it into account and to react to it. It has become a starting place for feminist conversation.

Jewish feminist theologian Judith Plaskow pursued Saiving's theme in her book, *Sex, Sin and Grace: Women's Experience and the Theologies of Reinhold Niebuhr and Paul Tillich.*[11] She, however, clarifies that her claim to work from women's experience is culturally specific and cannot be universalized as any woman's experience, biological motherhood notwithstanding. She is a Western, white, middle-class woman, and she draws on resources that disclose the experience of this group of women. Thus when Plaskow concludes, in a similar way to Saiving, that women have a fundamental problem in relation to self-actualization, she is referring to this specific category of women. For women who have lived out the pattern of self-sacrifice as continual accommodation to the needs of others, sin is not self-assertion and pride but failure to take responsibility for their own lives and decisions. Concomitantly, grace may not be this endless self-sacrifice, but might better be named in interdependent experience and language like friendship, solidarity, co-creation, and joy in relation.

Feminist theologians concerned to understand and heal women who have suffered from abuse have also taught us something more about the names of sin. One key article, representative of a wider literature, is that of Mary Potter Engel, "Evil, Sin, and Violation of the Vulnerable."[12] Potter Engel's larger project is a feminist liberation theology, especially for victim-survivors of domestic and sexual abuse. Within this framework she wants to focus on the doctrine of evil and sin, because this has been "one of the most powerful tools in the church's collusion with society in the victimization of women, children, and elders."[13] For Potter Engel, evil refers to the systemic structures or patterns of oppression in economic, political, and social life. Sin "refers to those free, discrete acts of responsible individuals that create or reinforce these structures of oppression."[14] In dealing with the perpetrator-victim relation, Potter Engel is clear that she wants to avoid any sense that they are equally responsible for the violence that occurs, and she does not want to blame the victim. Having said that, she also does not relinquish awareness that some victims have some responsibility for complicity in their own situation. In the case of both parties, Potter Engel suggests that social systems that oppress often play a part in the reproduction of violence. Evil and sin collude.

Potter Engel goes on to suggest four new ways of thinking about sin in the context of evil as it occurs in the situation of abuse. One normal, healthy response to abuse is anger. Yet women are socialized to deny their anger, even to name it as sinful, and victimized people, female or male, are often threatened into that same denial. Often both the victim and others who may be aware of the victimization deny their anger or "harden their hearts." The victim may respond to being abused by distorting her feelings or dissociating from herself, becoming numb or, in extremes, split off from herself. In the situation this response is frequently a necessary survival strategy, and insofar as it allows her to survive the violence it may be a form of life-seeking grace. Thus, Saiving's loss of self as sin cannot be applied in this situation. Yet this dissociation and numbing may block access to anger at the violation, and so to one's true self. It calls for healing that entails the ability to feel truthfully. For those aware of the victim's situation, or of wider situations of violation in our society, sin can be named as the failure to feel and be outraged; sin is hardening of the heart, moral callousness when righteous anger is demanded.[15]

Potter Engel also asks us to move away from any too quick identification of sin with disobedience. Too many children and wives are abused in the name of obedience. We might do better to name sin as betrayal of trust, especially in the covenant relationships of marriage or parenthood. This is the abuser's betrayal, not the victim's. Sin is precisely both this treachery and the fact that it destroys many victims' ability to trust anyone. This denies them the life-affirming trust so necessary to human well-being.

Because self-blame and self-hatred are such powerful responses to abuse, the description of sin as pride and self-love also becomes problematic. Here we see another of Saiving's themes, now raised from another vantage. Healthy self-love, like the ability to trust, is also necessary to our well-being. Potter Engel suggests that the situation of abuse allows us to see pride as an inflation of the boundaries of the self to annex another, again a mode of behavior in which men may be socialized. Alternatively, white middle-class women have often been socialized to deflate the boundaries of the self, to lose themselves in relationships, and so to become diffused. This form of diffusion parallels what Saiving described, but here the consequences may leave women more vulnerable to abuse and more lost when abused. Women's struggle toward creating a separate identity can be undercut by labeling this as sinful pride, self-love, or alienation from other. Only when each person's boundaries are appropriate and respected can there be real interdependence and care.

Finally, Potter Engel calls our attention to the dynamic tension between human freedom and our real dependence and fragility. The male/female pattern regarding this tension in white middle-class culture tends to be resolved toward male domination and female dependence. In either case, Potter Engel notes that we refuse to consent to our vulnerability by trying to avoid it. Perhaps this very failure to admit to the limits and gifts of our fragile situation shows us the face of sin.

At this juncture, it appears that she reintegrates the issue of anxiety which Saiving critiqued in a way that treats its gendered value, at least for many middle-class white people in this culture. Indeed, she has several times taken up and criticized or repositioned Saiving's original insight. She has suggested a more nuanced or multidimensional reading of sin that presses home the recognition that our definition of this (and other) key Christian theological symbol is tied to the way in which we describe the situation. Those situations in turn are read in light of the experience of particular groups of people. Therefore, it cannot surprise us to take up Plaskow's clarity that her definition of women's sin was pertinent to white middle-class women, herself and others like her. Potter Engel takes up the intersection of the socialization patterns of white middle-class people with the experience of violation.[16] Women in other situations, social locations, defined by gender, race, class, as well as other factors such as age or sexual orientation, are also working to redefine sin. Thus Saiving's original insight—that who is in what situation really counts—continues to be explored.

Before passing on to look at one further step in this rendering of experience, situation, and sin, we might note that Potter Engel's essay is partnered in *Lift Every Voice* by an essay conversation about grace in the situation of abuse, carried on by Susan Thistlethwaite and Mary Pellauer.[17] Like the suggestions in Saiving and Plaskow, the situation described leads to naming the alternative life-giving, healing, and creative moments as grace. Grace is first in the sheer survival of the trauma; grace is in seeking healing and the courage it takes to do this work; grace is in touching and feeling the anger and the grief; grace is in the process itself, and in the interruptions; grace is in the steps toward empowerment and work toward justice. While evocative and not systematic, the exploration of the harm of sin presses us to find the steps of life, healing and hope. These are the networks of grace we climb, holding each other's hands.

Another recent, powerful contribution, in *A Troubling in My Soul*, about the face of sin is offered by Delores Williams in her article "A Womanist Perspective on Sin."[18] This volume contains a wide range of essays on the experiences of evil, suffering, and sin, written by a broad group of womanist theologians and ministers. For Williams, womanist theology is sourced in the experience and faith of the African-American community. Its contexts are the struggles for liberation of her people, as well as of women. Specifically, her essay develops an historical perspective on the meaning of sin in the African-American community. To do this, she draws on the tradition of spiritual songs, the autobiographical statements of ex-slaves, and Black theology. She then turns to nineteenth-century narratives of African-American women for a sense of their understanding of sin. Finally she offers a constructive position for womanist theology today.

It is important to name the resources because they specify the experience, and so the situation(s), that shape this theological position. From the banal to the horrific, the violations of the middle passage, slavery, and post-Civil War racism that included and includes terrorism, shape the experience of African-American people. The women of the community suffered, in addition, the full gamut of sexual exploitation from harassment through gang rape, brutal beating, and murder. The narratives give power and depth to the abstract words *systemic oppression*. That is what Williams searches out—the systemic evil done unto a people and its effects on persons and the community, especially aware of the afflictions of the women. Here the issue Potter Engel raised, that systemic evil and personal sin intersect, comes sharply into focus.

One key symbol of sin that Williams names is the devaluation and defilement of the bodies of Black women, both through sexual violation and exploitative labor. For Williams, defilement is constituted by "atrocious action" taken against another person. Coupled with attack on women's spirits and self-esteem, this defilement constitutes grave social sin.[19] Following James Cone, she suggests that social sin is the very taking away of a people's humanity, especially here, the womanhood of Black women. Heightening this sinful process, she offers the biblical symbol that Black women are made in the image and likeness of God. Thus in the affirmation of themselves, their bodies, their culture, its food and songs and joy in community, she names the authentic and unyielding goodness of her people, grounded in the very creation of God. This symbol of the image and likeness of God serves to name the roots and branches of life and holiness elsewhere in this article named grace.[20]

In the situation of demonic social sin, Williams suggests that personal sin is in participation in those social structures, attitudes and expectations that continue their power. It is critical to note that personal sin is not in those acts the community calls "wrongdoing," when a person denied access to the means of sustaining life may be forced to steal bread. Nor is this sin in the sense of "unworthiness" that may denote diminished self-esteem. Williams is painstaking in her effort to distinguish the power of social sin from clarity about personal responsibility for the ongoing situation. Life is in the struggle for personal and social transformation.[21]

One last important note in this article that also links us to another wide area of womanist, feminist, and ethical concern is the parallel Williams draws between the defilement of the bodies of Black women and the defilement of nature through ecological destruction. Earth's body, gouged by those who own the means of production, and those who watch in silence, undergoes the atrocity of sin as Williams names it. Again, our hope is in the work for life.[22]

This limited review of a path of reflection about the connections among experience, the situation, and sin begins to illustrate the development of thought both about sin itself and about the growing care and complexity of women's reflection about our multiple experiences. Moreover, it illustrates the progressive awareness that we cannot presume a universal viewpoint but must attend to the particular contexts of different groups of women when we do theology. It also shows the way in which women have come to recognize that what we take to be our personal experience is consistently informed by social institutions, political, economic, legal, educational, and accompanying social attitudes, ideas, and expectations. The social context invariably informs the personal context, just as we as persons have some responsibility for shaping our social situation. Thus, in this area we can talk about the institutionalization and ideologies of racism, sexism, and classism in this culture, and we can also recognize if we ourselves are racists or buy into sexist attitudes and practices or the prejudices of access to wealth (class in this culture). It is also clear that these patterns intersect with each other: racism and sexism together diminish the persons of black women in white racist America. The economic institutions that have conspired to keep African-American people poor exacerbate the destructive effects of racism and sexism, yet the latter also support the former! Thus a network of social institutions and attitudes collude to demean, to disparage, to trap, to violate. So the demonic face of sin leers at us, and ravages.

THE FACE OF EVE

Another issue that surfaced early in the feminist discussion was the mythological or ideological[23] identification of woman with Eve, and so with sexuality and sin. In this we encounter a major ideological support of patriarchy in the Western tradition. For example, the text of 1 Tim. 2:9-14 makes clear that while Eve was made second, she sinned first, thus affording double reason for the subordination of women in patriarchy.[24] It is well beyond the scope of this essay to exegete the symbol of Eve or the debates about the creation stories that are multiple even among women scholars, let alone in the wider literature. However, the essays reviewed in the foregoing section indicate the growing awareness of systemic institutions of oppression that conspire to leave women subordinate, submerging her own will and identity to the needs of others, vulnerable to severe abuse and ready to blame herself for it, or again battered and defiled for being a woman in the augmented context of racial hatred. Such practices are supported by ideologies or cultural mythologies that not only allow them to continue, but even reinforce them. This means there are symbols and stories like that of Eve and Adam that are interpreted in a way that reinforces the practice of subordination of women. Women are imaged as inferior or as needing to be controlled, told to silence themselves or allow themselves to be violated because they are depicted as inherently evil or deserving of punishment for the evil they have wrought. While the relation between ideology and practice is repeatedly illustrated in this volume, it is the concern of this essay to offer a sense of the power of destructive ideologies/mythologies of woman in relation to the dynamics of sin.

The literature we have already explored indicates the progress women are making in renaming sin in terms of their own experiences and situations. However, that renaming is taking place in the context of Western, Christian, women attempting to name and break free from an identification with sin in their own cultural and religious world. One of the first feminist readers produced for college classrooms, *Women and Religion: A Feminist Sourcebook of Christian Thought*,[25] begins with the Bible and moves through the major theologians of the Western Christian tradition, reproducing an agonizing litany of misogynist texts. Many of these texts use the symbol of Eve, interpreted as the woman made from man and the one who first sinned, bringing havoc to us all.[26] Moreover, Eve is associated with sexual activity and sexual pleasure, for centuries suspect in the Christian tradition.[27] This volume and other recountings give us a painful portrait of women. From Tertullian's infamous dictum against Eve: "You are the devil's gateway. You are the unsealer of the forbidden tree. You are the first deserter of Divine law,"[28] through the horrifying text of the Inquisition's *Malleus Malleficarum*, its *Hammer against Witches*, which alleged that the sin of witchcraft entailed a woman's intercourse with the devil,[29] to recent Vatican arguments that women cannot be ordained because we do not bear a sufficient likeness to Christ (as male, a normative human),[30] there is a pattern of ideological devaluation and sometimes demonization of women.

Rosemary Ruether has repeatedly studied the misogynism of the tradition, from her early article, "The Descent of Woman,"[31] through her systematic work, *Sexism and God-Talk: Toward a Feminist Theology,* to her reader, *Womanguides: Readings toward a Feminist Theology.*[32] In her reading, Eve is one representation of the mythic "mother of all the living," whose power is undercut in the myth so that she is subordinated to the male (both God and human), which supports the growth of patriarchal civilization. She traces the male/female hierarchy as it matches the hierarchy of rational soul/subjugated body in Greek thought. She notes that early Christian attraction to virginity mirrors, in part, this desire to subject body to reason, and offers women as virgins the opportunity to overcome the liability of the body and its sexual capacities, to reverse the sin of Eve, and so to find redemption.[33]

Here the symbol of the Virgin Mary takes up the mythic counterpoint. Here is pure womanhood, unsullied by the bodily life of earthly women. She is the idealized, submissive and sexless virgin/mother, free of sin.[34] The parallel of sinful Eve, bodied, sexual, irrational, and sinless Mary, obedient to the Father, sexually innocent, immaculately conceived, assumed into heaven, indicates the powerful ideological play of symbols that inform and denigrate Christian women.[35] Neither symbol reflects the reality of women's lives, but both symbols, and the interpretations of their stories, can act to trap and confute women and create unreal images and expectations for both women and men. Moreover, while all women are blamed for the occurrence of sin in the mythos of Eve, none can match the unique role of Mary. Here women are not only caught between the poles of overidentification with sin or idealized sinlessness, but are then left struggling to find the truth of their own experience over against this damaging, indeed sinful, ideology, and against those institutions which draw strength from its perpetuation.

This brief reflection only offers a glimpse of the volumes of recent treatment of the mythos of woman in the Western tradition. Some of this is noted elsewhere in this volume. What is important here is to recognize that the struggle to rethink sin theologically goes hand in hand with the struggle to overcome the very naming of women ourselves as those who bring sin and embody sin, daughters of Eve, sexual and sinful. This mythic pattern has had a series of permutations both over the centuries and in recent American history; it has mystical, romantic, Victorian, and indeed racist variations. Against sinful ideologies we must struggle together toward the truth of our authentic selves, discovering life-giving symbols of womanhood for ourselves and our children, and living them. In this way we will all learn to discern better where real sin hides its damaging work and where sin's misnames are sinful, and grace shines beneath.

CONCLUSION

This essay has attempted to trace a few of the voices of women theologians who have been rethinking the names we give to sin in our lives. This entails critique of old names and, more painfully and powerfully, it entails the rejection of many names given to us, and often internalized over the centuries, that persist even today. Women theologians are clear that sin as death-dealing moral evil is all too present in social forms of oppression, institutional and ideological, and that we all, women and men, participate personally and knowingly in their harm, while also being harmed by them whether we will or no. We look for grace in the fundament of God's creation, in who we are, made in God's image, and in the steps each and all of us take to heal, to affirm life, and to give life to each other, to our children, and to the earth.[36]

NOTES

1. In Carol P. Christ and Judith Plaskow, eds., *Womanspirit Rising: A Feminist Reader in Religion* (San Francisco: Harper & Row, 1979), pp. 25-42. Originally published in the *Journal of Religion* (April 1960).

2. Ibid., p. 25.

3. Ibid., p. 26.

4. Ibid.

5. Ibid.

6. Ibid., pp. 26-27.

7. Ibid., pp. 36-39. This has been noted and discussed recently in Bonnie Miller McLemore, *Also a Mother: Work and Family as Theological Dilemma* (Nashville, TN: Abingdon Press, 1994), pp. 100-105.

8. Ibid., p. 37.

9. Catherine Keller, *From a Broken Web: Separation, Sexism and Self* (Boston: Beacon Press, 1986) discusses the "separate" and "soluble" selves of men and women in this culture in detail.

10. In Christ and Plaskow, p. 37.

11. Judith Plaskow, *Sex, Sin and Grace: Women's Experience and the Theologies of Reinhold Niebuhr and Paul Tillich* (Washington, DC: University Press of America, 1980). See also discussions of Plaskow in Anne E. Carr, *Transforming Grace: Christian Tradition and Women's Experience* (San Francisco: Harper & Row, 1988), esp. pp. 118-19 and 211-12, and in Susan Thistlethwaite, *Sex, Race, and God: Christian Feminism in Black and White* (New York: Crossroad, 1989), pp. 78-79.

12. In Susan Brooks Thistlethwaite and Mary Potter Engel, eds., *Lift Every Voice: Constructing Christian Theologies from the Underside* (San Francisco: Har-

per & Row, 1990), pp. 152-64. See Joanne Carlson Brown and Carole R. Bonn, eds., *Christianity, Patriarchy, and Abuse: A Feminist Critique* (Cleveland: The Pilgrim Press, 1989) for further reading and bibliography.

13. Potter Engel, p. 154.

14. Ibid., p. 155.

15. See also Beverly Wildung Harrison's famous article, "The Power of Anger in the Work of Love," in her *Making the Connections: Feminist Essays on Social Ethics* (Boston: Beacon Press, 1985), pp. 3-21.

16. This is not always clear in the article itself, but it is an important recognition. Note that the material on female socialization is also taken up from a psychological vantage in the Graff paper on that theme in this volume.

17. "Conversation on Grace and Healing: Perspectives from the Movement to End Violence Against Women," in Thistlethwaite and Potter Engel, *Lift Every Voice,* pp. 169-85.

18. In Emily M. Townes, ed., *A Troubling in My Soul: Womanist Perspectives on Evil & Suffering* (Maryknoll, NY: Orbis Books, 1993), pp. 130-49.

19. Williams, p. 145.

20. See also the article on *imago Dei* by Hilkert in this volume.

21. Williams, pp. 138, 143, 145-47.

22. Ibid., pp. 145, 147.

23. Myth and ideology will be used interchangeably here because the myths that identify women (here the focus is only on Eve and Mary) carry a map of symbols about women that masks the truth of our being and serves the interests of patriarchy, thus functioning both in a broad sense (cultural anthropology) and a narrow sense (Marx) as an ideology.

24. Rosemary Radford Ruether, *Womanguides: Readings toward a Feminist Theology* (Boston: Beacon Press, 1985), pp. 85-86.

25. Elizabeth Clark and Herbert Richardson, eds., *Women and Religion: A Feminist Sourcebook of Christian Thought* (New York: Harper & Row, 1977).

26. This essay cannot discuss the reconstructive work of Phyllis Trible, *God and the Rhetoric of Sexuality* (Philadelphia: Fortress Press, 1978), which is one key resource that clarifies that the original creation was of humanity—*adam* understood as an androgene whom God made into two sexes at once. Nor can we discuss the power of Augustine's interpretation of the creation and fall, which made sin the cause of all earthly suffering, so ably discussed by Elaine Pagels, *Adam, Eve, and the Serpent* (New York: Random House, 1988).

27. Pagels, *Adam, Eve, and the Serpent*, takes this on as a major issue throughout her text. Another very important scholarly contribution on the growth of Christian asceticism and the contribution of Augustine to it is Peter Brown, especially his *The Body and Society: Men, Women, and Sexual Renunciation in Early Christianity* (New York: Columbia University Press, 1988).

28. De Cult. Fem. 1.1. Cited in Ruether, *Sexism and God-Talk: Toward a Feminist Theology* (Boston: Beacon Press, 1983), p. 167.

29. Excerpted in Clark and Richardson, pp. 116-30.

30. See the "Declaration on the Question of the Admission of Women to the Ministerial Priesthood," in Leonard and Arlene Swidler, eds., *Women Priests: A Catholic Commentary on the Vatican Declaration* (New York: Paulist Press, 1977), pp. 37-49. This is based, in part, on Thomas's assertion that women are misbegotten males, following Aristotle, see ST I, q.92, a. 1, ad 1 and III, q. 39, a.1. This is also cited in Clark and Richardson, pp. 77-101.

31. Rosemary Ruether, "The Descent of Woman," in *New Woman, New Earth: Sexist Ideologies and Human Liberation* (New York: The Seabury Press, 1975), pp. 3-35.

32. In addition, Ruether also has worked extensively on Mary; see her *Mary: The Feminine Face of the Church* (Philadelphia: Westminster Press, 1977). There are chapters on Mary in many of her works. Another critical reading of the damage of the myth of Eve that appeared in the same period is in Mary Daly, *Beyond God the Father: Toward a Philosophy of Women's Liberation* (Boston: Beacon Press, 1973).

33. Ruether, "The Descent of Woman," esp. pp. 6-19.

34. Ibid., pp. 19-22. See also the accompanying chapter, "Mistress of Heaven: The Meaning of Mariology," pp. 36-62.

35. Ruether, *Sexism and God-Talk*, pp. 139-73.

36. As this book goes to press, a major contribution on evil from a feminist perspective has been offered by Susan A. Ross, "Evil and Hope: Foundational Moral Perspectives." See *Proceedings of the Catholic Theological Society of America* 1995 (forthcoming).

10

When Being Human Becomes Truly Earthly

An Ecofeminist Proposal for Solidarity

Anne M. Clifford

And then all that has divided us will merge
And then compassion will be wedded to power
And then softness will come to a world that is harsh and unkind
And then both men and women will be gentle
And then both women and men will be strong
And then no person will be subject to another's will
And then all will be rich and free and varied
And then the greed of some will give way to the needs of many
And then all will share equally in the Earth's
    abundance
And then all will care for the sick and the weak
    and the old
And then all will nourish the young
And then all will cherish life's creatures
And then all will live in harmony with each other
    and the Earth
And then everywhere will be called Eden once again
Judy Chicago[1]

    This poem expresses some of the greatest challenges of our age. Its lack of punctuation throughout, including the last line, is reflective of the profound interconnectedness of the longings of the human heart, longings for a future transformed by a guiding vision. The poem culminates with a call to cherish life's creatures, to live in harmony with each other and the Earth so that the desired transformation in which "everywhere will be Eden once again" will become reality.

As a whole, the poem poignantly raises the foundational question: What does it mean to be human? In times of crisis, this question becomes acute. In our present era of ecological crisis, we are challenged to respond anew to what, in many ways, has become *the* perennial question for theological reflection—the question of human meaning. If the crisis is to be remedied, if the hopeful vision of the poem is to be realized, we must change our perceptions of our selves and our relation to the Earth.

The faith traditions of Judaism and Christianity provide a succinct response to the question of human meaning. Humans are the creatures of God who, male and female, are made in God's own image and likeness (Gen. 1:27). An interpretation of this foundational belief in this era, increasingly called "postmodern," must be mindful of the fact that we participate in the life and health of a small blue planet in one galaxy among at least 193 others, that has been evolving to its present state for approximately 15 billion years. Like all the other forms of life that share Earth with us, we live within a five- to seven-mile-thick layer known to biologists as the "biosphere," an interconnecting network of ecosystems that is becoming ever more fragile with each passing day.

Earth's human inhabitants, more than any other, have contributed to the ecological crisis. The deterioration of the planet's ecosystems, however, has not necessarily been due to deliberate human malice. Rather, it is due to a much too narrow conception of nature, one that views the Earth's resources as the building material of human life.

In the 300-year drive to understand and gain control over nature, nature was stripped of its magical properties and became viewed as raw resources "there" for human use. In building North Atlantic industrial civilization, people with scientific and technological know-how adopted an adversarial stance vis-à-vis Earth. Its life forms, far from being cherished, have been treated as expendable objects for human use in the name of technological advance. Due to our exploitation of nature, harmony has given way to discord. The legacy of the modern vision of humanity's relationship to nature is a set of interrelated problems: the pollution of air, soil and water; the depletion of Earth's resources; the destruction of the ozone layer; deforestation with its accompanying displacement of indigenous peoples and the elimination of plant and animal species; and the unequal distribution of the necessities of life for peoples around the globe. Because these are the problems facing us today, it seems fitting that the question, "What does it mean to be human?" be restated, "When does being human become truly earthly?"

Fortunately, there is a growing recognition of the plight of the Earth. For the most part, however, ecologists and environmentalists, in their commitment to nature, have not attended to the connection of the domination of nature to the domination of women and of the poorer classes. In the industrial era, the fruits of the domination of Earth have been in the hands of the dominant class and sex. The unequal distribution of life's necessities has been more unequal for women, as has been the division of labor.

According to recent United Nations' figures, women make up slightly over 50 percent of the world's population, but over 75 percent of the starving people are women with their dependent children. The women of the world grow 50 percent of the world's food but own only 1 percent of the world's land, do most of the world's domestic work, make up 33.3 percent of the paid labor force and are concentrated in the lowest paid occupations, and earn 25 percent less than men who do similar work.[2]

ECOFEMINISM: THE INTERCONNECTION OF ECOLOGY AND FEMINISM

Ecofeminism recognizes that the domination of women and non-human nature are intimately connected and mutually reinforcing.[3] Ecofeminism offers Christian theology a foundational perspective for responding to questions about the meaning of human creaturehood. Unlike many of the other environmental movements of the 1990s, ecofeminism does not relate to the environment as the vast arena of nature outside ourselves which we humans can repair and restore. It challenges the claim to human autonomy from nature inherent in such a stance. True to the ecological paradigm, which by its very nature stresses the organic wholeness and interconnectedness of all forms of life, ecofeminism addresses the question of what it means to be human with stress on the earthliness of human existence. Ecofeminists recognize that we humans are, in effect, a force that threatens to push the Earth's biosphere dangerously out of balance. Therefore, it is vital for us to take a very careful look at what it means to be human participants in an endangered world.

Like all forms of feminism, ecofeminism is a movement to end the sexism of male power and privilege over women. In company with many other types of feminism, ecofeminism also opposes an oppressive patriarchal framework that legitimizes other forms of social domination, such as racism and classism. What sets ecofeminism apart from other feminisms, however, is its recognition of the connection between naturism, the domination of nonhuman nature, and the domination of women (and other supposedly inferior people) within North Atlantic patriarchal culture. Ecofeminist analysis draws attention to the logic used to justify the domination of humans on the basis of gender, race, class status or sexual orientation and notes that it is also used to justify the domination of nonhuman nature. In the words of Karen J. Warren:

> Because eliminating the logic of domination is part of the feminist critique—whether a critique of patriarchy, white supremacist culture, or imperialism—ecofeminists insist that naturism is properly viewed as an integral part of any feminist movement to end sexist oppression and the logic of domination which conceptually grounds it.[4]

Although there are important differences in the positions of individual ecofeminists, they universally agree that the domination of women and the exploitation of nonhuman nature are interconnected. There is a link between patriarchy and environmental destruction. Ecofeminists believe that we cannot end the exploitation of nature without ending human oppression, and vice versa. To achieve both, nothing short of a radical transformation of consciousness is needed. This transformation requires the acceptance of a conceptual framework that heretofore has not been a part of the predominant modes of North Atlantic thinking.

A conceptual framework is an interconnected set of beliefs, values, attitudes and assumptions that shape how we perceive ourselves and our relationship to one another and the world. In North Atlantic patriarchal culture, hierarchical dualism has been the predominant conceptual framework, a framework that divides reality according to gender, with higher value placed on those attributes associated with masculinity. Patriarchal hierarchies are problematic because they are dualistic. They presume "up/down" thought patterns that arbitrarily assign higher value, status and prestige to what is "up" at the expense of what is "down."[5] Hierarchical dualisms such as male/female, white/nonwhite, culture/nature must be challenged because they result in oppositional relationships and abusive behaviors. Historically, the elevation of what is associated with the white male creators of culture has been at the expense of females, nonwhites and nature.

In this era of ecological crisis, the culture/nature dualism is a particularly dangerous false construct. Our concept of nature is itself culture bound. This dualism treats nature as discontinuous from humans, who are the measure of all things. Nature—more correctly named nonhuman nature, since humans are participants in the Earth's processes—is treated as the external "other" of instrumental value for human use. Therefore, what is nonhuman can be exploited for the sake of human society and its progress.

Historically, the patriarchal hierarchical dualism that has placed higher value on human culture at the expense of nonhuman nature also encompasses other dualisms that value reason over emotion, mind over body, and male over female. In the logic of domination, rationality (especially value-neutral, scientific objectivity), freedom (especially, the autonomy of the individual), and transcendence of nature (especially the use and control of nonhuman nature for human ends) are valued. Since they are also culturally identified with "the masculine," the masculine is what is normative for being human. Those qualities associated with reproductivity, sensuality and emotionality—traits stereotypically associated with females—are the very qualities that make women identified with nonhuman nature and are, therefore, less valued and viewed as less authentically human. As a result, like nature, women have been treated as "the other."

ECOFEMINISM AND THEOLOGICAL ANTHROPOLOGY

In our era, an ecofeminist perspective is an important corrective for Christian theology that has made the human condition the centerpiece of its reflection. Since the Enlightenment, emphasis on theological anthropology has been North Atlantic Christianity's way of responding to the challenges posed to theology by the rising hegemony of the natural sciences, a hegemony that has contributed to the ecological crisis that we face today. When theology turned from the cosmos—and therefore from nonhuman nature—and appropriated a philosophical "turn to the subject" in response to this challenge, it also uncritically participated in the prevailing conceptual framework of hierarchal dualism that made nonhuman nature subordinate to human concerns.

As a result, for most of the modern period, theologians have directed their attention almost exclusively to human existence or human history, often with an emphasis on personal salvation or sociopolitical emancipation, and have implicitly treated nature as a timeless and static backdrop. In addition, not unlike the other modes of North Atlantic thinking, theological anthropology, while claiming a universality for its truth claims, has also been extensively androcentric, thereby ignoring the particularity of women's experience and relationship to God. As a result, males' experiences, values and images of God have been, and for the most part continue to be, elevated over females' experiences, values and images of God.

An ecofeminist perspective on contemporary theology gives direction to the process of bringing faith in God to understanding in a manner that calls for a radical conversion of mind and heart from hierarchical dualism to egalitarian holism. Such a conversion is required of us if we are to succeed in developing a conceptual framework for articulating what it means to be females and males in relationship to God, to one another, and to the nonhuman natural world in ways that mutually enhance these relationships.

The development of an ecofeminist theology of human earthly existence requires an examination of the historical, symbolic, theoretical and experiential manifestations of hierarchical dualism and domination. Due to the constraints of the limitations of length, it is impossible to treat all these areas as they deserve. Attention will be given to the logical starting point, the biblical texts foundational for creation theology. Our focus will be on the Genesis creation texts, because in the unfolding of the Christian tradition they have been interpreted in ways that have given the subordination of women and nonhuman nature a sacral legitimation.

It is important to note that from the standpoint of theological anthropology, the Bible, composed and edited over many centuries, presents no unified and systematic understanding of the human person or nature. Biblical stories, sayings and reflections are thoroughly theocentric. On the whole, in the Bible, God is the primary actor. What it means to be human is addressed in the context of God's activity as revealed in the course of the history of Israel and the life and message of Jesus Christ. The Bible confesses again and again that it is in God that the origin and ultimate meaning of creation are found.

By the same token, the concept of nature as a designation for organic and inorganic phenomena is derived from the modern sciences. The Bible does not focus on nature, per se. In fact, the Bible has no concept of nature, as it is understood today. In the language of the Bible, what we might refer to as nature may be simply equated with God's creation.

From the outset, it is important to bear in mind that, while the Bible is a source of divine revelation, it was composed by persons affected by patriarchal cultural attitudes. In addition, throughout the history of Christianity, its texts have been given patriarchal interpretations that have justified women's subordinate role in church and society. Biblical texts have also been drawn upon extensively to rationalize other forms of domination and hierarchical dualism, including the abuse of Earth and its life forms.

INTERPRETATION OF CREATION TEXTS, FROM ARCHETYPES TO PROTOTYPES

In response to the problem of patriarchal influence on the Bible, Elisabeth Schüssler Fiorenza has made a helpful distinction for interpreting biblical texts that will be applied here. Biblical interpretations can be guided by viewing a text as either an "archetype" or a "prototype." By making this distinction, she underscores the fact that while both archetype and prototype "denote original models," an archetype is typically understood to be an ideal form for an unchanging pattern. In contrast, a prototype is not a binding, timeless and unchanging pattern. It is always open to the possibility and, even at times, the necessity of its own transformation.[6]

The creation accounts in Genesis have been used extensively as sources for archetypes to legitimate the subordination of women and nonhuman nature. Without a doubt, for Judaism and Christianity, Genesis 2-3, the story of "Adam and Eve," is the most influential text for justifying the subordination of women. This ancient myth has been used as a basis for Western Christianity's hierarchical and dualistic interpretations of *imago Dei* (Gen. 1:27) that understood the male to normatively possess the image of God. Women, if they possessed the image of God at all, did so only derivatively under the males as their heads.[7]

Mary Catherine Hilkert, in her essay in this volume entitled "Cry Beloved Image: Rethinking the Image of God," surveys this traditional interpretation of *imago Dei*, noting the extent of its influence. The construction of gender difference, with its inherent subordination of women in the Christian tradition, is connected with the appropriation by Christian theologians (all of whom were male) of the hierarchical, dualistic thought patterns of Platonism, neo-Platonism and Aristotelianism and reading them into biblical texts.

The resulting interpretative synthesis contributed to Christianity's uncritical acceptance of the male/female and soul/body hierarchical dualism of Greek philosophy and culture. Christianity retained the symbolism of the rational soul as "masculine" and the body and its passions as "feminine," and gave them a sacral character. The soul/body division, of course, is also integral to the hierarchical dualism of the spiritual valued over matter, including not only the ground under our feet but also our bodily existence and all other forms of life. Thus living the properly "religious life" of the Christian required an asceticism of flight from the material world in order to insure the personal salvation of one's soul.

The dualistic conceptual framework "baptized" by Christian theologians was made the linchpin of modern thought by the most influential philosopher of the seventeenth century, Rene Descartes (1596-1650). His famous axiom, *Cogito, ergo sum*, resulted in the abstraction of the body from the mind and a virtual philosophical divorce between human beings and the Earth. The intellectual inheritance of this mode of thinking has resulted in the subject/object split and the mechanistic and instrumental construal of nature that has characterized North Atlantic thinking in the modern period.

In the past 300 years, many in the West have interpreted Genesis 1-3 as an archetype for a divinely sanctioned exploitation of nature, furthering and deepening the dualism of humans and nonhuman nature to the point of polarization. The text directing humans to exercise dominion over nonhuman nature and fill the Earth and subdue it (Gen. 1: 26-29) is often cited as the God-given basis for humans exercising power over nonhuman nature. Genesis 2: 20-21, in which the first human is directed by God to name all the animals in the garden, has also been cited to establish that all of creation was made to serve human purposes.[8]

From the standpoint of critical ecofeminism, a major contributor to the interpretation of the Genesis creation texts as legitimating the exploitation of nature is Francis Bacon (1561-1626), often cited as the "father of modern science." Carolyn Merchant's careful analysis of Bacon's writings reveals his extensive use of female imagery and metaphors as tools for adapting scientific methods of research to a form of power over nature. Bacon described nature as an unruly female that needed to be controlled and subdued.[9] He envisioned science as the work of the male scientific mind experimenting and testing until the secrets of female nature could be penetrated. The development of science to gain power over nature was given a religious interpretation by Bacon. He interpreted the Genesis 3 account of the "Fall of Man" and his expulsion from the garden of Eden caused by the temptation of a woman, as the reason man lost dominion over creation. In the pre-fall state of dominion, man was like God. Bacon concluded that because a female's inquisitiveness caused the first man's fall from his God-given dominion, man's interrogation of another female, nature, should be used to regain it.[10]

The question for theology is, do the Genesis creation texts warrant interpretations that justify the subordination of women and the domination of nonhuman nature, the unruly female? The short answer is no, they do not. These texts, given interpretations that have been treated as archetypes for attitudes about women and nonhuman nature, are also open to prototypical interpretations that can transform attitudes about women and nonhuman nature.

Since the Bible is theocentric, the basic message of the two accounts of creation in Genesis is the divine origin of the whole of creation. God created the universe, the Earth, its plants, birds, animals and humans. Each can be said to have a particular relationship with God. In the case of humans, however, this relationship is expressed in a unique fashion. In the earlier of the two stories found in Genesis 2-3, the metaphor for God's relationship to humanity is divine inspiration. Its author tells a story of God forming the human creature from the dust of the ground ('adamah) and breathing into this earthling ('adam) the breath of life (Gen. 2:7). In Genesis 1 this relationship is expressed in the ambiguous metaphor "the image of God" (Gen. 1:26-27). In both accounts, humans, although they share much with other creatures, have a special relationship with God, a certain affinity for God.

The story in Genesis 2:4b-3:24 reflects the concerns of the united kingdom of David and his successor Solomon (ca. 1010-930 B.C.E.). The Yahwist tradition, of which this text is a part, reveals Israel's appropriation of an ideology that both legitimized the monarchy and at the same time held it accountable to the law of the Mosaic covenant.[11]

This account is widely regarded as an etiology, a story rich in symbolism that attempts to locate and give expression to the situation of the people at that time. This etiology encompasses the experience of goodness and intimate relatedness with God, the benevolent Creator, and the contrast experience of sin and estrangement from that God. The creation of the human from the dust of the Earth makes it clear that the human person is bound to the Earth. However, the gift of life-breath that God breathed into the human earthling also expresses the special bond with the Creator that humans enjoy as gift.

The story unfolds with God placing the earthling in the garden of Eden, which this creature is to cultivate and care for (Gen. 2:15). God declares that it is not good for this creature to be alone. An attempt is made by God to provide a suitable companion. God creates the animals, and the human earthling is directed to name them. Naming is not a sign of domination but rather reflective of how the human earthling establishes relationships with other creatures. Put simply, naming expresses the bond between humans and animals, not a divinely ordained domination of animals by humans.

Although the presentation of the animals begins by stressing their similarities to the human earthling—both are made from the dirt of the Earth—it does end up focusing on their differences. Difference, however, is value neutral. According to Phyllis Trible's analysis, although the earthling and the animals are both living beings (*nephesh*), it is through the God-given power of naming that the earthling is distinct from the animals. The charge to name the other creatures results in a hierarchy of harmony planned by God.[12] This hierarchy is a harmony of differentiation. The difference between the human earthling and the other species placed in the garden by God is illustrated by the fact that the animals prove to be inappropriate companions for the first earthling.

God, in an act of compassion, creates woman out of the earthling's own body. This one at last is suitable (Gen. 2:23). Trible points out that the creation of woman is a second full creation. Through God's activity of fashioning this creature from the first human earthling, *'adam*, becomes male *'is* and female *'issa*. She asserts:

> In the very act of distinguishing female from male, the earth creature describes her as "bone of my bones and flesh of my flesh" (2:23). These words speak unity, solidarity, mutuality and equality. Accordingly, in this poem the man does not depict himself as either prior to or superior to the woman. His sexual identity depends on her even as hers depends upon him. For both of them sexuality originates in the one flesh of humanity.[13]

In the chapter that follows, the pair falls to temptation and sins, with the result that the harmonious relationship between humanity and nature undergoes a rupture from which both sides suffer. The rupture in nonhuman life is symbolized by the curse directed to the serpent. From the human side, the rupture is the bond of equality between women and men. Due to the role assigned to Eve as the first of the pair to succumb to temptation, man will rule over her and her female descendants. The punishment laid on her and the women who come after her is bearing children in pain. In reflecting on this text, Trible points out:

> His supremacy is neither a divine right nor a male prerogative. Her subordination is neither a divine decree nor the female destiny. Both their positions result from their shared disobedience.[14]

What is narrated in Genesis 3 is more than an etiological explanation of the difference in sex roles; it is a legitimation for the inequality of women in the Israelite community. This text encapsulates the hierarchical dualism of Israel's society during the monarchy. The subordination of women prevents them from participating in defining the communal values of society. Woman becomes "the other," systemically excluded from Jewish religious life and practice.[15]

Genesis 1, likely a protest against the notions of creation held by Israel's Babylonian oppressors, is written in a very different literary style. This Priestly account of creation was formulated in the historical context of the exile of Jews in Babylon in the sixth century B.C.E. The exile was a devastating experience for Israel, politically and theologically. Those who survived the trauma reasserted their belief in God's power over chaos. They did this by developing their own creation narrative. This narrative, greatly influenced by the epic poem of their Babylonian enslavers, *Enuma elish*,[16] has some elements of obvious correspondence to it. Both stories have the same general succession of events: chaos at the beginning, creation of the firmament, of dry land, of the heavenly bodies, and of people.

There are, however, major differences. In *Enuma elish*, the "stuff" of creation comes from a terrible conflict in which the goddess Tiamat is slain by the young god, Marduk, in an act of violent vengeance. It is from the carcass of this slain matriarchal goddess that the world is made. In contrast, Genesis 1 depicts God creating planet Earth simply by a word that brings order out of chaos. When it comes to the creation of humans, in the Babylonian myth the first human is created from the blood of the most evil of the gods, who is slain by the others. This creature, designated as "the savage," is to be in the service of the gods. In contrast, in Genesis 1 the human earthling is made by God along with the animals, their earthly co-inhabitants, in God's own image. It is this creation that is proclaimed to be "very good." There is no consensus among biblical exegetes about the precise meaning of the phrase "in the image of God." Since human creatures enjoy a special relationship to God, their purpose within the order of creation is said to be the exercise of dominion over the other orders of animals with whom humans share the same habitat.

Many scholars interpret the language of image and dominion as royal in origin. The words *image* and *likeness* echo language used of ancient Middle Eastern kings, the sovereigns who represented their gods as rulers in theocratic societies. If this is true, then the nobility of being an exiled Jew oppressed by slavery sharply contrasts with and is pointedly critical of the Babylonian picture of humans as the slaves of the gods.

For many feminist readers of the words "So God created human-kind in his [sic] image, in the image of God he created them; male and female he [sic] created them" (Gen. 1:27), the claim for equality of women with men and of full human dignity is given divine approba-tion. Given the patriarchal treatment of women in the Priestly tradi-tion as a whole, however, the inclusion of women in the phrase "in the image of God" evokes a feminist hermeneutics of suspicion. The treatment of women in other texts of the Priestly tradition, such as the laws of uncleanness for menstruation and childbearing in Leviticus 12 and 15, effectively separate women from the sacred realm. In the light of these texts, does Genesis 1:27 assert the equality of women with men?

Phyllis Bird has argued that the inclusion of women as imaging God may be merely a part of the logic of the accompanying command to "be fruitful and multiply, and fill the earth" (Gen. 1:28).[17] Since the Priestly writers probably had no experience of an egalitarian society, it is unlikely that *imago Dei* is an explicit claim for women's equality with men. However, this need not and certainly has not prevented a prototypical interpretation of the *imago Dei* symbol for women's full equality and human dignity. The inclusion of women as "made in the image of God" in Genesis 1:27 has been given emphasis by feminists due to women's experience. In many ways the recognition that fe-males are *imago Dei* has been transformed by women in their struggle against the dehumanizing forces of patriarchy. This symbol, proto-typically transformed as a claim for equality and full human dignity, continues to evoke the further transformation of patriarchal struc-tures and the interpretations of reality that accompany them.

The directive for dominion in Genesis 1:26-30 obviously must be addressed because it has been used as an archetype for human domi-nation of the Earth in North Atlantic culture, as is illustrated by the influential position of Bacon. Richard Clifford argues that the full meaning of "to have dominion" only emerges later in the biblical story. As people became more numerous, they also became more sinful. Noah and his family alone are found to be righteous by God and excepted from the flood that destroyed all other humans. Noah is told "to bring two of every sort of living things into the ark; they shall be male and female" (Gen. 6:19). Clifford reflects, "Noah's gathering of the animals to save the species makes clear at last what having dominion over animals means: seeing to their survival."[18]

What this text also illustrates is the belief, recognized implicitly by the biblical authors, that all human offenses potentially imperil nature. This is the strongest statement about what dominion means. It gives a potentially ecological understanding of the Deuteronomic directive, "Choose life, so that you and your descendants may live" (Deut. 30:19). If we fail to love and obey God, not only we, but also all that lives on the Earth, shall perish.

The other problematic directive to the first pair is "fill the earth and subdue it" (Gen. 1:28). Again Richard Clifford is helpful. His examination of the use of *subdue* in other biblical texts, for example in Numbers 32:21-22, indicates that *subdue* is meant in the sense of establishing a territory on which a godly life can be built. He concludes that subduing the land means to inhabit the land that God gives, transforming it into a home. Clifford asserts, "It does not mean to exploit it but rather to receive it as a gift and live on it."[19]

AN ECOFEMINIST THEOLOGY OF SOLIDARITY WITH GOD AND THE EARTH

Some environmentally concerned theologians are arguing today for a stewardship typology in which humans live out their divinely ordained *imago Dei* as caretakers of the Earth and all its creatures.[20] Stewardship, however, is a concept with shortcomings worthy of consideration. Solidarity, therefore, will be explored as a viable and more desirable alternative for an ecofeminist theology of creation.

To its credit, stewardship pointedly critiques the interpretation of *imago Dei* that envisions humanity as absolute sovereigns over the Earth, as if all nonhuman creation was made for the disposal of divinely appointed royal despots. In the stewardship typology, to be *imago Dei* is to be called to represent God in relationship to the rest of creation as the divinely appointed trustees of God's property. The assumption is that the steward is given the responsibility to look after his superior's property in that superior's absence. Care for God's property is to be benevolent through and through. However, since stewardship interprets the garden of Eden as made for human use, it implies a divinely sanctioned instrumental management of nonhuman nature for human benefit.

The stewardship typology for *imago Dei* is an inadequate interpretation for the crisis we face today. Like the sovereignty typology, it perpetuates the conceptual framework of hierarchical dualism. Human mastery of nonhuman nature, whether it is destructive or benevolent, is still a claim for mastery. Stewardship falls into the conceptual trap of the hierarchical otherness of humans vis-à-vis nonhuman creation. Thus the interdependence of humans with all of creation is neglected.

For a more holistic solution to what is lacking in the stewardship typology, I am proposing a typology of solidarity. Solidarity is predicated on a unified effort of distinct groups to achieve a common good, a healthy planet on which all life forms can flourish. The unified effort that solidarity seeks does not erase difference, be that the differences among peoples of different cultures, races and classes or the differences between humans and other life forms.

My North Atlantic ecofeminist theological application of solidarity to *imago Dei* treats this symbol prototypically as an affirmation of humanity's profound bondedness with God, with peoples of different cultures and with the other life forms on Earth. It challenges the archetype that holds that the God of Genesis 1 is rightly interpreted as a distant sovereign ruling from afar. God is not the king of human beings, but rather the source and goal of the whole of creation. The emphasis is on God as the Creator who neither originated out of cosmic conflict nor created the cosmos out of conflict with other deities. The meaning and significance of this for *imago Dei* is that it indicates how God and humans are to be co-creators.

Our solidarity with God as *imago Dei* does not set us apart from creation, as the anthropocentric archetypical interpretation of this symbol did. Rather it decenters human beings of North Atlantic culture as the apex and goal of creation. Like the rest of creation, we are made of the same dirt—the same elements that are in the rocks of the hills, the birds of the air and the fish of the seas are in us. Our relationship to all the other creatures of Earth is, however, not one of simple sameness, but rather one of interdependent kinship with respect for diversity. In an ecofeminist understanding of solidarity, the hierarchy of biological complexity of living and nonliving creation is not dismissed. It is tempered with an emphasis on harmony and mutual connectedness. The biological hierarchy of complexity is not a basis for valuing one part of creation over another, but rather a basis for appreciating every aspect of creation as reflecting the glory of God in distinct ways.

The praxis of an ecofeminist theological solidarity of humans with the Earth is to make one's relationship with the rest of creation, a relationship that eschews conflict and competition with other peoples and other life forms on Earth. The relationship seeks to bring harmony with God and with all of creation into our daily life choices.

To embody an ecofeminist theology of solidarity requires a conscious affirmation of the common sense reality that humans belong to the Earth and are dependent on the great matrix of Earth's life forms.

Obviously to be human is to exercise responsibility for plant and animal life in ways that they cannot. Certainly, a commitment to an ecofeminist theology of solidarity also recognizes that the responsibility for Earth healing by industrialized North Atlantic peoples, who have unjustly exploited both human and natural resources of poor Southern nations, is much greater than for those people who live in "Third World" countries of the Southern hemisphere.

The call for the praxis of a responsible solidarity is not based simply on duty, although our duty to right the wrongs humans have inflicted on the earth in the name of progress is real. Responsible ecological solidarity calls for an ongoing discernment about the life choices we make, informed by an empathy that is rooted in the belief that God is love and that in our affinity with God as *imago Dei*, we are called to incarnate that love in how we relate to the whole of creation. This is essential if we are going to be motivated to move beyond the patriarchal framework and its hierarchical dualism that keep us cut off from people who are different from us or from nonhuman life forms. The empathy of an ecofeminist solidarity with God and creation is not simply a generalized feeling of good will and benevolent care for the Earth. The empathy of ecofeminist solidarity is cognitive as well as affective. It is a felt knowledge that informs our specific responses to those creatures of God most profoundly endangered by the ecological crisis.

Experientially, empathy is expressed in solidarity with those humans, animals and plants at risk due to the choices made by those who, without questioning, participate in the patriarchal conceptual framework characterized by patterns of domination. Empathetic ecological solidarity requires us to devote time and effort to become informed about the plight of others, for example, becoming aware of the life struggles of "Third World" persons burdened by poverty, such as the indigenous women and men of the Amazon who are losing their homes and way of life by indiscriminate burning of the rain forest. It also requires us to be informed about the plight of plant and animal life forms that are endangered.

Certainly the loss of the rain forest negatively affects the whole planet, but the empathy of solidarity calls forth more from us than being informed about how the destruction of the rain forest might affect us. It calls us to risk setting aside our elevated sense of differences from indigenous peoples and other life forms and owning our profound connectedness with those people whose homes and cultures are being destroyed, and the plants and animals that are being driven to extinction. Empathetic solidarity requires information, but it is embodied in the formation of our life choices, choices that affirm that each and every creature has value in and for itself as a creation of God.

CONCLUSIONS

The ecological crisis plaguing Earth is a life-and-death matter. Ecofeminism recognizes this and argues that the domination of non-human nature and of women are intimately connected and must be remedied. An ecofeminist theology of the human person critiques the archetypal interpretations of scripture that have been used to legitimate these forms of domination. The ecofeminist prototypical interpretation of the Christian biblical symbol *imago Dei*, which I have proposed, not only affirms the full human dignity of women and men, it also affirms the solidarity of humans with God, the Earth, and all its life forms. This solidarity calls for an ongoing discernment that embodies empathy in connectedness with the earth in ways that are responsive to the many manifestations of our ecological crisis and appropriate to biblically rooted creation faith.

Certainly, adoption of an ecofeminist theology of creation will not restore Earth to an Eden-like state. Eden is a utopian symbol, a product of the human religious imagination. However, an ecofeminist interpretation of solidarity of humans with all of creation may help us recognize the implications of the fact that we are not the elevated center of creation. The anthropocentricism of North Atlantic culture is something that planet Earth cannot afford. To truly be earthlings, we must live in harmony with the Earth and embody an empathy with the plight of all of its peoples and with all of its life forms in our life choices.

> AND THEN BOTH WOMEN AND MEN WILL
>   BECOME TRULY EARTHLY
> KNOWING THAT NOT ONLY WE HUMANS,
> BUT ALSO ALL OF CREATION LIVES AND MOVES
> AND HAS ITS BEING IN GOD

NOTES

1. Judy Chicago, "Untitled Poem from 'The Dinner Party'," in Marilyn Sewell, ed., *Cries of the Spirit: A Celebration of Women's Spirituality* (Boston: Beacon Press, 1991), p. 235.

2. These United Nations statistics are taken from the "World Women Data Sheet on the Occasion of Decade for Women, Equality, Development and Peace, 1975-85," cited in Patricia H. Cancellier and Kimberly A. Crews, *Women in the World: The Women's Decade and Beyond* (Washington, DC: Population Reference Bureau, Inc., 1986), p. 1.

3. Francoise d'Eaubonne introduced the term *ecoféminisme* (ecofeminism) in *Le féminisme ou la mort (Feminism or Death)*(Paris: Pierre Horay, 1974), pp. 213-52, to emphasize women's potential for bringing about major changes in ecology. Recent collections of essays of interest related to what I am proposing in this essay are Carol J. Adams, ed., *Ecofeminism and the Sacred* (New York:

Continuum, 1993) and Greta Gaard, ed., *Ecofeminism, Women, Animals, Nature* (Philadelphia: Temple University Press, 1993).

4. Karen J. Warren, "The Power and the Promise of Ecological Feminism," *Environmental Ethics* 12 (1990): 132.

5. I am emphasizing hierarchical dualism and not hierarchy *per se*. I believe that it is possible to acknowledge a hierarchy of biological complexity without making value judgments about it. I am, therefore, taking a different position from that of highly influential ecofeminists who reject hierarchy out of hand, namely Ynestra King in "The Ecology of Feminism and the Feminism of Ecology," in Judith Plant, ed., *Healing Our Wounds: The Power of Ecological Feminism* (Boston: New Society Publishers, 1989), pp. 18-28, and Elizabeth Dobson-Gray, *Green Paradise Lost: Remything Genesis* (Wellesley, MA: Roundtable Press, 1979).

6. Elisabeth Schüssler Fiorenza, *Bread Not Stone: The Challenge of Feminist Biblical Interpretation* (Boston: Beacon Press, 1984), p. 61.

7. See in particular Augustine, *On the Trinity*, 12.7.10.

8. Lynn White, "The Historical Roots of Our Ecological Crisis," *Science* 155 (1967): 1206. This essay, widely cited in environmental literature, argues that the root of Western arrogance toward nature lies in the Christian belief that nature has no reason for existence save to serve humans. The source of the ecological crisis is Christian anthropocentrism.

9. Carolyn Merchant, *The Death of Nature* (San Francisco: Harper and Row, 1980), pp. 164-72. Merchant draws attention to the influence of the interrogation of witches, in which Bacon was involved as an officer in the court of James I, on his choice of metaphors for the interrogation of nature.

10. Ibid., p. 170. Merchant cites "Novum Organum," Part 2, in Francis Bacon, *Works*, vol. 4, p. 247, and "Valerius Terminus," *Works*, vol. 3, pp. 217, 219, ed. James Spedding, Robert Leslie Ellis, and Douglas Heath (London: Longmanns Green, 1870), and "The Masculine Birth of Time," in Benjamin Farrington, ed., *The Philosophy of Francis Bacon* (Liverpool, England: Liverpool University Press, 1964), pp. 62 and 317 n. 13.

11. Diane Bergant with Carroll Stuhlmueller, "Creation According to the Old Testament," in Ernan McMullin, ed., *Evolution and Creation* (Notre Dame, IN: University of Notre Dame Press, 1986), p. 156.

12. Phyllis Trible, in *God and the Rhetoric of Sexuality* (Philadelphia: Fortress Press, 1978), p. 92.

13. Ibid., pp. 98-99.

14. Ibid., p. 128.

15. For an excellent treatment of the "otherness" of women in Judaism, see Judith Plaskow, *Standing again at Sinai; Judaism from a Feminist Perspective* (San Francisco: Harper and Row, 1990).

16. For a translation of *Enuma elish*, see Alexander Heidel, *The Babylonian Genesis Story of Creation* (Chicago: University of Chicago Press, 1951), pp. 18-60.

17. From a very careful analysis of Genesis 1, Phyllis A. Bird argues that *imago Dei*, in reference to 'adam and the sexual differentiation that accompanies it, cannot be understood apart from the command "Be fruitful and multiply..." Sexual differentiation anticipates God's blessing and prepares for it. See "'Male and Female He Created Them': Gen 1:27b in the Context of the Priestly Account of Creation," *Harvard Theological Review* 74 (1981): 146-47.

18. Richard J. Clifford, S.J., "Genesis 1-3: Permission to Exploit Nature?" *Bible Today* (1988): 135.

19. Ibid., p. 136.

20. Some recent works on the environment and/or ecology with emphasis on stewardship include Robert Faircy, *Wind and Sea Obey Him* (Westminster, MD: Christian Classics, 1988); Douglas John Hall, *Imaging God: Dominion as Stewardship* (Grand Rapids, MI: Eerdmans, 1987), and idem, *The Steward: A Biblical Symbol Come of Age* (Grand Rapids, MI: Eerdmans, 1990).

11

Cry Beloved Image

Rethinking the Image of God

Mary Catherine Hilkert

Where is "me"
   a part of me is missing
   aborted—stillborn—
      since that Garden time

      yet without plan or warning
      ever and ever again moving
      deep within my body
         and soul
      a person "image of God"
         WOMAN
      comes grasping, grasping
      for the breath of life
      struggling to be born
      and live—free

pushed back, covered over by
myriads of words—intoned word
   you are not man
   you are woman
   created for a man's pleasure
      and comfort
   created to bear man-child
      to rule you

created to bear woman-child
    to be subject to man-child

Man-child, oh man-child,
my father, husband, brothers, sons
  do you feel a deep stirring
      rebellion
  at the intoned word for you?
      You are man, be big
      be strong, powerful
      never surrender; succeed
      let no tears break through
      be mind, not heart
          heart is for the weak
      be arrogant-aggressive

CRY, CRY BELOVED IMAGE
Who calls us both?[1]

Commenting on this poem by Anne McGrew Bennett and similar calls for liberation from the voices of Asian women, Choan-Seng Song observed:

> Reading these words, whether from East or from West, one feels as if a volcano is erupting, the earth is shaking, and an abyss is breaking open. For what we—women and men—are going through today is the pain of a new creation, the birthpangs of a new image of woman and a new image of man in God. A revolution of a most radical kind is in the making here.[2]

This revolution involves not only our understanding of what it means to be human and of our appropriate relationship to the rest of creation, but also deeply held images and convictions about the very mystery of God.

In the last chapter, Anne Clifford called for conversion to an ecofeminist conceptual framework that opposes all forms of hierarchical dualism and embraces a holistic view of reality. Criticizing patriarchal interpretations of what it means to be created in the image of God that legitimate male domination and female subordination as well as human domination of the earth as "divinely intended," she proposed a theology of creation as a network of interdependent kinship that stresses solidarity with the earth, rather than "good stewardship" as the appropriate relationship of human beings to the rest of creation.

As Clifford noted, the unique relationship of human beings with God as described in Genesis and handed on through the Christian tradition is expressed in the ambiguous metaphor "image of God." In view of the effective history of the symbol's use to subordinate nature to human control and subordinate women to men, the question has been raised whether the symbol is an inherently imperialistic one that should be discarded in our day.

Yet the symbol is foundational not only to all Christian anthropology, but explicitly to feminist and womanist theology. As Janet Kalven once noted, "religious feminists are simply drawing out the implications of affirming that women are fully human beings made in the image of God."[3] Katie Cannon has argued that the symbol is central to ensuring African-American women's dignity as persons.[4] In the Roman Catholic tradition, an understanding of the human person as created in the image of God undergirds the social teaching of the church protecting the most vulnerable members of society from extinction or harm. The symbol remains essential to our understanding of what it means to be human, but it clearly needs a critical and creative retrieval in our day.

Since critical analysis of the effective history of the use of the symbol to subordinate women to men is available elsewhere, that will be reviewed only briefly here. More crucial are attempts to retrieve the symbol in ways that promote human dignity and the flourishing of all creation. Clifford's chapter emphasized the essential ecological framework for the retrieval of the symbol. The focus of this chapter will be to reflect on the personal, interpersonal, and social importance of the claim from Genesis that became central to Christian anthropology: humankind is created in the image and likeness of God.

CRITICAL REVIEW OF THE TRADITION

The persistence of the question in the Christian tradition of whether women were created in the image of God is revelatory in itself. There was no question as to whether "man" was created in the divine image, only whether "woman" was included. In the early church, some argued that only the male was in God's image, since woman was divinely intended to be subject to man.[5] In the Middle Ages, Peter Abelard (1079-1142) concluded from 1 Cor. 11:7 that "Certainly man, according to the Apostle is in the image of God and not woman."[6] Gratian (c. 1140) further reinforced the notion that "woman was not made in God's image." [7]

Problematic passages from Augustine (*De Trinitate*, 12.7.10) and Aquinas (ST 1, q. 93, a.4) are most frequently cited as evidence that the Christian tradition taught that women did not image God as fully as did men. To their credit, both Augustine and Aquinas moved beyond earlier traditions that held that only the male was created in God's image. Using a trinitarian framework, both taught that the image of God is found primarily in the human soul. In knowing and loving, the human mind images the trinitarian God's self-knowing and self-loving. Augustine and Aquinas agreed that in that primary way women and men were both created in the image of God.[8]

Nevertheless the story of the creation of woman in Gen. 2, particularly as interpreted by Paul in 1 Cor. 11, remained problematic: "woman was made *for* man and *from* man." Given his understanding of those texts, Augustine concluded that as man's helpmate, woman is *not* the image of God. In a highly allegorical passage, he suggests that the man alone can image God, but woman images God only when she is joined with her mate. He was so convinced that the subordination of woman to man in the social order was part of the divine creative plan that he could assert, "In paradise, men will rule, women will obey, and both will be perfectly happy" (*De Trinitate* 12.7.10).

Grappling with the same problematic biblical passages, Aquinas, too, conceded that "in a secondary sense" God's image is found in a man in a way it is not found in a woman, "for man is the beginning and end of woman, just as God is the beginning and end of all creation" (ST 1, q. 93, a. 4, ad. 1). While Aquinas granted that some forms of subjection or subordination are the result of sin, he argued that there is a kind of domestic or civil subjection in which "the ruler manages his subjects for *their* advantage and benefit." This latter form of subordination for the "good order" of society, Aquinas maintains, is part of the divine creative plan.

[T]his sort of subjection would have obtained even before sin. For the human group would have lacked the benefit of order had some of its members not been governed by others who were wiser. Such is the subjection in which woman is by nature subordinate to man, because the power of rational discernment is by nature stronger in man. (ST 1, q. 92, a. 1, ad. 2)

Aquinas' conclusion that the power of rational discernment is "by nature" stronger in man derives from his acceptance of Aristotle's characterization of the female as a defective male (male manque) and as the "passive cause" rather than the "active cause" in procreation (ST I, q. 92, a. 1). John Calvin argued from the basis of a "divine social mandate" rather than the divine plan discovered in the nature of things, but nonetheless concurred that men were divinely destined to rule and women to obey.[9]

Even this very brief survey of some of the major figures in the classic Christian tradition gives ample evidence of why not only feminists, but also a recent consultation of the World Council of Churches, have concluded that "the doctrine of God's image (*imago Dei*) has by tradition been a source of oppression and discrimination against women."[10] Further, the patriarchal lens through which the image of God was focused at various times and cultures in the history of the Christian Church excluded a full picture not only of women, but also of other nondominant groups, including slaves and servants, Native Americans and African Americans, the disabled, and gays and lesbians.

THE SYMBOL GIVES RISE TO JUSTICE

While Christian teaching, preaching, and practice have at times reflected and even reinforced the sinful biases of various cultures and periods of history, the claim that human persons are created in the image of God and endowed with fundamental human dignity has been central to prophetic preaching and the church's defense of basic human rights. As Lisa Cahill has noted, "image of God" is "the primary Christian category or symbol of interpretation of personal value."[11] Creation in the image of God serves as a root metaphor for the Christian understanding of the human person that grounds further claims to human rights.

The history of Christian preaching and teaching offers multiple examples of the symbol of creation in the image of God fostering social transformation and personal conversion. In our own day, the Roman Catholic bishops' pastoral letter "Brothers and Sisters to Us" condemns racism as sin precisely because it

> divides the human family, blots out the image of God among specific members of that family, and violates the fundamental human dignity of those called to be children of the same Father . . . God's word in Genesis announces that all men and women are created in God's image; not just *some* races and racial types, but *all* bear the imprint of the Creator and are enlivened by the breath of his one Spirit.[12]

In a similar vein, the Administrative Board of the United States Catholic Conference, when reflecting on a Gospel response to "the many faces of AIDS," insisted that "Made in God's image and likeness, every human person is of inestimable worth."[13]

Official statements of all Christian churches today unconditionally affirm that women and men are created equally in the image of God and are to be accorded equal human dignity with men. This is true even of those churches who deny ordination to women or argue that women are divinely intended to be subordinate to men. Thus the most recent document of the Missouri Synod Lutheran Church, which defends women's subordination to men as part of the original purpose of God in creation, nevertheless insists that "[the woman] is in every way [the man's] equal before the Creator. . . . The clear principle laid down in the inspired record of creation [is]: *Man and woman are equal in having the same relationship to God and to nature.*"[14] The fourth draft of the Roman Catholic Bishops' proposed pastoral response to "women's concerns" likewise cites as basic truth from the church's teaching that "both women and men are made in God's image. There is no hint of superiority of men or the inferiority of women." In reflecting on marriage, the bishops further clarify: "Each of the two, the man and the woman, is individually made in the image and likeness of God. They are also an image of God together, in their mutual love, in becoming 'one Flesh' (Gen. 2:24). Their communion of love mirrors the Trinitarian life, the communion of love in God."[15]

While the Christian churches are clear in their contemporary statements about the equal dignity of every human person, biases—including those of racism, sexism, heterosexism—continue in both church and society. Reaffirming that every human person is created in the image and likeness of God and endowed with inviolable human dignity is not enough. The symbol of basic human dignity is intended to give rise not only to right thinking, but to right relations. The Christian proclamation that human beings are created in the image of God underscores the fundamental human dignity of every person. At the same time, however, that proclamation sets a moral agenda for both church and society. As David Tracy has remarked:

> Christians continue to believe that all human beings are made in the image and likeness of God. They have become far more sensitive, however, to the fact that this theological indicative, in the present world, must also function as an imperative. The task of human beings, on this newer reading, is to actualize what they are potentially, and to actualize that reality in the struggle for a *not-yet* acknowledged dignity of every human person: for the need, in sum for human rights in their full social, economic, cultural, political, civic, and religious dimensions.[16]

The problem is, of course, that in practice as well as theory, we disagree about what constitutes human dignity, fundamental equality, human rights, and just social structures. Within the Christian community, we further disagree about whether the teaching regarding divinely intended distinct "proper roles" for women and men is compatible with the teaching that both image God equally and share equal dignity, whether and how women can image Christ in roles of leadership and particularly in the Eucharistic assembly, and whether the call to image the trinitarian God by being the Body of Christ requires divinely intended hierarchical structures or a radical refashioning of a community of equal discipleship.

Part of the reason we do not have a unanimous judgment about what constitutes human dignity and just social and ecclesiastical structures is that the fullness of human life, of the church, and of the reign of God lies ahead of us, not behind us. Creation, anthropology, and ecclesiology all need to be rethought in eschatological terms. An eschatological approach to creation reminds us that the image of God describes not a primordial state from which the first human beings fell, but the destiny toward which the human community is called. In a similar way, the call to "be conformed to the image of Christ" is the mission of the church shared by all the baptized, a vocation that constantly summons the pilgrim people of God to deeper conversion. In a real sense, the full meaning of what it means to "image God" or "image Christ" remains in the future.

Both imagination and concrete ethical action are needed as a basis for a renewed theology of *imago Dei* or *imago Christi*. But imagination is always linked to memory. In both the Jewish and Christian traditions, stories and symbols from the past form the basis of renewed hope and prophetic action in the present. This is true in a unique way for Christians, who believe that the future of humanity and the world has already begun in the life, death, and resurrection of Jesus. What can the symbols *imago Dei* and *imago Christi* contribute to contemporary efforts to reimagine what it means to be human?

REIMAGINING RIGHT RELATIONS

Remembering the Garden

If we turn first to the basic anthropological symbol of *imago Dei*, we might ask how it can lead to a new future in terms of both interpersonal relationships and social and political structures. Feminist biblical scholar Phyllis Trible proposes that a creative rereading of Genesis 2, the creation story that was at the root of much of the patriarchal legitimation of women's subordination, can offer some surprising new insights about God's vision of right relationship.[17] Trible interprets the myth as subverting, rather than legitimating, patriarchal structures and relationships. Noting that *'adham* is the generic term for humankind, she undercuts the traditional argument that woman was created for man and from man by pointing out that the two sexes come into existence simultaneously. In terms of the traditional argument that man was created first and woman last, Trible's literary analysis of the creation suggests that "the last may be first" in the literary or theological structure of a story or that, viewed as a literary inclusion device, the creation of man first and woman last suggests that the two are in fact equal. The characterization of woman as subordinate to man because she is man's helpmate *(ezer)* is similarly undercut when one realizes that the same term is used to describe God as helpmate to Israel.

Prior to Genesis 3, where radical rupture in all relationships is introduced into the story, the myth's vision of relationship between human persons, humankind and the earth, and human beings and

God is one of friendship and harmony. The "order of creation" suggests equality and mutuality between women and men. Only after their shared failure to observe the divine "limits" disrupted the "right order" of creation are man and woman portrayed as ashamed of their nakedness, failing to take responsibility for their actions, and hiding from God out of fear. The domination of male over female is clearly identified as a consequence of sin rather than the divine creative plan.[18]

Further, as Trible delineates, "This sin vitiates all relationships: between animals and human beings (3:15), mothers and children (3:16); husbands and wives (3:16); people and the soil (3:17-18); humanity and its work (3:19)."[19] Far from legitimating patriarchy, Trible's analysis of Genesis 2-3 concludes, "The Yahwist narrative tells us who we are (creatures of equality and mutuality); it tells us who we have become (creatures of oppression); and so it opens possibilities for change, for a return to our true liberation under God. In other words, the story calls female and male to repent."[20]

In the context of the Hebrew worldview, the creation stories in Genesis 1 and 2 suggest that the image of God comprises the goodness of the whole person, human relationships of equality and mutuality, a relationship of harmony between human beings and the earth, and a call to friendship with God. Each of those dimensions is important for a retrieval of the symbol that can contribute to a contemporary understanding of what it means to be human.

The Body-Self as Image

To say that human beings are created in the image of God is to say something about the dignity and goodness of all aspects of the human person. Early Christian theology, developed within a Platonic and neo-Platonic culture, located the image of God within the spiritual soul of the individual human person and/or man's role of dominion over woman and the earth. The image of God within human embodiment, human relationships of mutuality, human community, and humankind's kinship with the earth were either neglected or negated.[21]

A contemporary retrieval of the symbol of *imago Dei* rejects the Platonic-Cartesian split of body and soul. Our body is not something we have; rather, we are body-self. As feminist ethicist Beverly Harrison describes it, our body-self is "the integrated locus of our being-in-the-world. We are related to everything through our body-selves."[22] Even our relationship with God is possible only through our body-selves. This claim is at the heart of any incarnational or sacramental theology. God has communicated Godself most fully in and through the *incarnate* Word. And because as human beings we are constituted as body-spirit, our relationship with God or any form of spiritual experience is always mediated. Taking a clue from Irenaeus, who wrote against the gnostic heresies in the early church, we need to refashion a theology of how human persons image God that emphasizes that the only one who fully imaged God was a concrete, enfleshed human being.

Sexuality, a central aspect of embodiment that the church fathers were most loathe to include in the image of God, has become central to a contemporary understanding of how the human person images the trinitarian God whose being is to-be-in-relationship. As Catherine LaCugna states:

> Sexuality lies at the heart of all creation and is an icon of who God is, the God in whose image we were created male and female (Gen. 1) . . . Sexual desire and sexual need are a continual contradiction to the illusion that we can exist by ourselves, entirely for ourselves . . . Sexuality can be a sacred means of becoming divinized by the Spirit of God . . . Sexual practices and customs can be iconic of divine life, true images of the very nature of the triune God.[23]

LaCugna defines the term *sexuality* broadly as the capacity for relationship, for ecstasis, for self-transcendence. Pope John Paul II identifies this orientation toward giving oneself to the other in love as "nuptial symbolism." He affirms that "human beings image God then, not only in their spiritual capacities of knowing and loving, but also in their bodiliness, as masculine and feminine persons oriented to self-giving, communion, parenthood, and fruitfulness."[24]

GENDER, COMPLEMENTARITY, AND FEMALE IMAGING OF THE DIVINE

At this point, however, John Paul II and others argue that sexual differences point to distinct "proper qualities" and distinct vocations and roles for women and men. Specifically, John Paul identifies virginity and motherhood as "two particular dimensions of the fulfillment of the female personality . . . two dimensions of the female vocation."[25] Not only the physical constitution of women, but also the "psychophysical structure of women" is "naturally disposed" to motherhood. This "naturally spousal predisposition of the feminine personality" can also be realized, he maintains, in virginity . . . which makes possible another kind of motherhood, motherhood "according to the Spirit."[26] The mystery of women is explicitly identified as "virgin-mother-spouse."[27]

Feminist theologians explicitly reject a dualistic anthropology that reduces women to their maternal function.[28] They do, of course, recognize and celebrate the uniqueness of women's experience of birthing and nurturing. Further, they underline the importance of retrieving the female metaphor of God as Mother in order to break the "stranglehold" of male imagery over the religious imagination.[29] At the same time, they recognize that the concept of motherhood is socially constructed and needs to be critically appropriated in a way that does not reinforce patriarchal roles and assumptions. While women's bodily experience and female sexuality provide appropriate images and metaphors for the divine, the way that women image God or the destiny and vocation of women cannot be extrapolated solely from biology. One can recognize and celebrate the sacredness of women's bodies without falling into the error of "anatomy is destiny."

Some proponents of a theology of distinct and proper roles and a necessary "complementarity" between women and men claim support for their views in trinitarian symbolism. Benedict Ashley argues for a "defining relation between woman and man that is not only one of mutuality, but also of complementarity, so that not every social differentiation based on gender is unjust, but in some cases (e.g., family relations) for the common good of all."[30] He grounds his anthropology in what he interprets as a "hierarchical order" among the persons of the trinity, but insists that "the total receptivity of the Son and Spirit with respect to the Father in no way makes them inferior to the Father, and the obedience of a member of a human community to its legitimate authorities in no way makes them personally inferior to those authorities."[31] Yet any form of subordination among the persons of the trinity is precisely what orthodox trinitarian theology precludes. Further, as LaCugna has remarked, "there is no intrinsic reason why men should be correlated with God the Father and women with God the Son."[32]

IMAGING THE TRINITARIAN GOD

Rather than giving a theological basis for women's "subordinate but equal" role in family, society, and church, the doctrine of the trinity challenges us to rethink radically our understanding of what it means to be human. If we are created in the image of a God who is not an isolated monad but a dynamic community of love, then human existence is fundamentally social. If human destiny is finally participation in the very life of the trinity, then human persons are created as essentially relational. If human relationships, including those between women and men, are meant to mirror the relationality that constitutes the trinity, then they must be characterized by radical equality and mutuality. If the trinitarian model offers the ideal paradigm for social and political relations, then unity-in-diversity and radical equality become ethical and political mandates.

The earliest Christian reflection on what it meant for human beings to be created in the image of God developed before the trinitarian doctrine had been forged. Strongly influenced by Greek philosophical presuppositions about the nature of God and a necessary hierarchical social order, early Christian writers located the image of God in the spiritual and rational soul of individual human persons or within patriarchal social relationships. Later, when Augustine and Aquinas did describe the image of God in trinitarian terms, they continued to locate the image of the trinity primarily in the faculties of the soul of the human person.[33] Augustine used the analogy of human relationships as imaging God, but given his understanding of Genesis 2 and 1 Cor. 11, he concluded that man and woman image God together when woman is in the "right relation" of subordinate helpmate (*De Trinitate*, 7, 7, 10).

Contemporary theology offers a very different view of the implications of saying that the human person is created in the image of God. Catherine LaCugna, Walter Kasper, Jürgen Moltmann, and others have argued that recognition that the very essence of God is "to-be-in-relation" calls for a rethinking not only of the human person and social relationships, but of all reality. The very nature of existence is relational; being is always being-in-relation. The mystery of what it means to be a human person and what constitutes authentic human, social, and political relationships is grounded in the deeper mystery of God: At the heart of reality is relationship, personhood, communion.[34] The trinitarian foundation of all of reality calls for human societies that are characterized by mutuality, interdependence, inclusiveness, equality, and freedom. As Elizabeth Johnson has written, "The Trinity as pure relationality . . . epitomizes the connectedness of all that exists in the universe. Relation encompasses and constitutes the web of reality and, when rightly ordered, forms the matrix for the flourishing of all creatures, both human beings and the earth."[35]

Given this trinitarian perspective, a new emphasis emerges. While the dignity of every human being needs to be respected and protected, human persons do not image God primarily as individuals, but rather in "right relationship" with one another. The image of God is reflected most clearly in communities characterized by equality, respect for difference and uniqueness, and mutual love. Highlighting the social character of the doctrine of the trinity, Jürgen Moltmann maintains that "Human beings are *imago trinitas* and only correspond to the triune God when they are united with one another . . . The isolated individual and solitary subject are deficient modes of being human because they fall short of likeness to God . . . Socially open companionship between people is the form of life which corresponds to God."[36]

But how do we know what is the right ordering of reality? And what is the origin of this Christian conviction that the trinitarian mystery of love is the very heart of reality? Both questions lead us back to the history of Jesus of Nazareth, whom Christians confess to be the very image of God enfleshed.

JESUS AS "PERFECT IMAGE" AND HUMANS AS "IMAGING CHRIST"

In a world of finitude and sin, the vocation of humankind to live in "right relationship" with one another, with the rest of creation, and with God remains a destiny we hope for and work toward. From a Christian perspective, only one human being can be said to be the very icon of God among us—Jesus the Christ. The life, ministry and death of Jesus of Nazareth reveal what it means concretely for human beings to image the divine love that is the very life of the trinity. God's "right order" of relationships can be glimpsed in the world of parables that Jesus preached, lived, and embodied—where the last and the least are the privileged, where no one is excluded from the common table, where leaders wash feet and seek the lost, where children are welcomed and cared for, where women and men are partners, friends, and equal disciples, where enemies are reconciled and sinners pardoned, where the created world is respected and celebrated, and where fidelity and love defeat betrayal and death.

In the life, ministry, death, and resurrection of Jesus, a new communion was sealed between the divine and the human. God shared human history even unto death and destroyed the bondage of sin and death. Christians believe that not only the mystery of the divine, but also the deepest truths about human life and destiny, have been revealed in Jesus Christ. But the incarnational principle extends further. The mystery of Christ who is the very icon of God includes the community, which is called "to be conformed to the image of Christ" (Rom 8:29). Given the realities of finitude and sin, Christian communities as well as individual Christians often fail to witness to the mystery of God-among-us. Sin and division betray the community's deepest identity and vocation and cause stumbling blocks for others who fail to see in the Christian church the Body of Christ in whom "there is neither Jew nor Greek, slave nor free, male nor female" (Gal. 3:28).

At the same time, it is precisely in and through the concrete contours and challenges of daily life, including our failures, that the power of the Holy Spirit is active, conforming us into the image of Christ. Convinced that "where sin abounds, grace abounds still more" (Rom. 5:20), Paul can say of the Christian community: "All of us are being transformed into that same image from one degree of glory to another" (2 Cor. 3:18). The christological creation hymns make even broader claims, proclaiming that the entire universe is created in Christ and destined to share in the reconciliation between creation and God brought about through Christ (Col. 1: 15-20).

Given the maleness of Jesus, however, the question of whether women can image Christ as fully as men remains problematic, particularly in debates about the possibility of women's ordination. The 1976 Vatican "Declaration on the Question of the Admission of Women to the Ministerial Priesthood" (*Inter Insignores*) argued that

> when Christ's role in the eucharist is to be expressed sacramentally, there would not be this "natural resemblance" which must exist between Christ and his minister if the role of Christ were not taken by a man: in such a case it would be difficult to see in the minister the image of Christ. For Christ himself was and remains a man.[37]

That passage and its underlying assumptions regarding sacramental symbolism, the theological significance of the maleness of Jesus, the theology of ordained ministry and the presider's role at Eucharist, are all problematic and have been critically analyzed elsewhere. Fundamental to the discussion here is the central point that Christians are conformed to the image of Christ through baptism and the living of the Christian life. The image of Christ is reflected in the ethics and lives of Christian communities and individual Christians who tell the story of Jesus with their lives. It is lack of fidelity to the gospel, rather than gender, that makes it difficult to see the image of Christ in a human person or community. As Elizabeth Johnson has stressed, "The image of Christ does not lie in sexual similarity to the human man Jesus, but in coherence with the narrative shape of his compassionate, liberating life in the world through the power of the Spirit."[38]

The global context of senseless and radical suffering provides the contemporary horizon that challenges any attempt to retrieve the symbols of *imago Dei* and *imago Christi.* In an age when basic human dignity is systematically ignored and violated through horrors that include "ethnic cleansing," rape as a weapon of warfare, and the abuse and deprivation of children throughout the world, the "image of God" in human persons is revealed as an image desecrated, the image of Christ crucified. Only if human communities and individuals rise up in indignation, protest, solidarity, and action on behalf of those whose basic human dignity has been violated can the image of God also be revealed as compassionate love in solidarity with us even unto death.

Like the basic anthropological symbol *imago Dei*, the explicitly Christian anthropological symbol *imago Christi* grounds our identity and points to our destiny and our vocation. Created in the image of God and baptized into the image of Christ, we have been given an inviolable dignity and an irreversible mandate. Every human person is endowed with radical dignity, every aspect of humanity as created by God shares in the human potential to image the divine. As fundamentally social and relational beings, we image God most profoundly when our human relationships, our families and communities, and our social, political, economic, and ecclesiastical structures reflect the equality, mutuality, and love that are essential to the trinitarian God revealed in Jesus and in communities living in the power of his Spirit. In a world of violence, hatred, radical suffering, competition, and oppression, Christians believe, proclaim, and strive to give testimony with their lives to the conviction that humankind is created in the image of, and destined for full participation in, the divine mystery of love.

NOTES

1. Anne McGrew Bennett, "A Part of Me Is Missing," in Clare Benedicks Fischer, Betsy Brenneman, and Anne McGrew Bennett, eds., *Women in a Strange Land: Search for a New Image* (Philadelphia: Fortress, 1975), pp. 7-8.

2. C. S. Song, *The Compassionate God* (Maryknoll, NY: Orbis Books, 1982), pp. 15-16.

3. Janet Kalven, "Women's Voices Begin to Challenge...," *National Catholic Reporter,* April 13, 1984, p. 20. Note also Rosemary Radford Ruether's observation that the source of the Women-Church movement is the deep alienation that many Christian women feel toward Christianity as a religion that fails to affirm them as women, both their leadership talents and their female humanity as "image of God." "Women-Church: A Way to Stay While Patriarchy Wears Away," *National Catholic Reporter,* August 13, 1993, p. 22.

4. As noted in Jacqueline Grant, *White Women's Christ and Black Women's Jesus* (Atlanta: Scholars Press, 1989), p. 208. Grant is referring to Cannon's dissertation, *Resources for a Constructive Ethic for Black Women with Special Attention to the Life and Work of Zora Neale Hurston* (Ph.D. dissertation, Union Theological Seminary, 1983).

5. See, for example, Diodore, *Commentary on Genesis,* in *Patrologia Graeca,* PG 33, 1564d. See also John Chrysostom, *In Gen. Chap. I hom.* 3.2; 8.4; 9.4. In the Latin tradition, Ambrose, Augustine's teacher, did not directly discuss the question. However his commentary on the six days of creation refers to women as a source of temptation for "man" and describes the beautiful human body as including male genitals (*Hexaemeron* 6.8. 49-50; 6.9). See Maryanne Cline Horowitz, "The Image of God in Man—Is Woman Included?" *Harvard Theological Review* 72 (1979): 175-206.

6. *Intr. ad. theol.* 1.9.

7. As cited in Horowitz, "The Image of God in Man—Is Woman Included?" p. 177.

8. *De Trinitate,* 14.3.6 and 14.8.11; ST 1, q. 93, a.4, ad. 1.

9. On this point, see Rosemary Ruether, *Sexism and God-Talk* (Boston: Beacon, 1983), p. 98.

10. Quoted in *The Ecumenical Review* 33 (1981): 77.

11. Lisa Sowle Cahill, "Toward a Christian Theory of Human Rights," *The Journal of Religious Ethics* 8 (1980): 279. For development of the notion of image of God as "root metaphor," see Lucien Richard, "Toward a Renewed Theology of Creation: Implications for the Question of Human Rights," *Eglise et Theologie* 17 (1986): 149-70.

12. National Conference of Catholic Bishops, "Brothers and Sisters to Us: A Pastoral Letter on Racism, November 14, 1979," in J. Brian Benestad and Francis J. Butler, eds., *Quest for Justice: A Compendium of Statements of the United States Catholic Bishops on the Political and Social Order 1966-1980* (Washington, DC: U.S. Catholic Conference, 1981), pp. 375, 378.

13. USCC Administrative Board, "The Many Faces of AIDS: A Gospel Response," *Origins* 17 (December 24, 1987): 483.

14. "Women in the Church: Scriptural Principles and Ecclesiastical Practice" (Commission on Theology and Church Relations of The Lutheran Church—Missouri Synod, September 1985), p. 20. For the discussion of woman's subordination to man as divinely intended, see pp. 21-37.

15. "One in Christ Jesus," *Origins* 22 (September 10, 1992): 224-25.

16. David Tracy, "Religion and Human Rights in the Public Realm," *Daedalus* 112 (1983): 248.

17. Phyllis Trible, "Eve and Adam: Genesis 2-3 Reread," in Carol P. Christ and Judith Plaskow, eds., *Womanspirit Rising* (New York: Harper and Row, 1979), pp. 74-83.

18. This insight is now broadly accepted beyond the parameters of feminist theology. See, for example, John Paul II, *Mulieris Dignitatem*, no. 10.

19. Trible, "Eve and Adam: Genesis 2-3 Reread," p. 80.

20. Ibid., p. 81. See also Mary Aquin O'Neill, "Imagine Being Human: An Anthropology of Mutuality," in Priests for Equality, ed., *Miriam's Song II* (West Hyattsville, MD: Priests for Equality, 1988), pp. 11-14. For creative reflection on right relations between women, see Judith Plaskow's Jewish feminist midrash, "The Coming of Lilith," in Rosemary Ruether, ed., *Religion and Sexism: Images of Women in the Jewish and Christian Traditions* (New York: Simon and Schuster, 1974), pp. 341-43.

21. There were exceptions, of course. Refuting gnosticism's denial of the goodness of material creation and of the full humanity of Jesus, Irenaeus, for example, emphasized that we are created in the image of the *incarnate* Word (*Adv. Haer.* 5.16. 2). More frequent, however, were statements like that of Clement of Alexandria: "Conformity with the image and likeness is not meant for the body (for it were wrong that what is mortal be made like what is immortal), but in mind and reason, on which the Lord impresses the seal of likeness, both in respect of doing good and of exercising rule" (*Stromata* 2.19. 370).

22. Beverly Wildung Harrison, *Our Right to Choose: Toward a New Ethic of Abortion* (Boston: Beacon, 1983), p. 106, quoted by Susan A. Ross in "Then Honor God in Your Body (1 Cor. 6:20): Feminist and Sacramental Theology on the Body," *Horizons* 16 (1989): 21.

23. Catherine M. LaCugna, *God for Us: The Trinity and Christian Life* (San Francisco: Harper San Francisco, 1991), p. 407.

24. Quoted in the fourth draft of the proposed U.S. Bishops' Pastoral on women's concerns, "One in Christ Jesus," no. 20. See also John Paul II, "Marriage Is One and Indissoluble in the First Chapters of Genesis," General Audience Address, Nov. 21, 1979.

25. *Mulieris Dignitatem*, nos. 17 and 21, refers explicitly to "the two different vocations of women."

26. Ibid., no. 21.

27. Ibid., no. 22.

28. See Mary Buckley, "The Rising of the Woman Is the Rising of the Race," *Proceedings of the Catholic Theological Society of America* 34 (1979): 48-63; Mary Aquin O'Neill, "Toward a Renewed Anthropology," *Theological Studies* 36 (1975): 725-36; Rosemary Radford Ruether, *Sexism and God-Talk* (Boston: Beacon, 1983), ch. 3, 4, 7, 9, and postscript; Anne Carr, *Transforming Grace*, pp. 49-51 and 117-28.

29. See Johnson, *She Who Is: The Mystery of God in Feminist Theological Discourse* (New York: Crossroad, 1993), esp. pp. 170-87. See also Sallie McFague, *Models of God: Theology for an Ecological, Nuclear Age* (Philadelphia: Fortress, 1987) and Sandra M. Schneiders, *Women and the Word* (New York: Paulist, 1986).

30. Benedict Ashley, "Appendix to the McGivney Lectures, 1992," *Justice in the Church*, typewritten manuscript, forthcoming, from The Catholic University of America Press, p. 22.

31. Ibid., p. 21. See also Joyce Little, "Sexual Equality in the Church: A Theological Resolution to the Anthropological Dilemma," *Heythrop Journal* 28 (1987): 165-78.

32. Catherine Mowry LaCugna, "God in Communion with Us," in Catherine Mowry LaCugna, ed., *Freeing Theology: The Essentials of Theology in Feminist Perspective* (San Francisco: Harper San Francisco, 1993), p. 98. See pp. 94-99 for further analysis and critique of the theology of complementarity from a trinitarian perspective.

33. This approach to trinitarian theology dominated in the Western (Latin) tradition. In the East, some of the very thinkers who helped forge trinitarian doctrine also emphasized that the image of God is found in the primal human community. See Jürgen Moltmann's discussion of Gregory of Nazianzus et al., in *God in Creation*, trans. Margaret Kohl (San Francisco: Harper and Row, 1985), p. 242.

34. See LaCugna, *God for Us*, pp. 243-317. See also Walter Kasper, *The God of Jesus Christ* (New York: Crossroad, 1984); Johnson, *She Who Is*, pp. 191-223; Moltmann, *The Trinity and the Kingdom*, trans. Margaret Kohl (San Francisco: Harper and Row, 1981).

35. Johnson, *She Who Is*, pp. 222-23.

36. Moltmann, *God in Creation*, pp. 216, 223.

37. "Declaration on the Question of the Admission of Women to the Ministerial Priesthood," *Origins* 6 (February 3, 1977): 522. See Elizabeth A. Johnson, "The Maleness of Christ," in Anne Carr and Elisabeth Schüssler Fiorenza, eds., *The Special Nature of Women? Concilium 1991/6* (Philadelphia: Trinity Press International, 1991), pp. 108-16.

38. Johnson, *She Who Is*, p. 73. See pp. 246-72 for an excellent discussion of how women's suffering is a participation in the suffering of Christ in a context that stresses resistance and hope and critiques the ideological use of the cross to legitimate or perpetuate suffering.

12

Woman and the Last Things

A Feminist Eschatology

Peter C. Phan

The intention of this essay is to envisage a possible shape of Christian eschatology from the feminist perspective.[1] Feminist theology, like liberation theology, it has been claimed, is not just a regional theology, a theology *of* a particular aspect of Christian existence, but a radically new *way* of doing theology. To make good this assertion, feminist theologians, using the hermeneutics of suspicion, proclamation, remembrance, and creative actualization,[2] have been engaged in critiquing and reformulating the very nature and method of theology as well as the whole gamut of Christian doctrines.

It is common knowledge that eschatology, long an uncontroversial theme in Christian theology, at least since Benedict XII's constitution *Benedictus Deus* (1336), has been in recent years, to use Hans Urs von Balthasar's famous dictum, working overtime since its office was shut down in the nineteenth century.[3] Despite this renaissance, however, and despite the profound impact of feminism on theology in general, current monographs on eschatology have scarcely raised the question of whether and how the doctrine of the last things might be challenged by feminist thought.[4] On the other hand, while feminist theology has rearticulated almost all fundamental Christian doctrines, from hermeneutics and theological method to the doctrine of God and the Trinity, christology, ecclesiology, anthropology, ethics, and spirituality,[5] it has not given a systematic treatment to what Ernst Käsemann called "the mother of all Christian theology."[6] Even recent comprehensive expositions of feminist theology have ignored eschatology as a special theme altogether.[7] The two exceptions, to my knowledge, are Rosemary Ruether and Sallie McFague, but even their writings on the subject are to date quite meager.[8]

In what follows I will first of all delineate the connections between eschatology and (eco)feminist theology. Secondly, I will critically review the works of Ruether and McFague on eschatology. Finally, I will make some constructive proposals toward an ecofeminist eschatology.

ESCHATOLOGY AND FEMINIST THEOLOGY

In a pithy sentence, Karl Barth underscores the centrality of eschatology for Christianity: "Christianity that is not entirely and altogether eschatology has entirely and altogether nothing to do with Christ."[9] By eschatology (the doctrine of the *eschata* or the last things) is meant the study of realities that occur both to the individual—called "individual eschatology"—(i.e., death, particular judgment, purgatory, heaven and hell) and to humankind as a whole—called "collective eschatology"—(i.e., the end of the world, the Parousia, the resurrection of the dead, and the general judgment).

It is a consensus among historians of dogma that while collective eschatology, centered on the Christ-event, was dominant in the early Church, the focus was gradually shifted almost exclusively to individual eschatology. From the twelfth century, with the emergence of the doctrine of purgatory as a place between heaven and hell, then with the teaching of the Second Council of Lyons on purgatory (1274), next with the teaching of Benedict XII on the beatific vision by the souls just immediately after death and on the concomitant notion of the intermediate state (1336), and lastly with the teaching of the Fifth Lateran Council on the immortality of the soul (1513), Christian eschatology acquired a distinctively individualistic and otherworldly cast. The "last things" were seen as objects and events occurring to each individual soul in the world beyond, and the eschatology that was shaped by this view was characterized by what Yves Congar called "the physical style."[10]

Besides narrowing the scope of eschatology, this physical style produced unfortunate effects on theology and spirituality as a whole. Eschatology, appended at the end of dogmatics, became an object of curiosity and idle speculation and was stripped of any relevance for Christian life. Theologians expended their mental energies arguing about the nature of purgatorial fire, the possible maximum length of the stay in purgatory, the nature of limbo, the kinds of pains in hell, the characteristics of the risen body, the location of hell and heaven, and so on.

Furthermore, this otherworldly eschatology introduced a sharp separation between body and soul, between the self and the cosmos, between the immortality of the soul and the resurrection of the flesh, between earthly realities and the world beyond, between time and eternity. This dualism destroyed the ontological unity of the human person, bifurcated the destiny of history into natural and supernatural, and drove a wedge between nature and grace.

Eschatology also became divorced from other parts of theology, such as christology, ecclesiology, anthropology, and the theology of grace and of the sacraments. As a result the theology of these realities was truncated and impoverished. For instance, without the eschatological dimension, the role of Christ as the "Absolute Savior," to use Rahner's expression, is obscured; the church loses its character as a pilgrim people of God; humans are deprived of their existential orientation toward death, their *sein zum Tode,* to use Heidegger's phrase; grace is no longer seen as anticipation and foretaste of the beatific vision; and the sacraments forfeit their nature as *signa prognostica,* to use Thomas Aquinas's expression.

In reaction to this sterile eschatology, there were two important shifts in Roman Catholic eschatology in recent times. The first occurred in the wake of the definition of the dogma of the Assumption in 1950. New studies appeared that highlighted the personal and interpersonal character of all human actions. This trend is most visible in Karl Rahner, whose *anthropologische Wende* in theology is well-known.[11] Thus, for instance, death is now seen not only as a consequence of sin, as something imposed upon the human person to be passively endured, but also and primarily as an act of freedom which a person performs to bring his or her history to a final and definitive end. An anthropology was developed to overcome the age-old dualism between body and soul, immortality and resurrection, time and eternity, the self and the cosmos, the individual and the collective, the immanent and transcendent consummation of the world. In this anthropology, the relationship between these pairs of polarities is seen in direct rather than inverse proportion. For example, matter and spirit are not seen as opposites but as mutual correlates and conditions of possibility: the human spirit is the immanent product of the becoming of matter through active self-transcendence so that matter becomes itself by being spiritualized and spirit actualizes itself by being materialized.[12] As a result of this anthropological view, the unity between individual and collective eschatologies is also restored.

The second shift that has momentous implications for eschatology occurred during and especially after the Second Vatican Council. In addition to the personal and interpersonal aspects of human existence, emphasis was also laid on its sociopolitical dimension. Questions were raised about the relationship between Christian hope and innerworldly (e.g., Marxist) utopia, between salvation from sin and liberation from sociopolitical and economic oppression, between worship and social activity, between church and world, between history and the Kingdom of God.[13] Rahner's eschatology itself illustrates the trajectory from a personal to an intersubjective to a so-ciopolitical perspective.14

It is in the context of these two shifts toward the subject and society, toward the human as "spirit in the world" (Rahner), that feminist theology as liberation theology as well as a feminist eschatology should be located. As is well known, feminism is a complex move-ment with an equally complex history. As Sandra M. Schneiders summarizes it, it can be classified into four broad types, each with its distinct emphasis on various aspects of the liberation of women from patriarchal oppression: liberal, cultural, socialist, and radical.15

Liberal feminism is concerned with the political and legal rights of women but does not question the social system as such. Cultural feminism does question the sociopolitical and economic order but rather than attempting to transform it, tries to humanize it by incor-porating the distinctive contributions of women as women to a better world. Both social feminism and radical feminism aim at a total transformation of the social order but perceive the root cause of women's oppression differently. For social feminism, the root cause is economic oppression; for radical feminism, it is patriarchy, that is, the system of universal hierarchical dualism that is embodied primarily in the domination of the male household head over all other members of the family and is found in all forms of oppression such as sexism, classism, clericalism, colonialism, racism, ageism, and heterosexism. Despite its manifold differences, feminism is characterized by a com-mon "commitment to the equality of women with men,"16 to the full personhood of woman.

Christian feminist theology, largely Roman Catholic, emerged from this women's movement for liberation. As has been mentioned above, it has attempted to reconceptualize all the basic doctrines of the Christian faith by means of a critique of past patriarchal theologies and practices, a recovery of the neglected or suppressed history of women in the Christian tradition, and a reformulation, based on women's experiences, of the Christian faith in categories that promote the emancipation of women and their full equality with men in both church and society.

In this effort at constructing a feminist theology, what are the basic issues in eschatology that require reformulation on the basis of women's experience? Along the line of feminist hermeneutics, these issues can be grouped in three categories. First, are there any doctrines in past eschatologies that are patriarchal and androcentric, that regard women as inferior to men, that are misogynist, to which a hermeneu-tics of suspicion must be applied? Secondly, are there forgotten or suppressed resources in past eschatologies, both within and outside of orthodox Christianity (e.g., gnosticism and Montanism), which a hermeneutics of recovery must be exercised to retrieve? Thirdly, in the hermeneutics of creative actualization, does women's experience have anything specific to say about the last things, in terms of both the individual and collective human history? For instance, do women perceive death and dying, sin and punishment, heaven and hell, immortality and resurrection, the reality of the Reign of God, and the consummation of history, including the cosmos, in a distinctive way, different from men's? Can women's experience of conception and birthing, of the body, of the relationship between the self and the other, between human history and the cosmos, help contemporary eschatology overcome the dualistic split between body and soul, eternity and time, the individual and the society, the personal and the political? More narrowly, what contribution can an ecological theology bring to a renewed understanding of the last things? Underlying these questions is the attempt to bring ecofeminist insights to bear on certain basic themes in Christian eschatology. Among feminist theologians, Rosemary Radford Ruether and Sallie McFague have begun to carry out this task, and to their works I now turn.

EMERGING FEMINIST ESCHATOLOGIES

Rosemary Radford Ruether

Ruether, to the best of my knowledge, is the first feminist theologian to write explicitly on Christian eschatology. In what can be called the first *summa* of feminist theology, *Sexism and God-Talk*, she dedicates, somewhat in a traditional fashion, the *last* chapter to eschatology.[17] Some seven years later, she contributed an essay on feminism and eschatology to a reader, in which she incorporated some of the materials of the earlier piece. This time, however, there is a self-conscious choice, at least on the part of the editors (and presumably at least with the tacit agreement of Ruether), to place the essay at the *beginning* of dogmatics, right after the doctrine of God.

This decision, it is said, is made to underscore two points which Ruether herself makes in her essay: first, to stress that the tendency toward dualism and the denial of death lie at the root of the lack of concern for social justice in western societies; and, secondly, to underline that the vision of justice affects all our activities in the present.

By "eschatological," Ruether means the "view that believes in the possibility of human transcendence of mortality."[18] She begins her exposition on eschatology with a pointed question: "Does feminism have a stake in immortality?"[19] or "Does feminism have a doctrine of eschatology?"[20] To answer that question, Ruether appeals to women's past and present experiences and uses the critical principle of "promotion of the full humanity of women,"[21] which is itself derived from the prophetic tradition, to judge received doctrines and practices.

With reference to women's experience, Ruether adopts Charlotte Perkins Gilman's analysis of the different ways in which religion's attitudes toward immortality were shaped by the experiences of the male and the female.[22] For the male, so Gilman argues, the pivotal experience was *death* and the egoistic fear of death, given his role as hunter and warrior. The male religion, then, is built on the blood mystery of death, and its purpose is to help him escape death and to achieve survival in immortality. By contrast, woman's experience was *birth*, which is also a blood mystery threatening her with death, but which is in service of the immediate creation of new life. The female religion is oriented to the altruistic service to life for the next generation. Though somewhat critical of Gilman's dated anthropological history, Ruether sees in her theory a powerful challenge to the eschatological focus of religion in general and to Christianity in particular, which has defined salvation primarily as victory over death and attainment of immortality and eternal life.

As might be expected, Ruether delivers a sharp critique of traditional eschatologies, especially because they were formulated primarily by males and because they denigrated women and their bodies as mothers and birthgivers. She pointed out how Platonic conceptions of eschatology, built on body-soul dualism, were negative toward women as sexual persons and mothers. The corruptible body (*soma*) was seen as the prison (*sema*) of the soul, which can achieve immortality only if it is liberated from the body. Women were typically seen as more "fleshly" than men, less capable of rationality and hence of immortality. According to Plato, the soul was incarnated first into the male. Only when it failed to control its passions did the soul fall down into a lower state of life.

Early Christianity, in Ruether's view, incorporated much of this Platonic view of the female flesh as inimical to eternal life. This hostility to women was most visible in the male ascetic movement, which regarded women as the embodiment of corruptible flesh and considered physical contact with them as conducive to decay. This opposition between eternal life and female flesh took two contrasting but related forms. On the one hand, some early Christians wondered whether women's bodies could be redeemed at all in the resurrection of the dead. Female sexuality and life processes—menstruation, pregnancy, birthing, and suckling—were considered impure and leading to decay and death.

Some of them, e.g., Origen and Gregory of Nyssa, opined that originally humanity was created with a "spiritual body" without sexual distinction; only after the Fall did it take on the "coats of skin" (Gen. 3:21) burdened with sexual intercourse and reproduction and other shameful acts.[23] It follows then that in the resurrection of the dead the female body, as Leander of Seville seemed to suggest, will become male,[24] or, should the human body rise as male and female, the female body at least must be purged of all its reproductive functions and its sexual organs will no longer be, as Augustine says, "suited to their old use," but will be mysteriously transformed into "a new beauty, and this will not arouse the lust of the beholder, for there will be no lust, but will inspire praise of the wisdom and goodness of God."[25]

On the other hand, Ruether points out, the phobia toward female carnalness can take the form of sublimation of the female body as the substratum of spiritual rebirth and transcendence of material existence and death. This sublimation occurred in the church's view of Christian virgins, especially of Mary. Mary represents the virginal body of the eschatological church (the "male feminine"), and her Assumption is an anticipation of the universal sublimation of the flesh in the general resurrection, in which the mortal flesh is reunited with the immortal soul.[26] In this process of sublimation, the male leadership in the church appropriated to itself all the female activities, now spiritualized and raised to a higher realm, of conception, birthing, and nurture.

In sum, Ruether's judgment of traditional eschatology is peremptory:

> Male eschatology is built on negation of mother. Rejection of sexuality and procreation is not merely a function of prudery. Or, rather, antisexual asceticism is itself based on the fantasy that, by escaping the female realm of sexuality and procreation, one can also free oneself from finitude and mortality. The escape from sex and birth is ultimately an attempt to escape from death for which women as Eve and Mother are made responsible. Male eschatology combines male womb envy with womb negation.[27]

As women increasingly claim the right to be autonomous "selves" and refuse the role of ancillaries to males, they must question and reject the androcentric eschatologies crafted by male intelligentsia. In reformulating an eschatology that is liberating for women, Ruether agrees with Charlotte Perkins Gilman that the "first responsibility lies in building the powers of birth," that is, "creating and raising children, the pledge of the continuation of human life in the finite future, and shaping a just and sustainable human society to bequeath to that next generation."[28]

Feminist eschatology, as any holistic eschatology, must consider both the collective and individual aspects of human existence. Indeed, given the feminist emphasis on the human person's relationality with and radical interdependence between both other humans and the nonhuman cosmos, it is not surprising that Ruether, in constructing a feminist eschatology, as we shall see, gives priority to collective and even ecological eschatology.

With regard to collective eschatology, she insists that in contrast to Hebrew and Christian messianisms and their secular stepchildren in liberal and revolutionary ideologies, feminist eschatology does not espouse a linear view of history as a universal project leading to a final, all-perfect consummation either at the end of history or beyond, by way of either evolution or revolution. At such a final salvific end point, all contradictions and evils of history will be overcome and universal goodness reign. Such an end point, Ruether argues, either fails to provide a point of reference for historical hope, if it occurs outside of history, or is identified with a particular social movement, should it occur inside history. Even the Christian critique of the immanent messianism by means of the concept of "eschatological proviso" (e.g., J. B. Metz) to keep history constantly open and to relativize all human endeavors fails to pass muster because, in Ruether's view, it is still based on a model of endlessly stretching forward into the future. This endless flight into the future contradicts the finite nature of human beings and cosmic resources.[29]

In lieu of this historical eschatology, Ruether proposes a different model based on conversion.

> Conversion suggests that, while there is no one utopian state of humanity lying back in an original paradise of the "beginning," there are basic ingredients of a just and livable society. These ingredients have roots in nature and involve acceptance of finitude, human scale, and balanced relationships between persons and between human and non-human beings . . . All these ingredients contribute to what we spontaneously recognize to be a livable, as distinct from an unlivable environment.[30]

Unlike historical eschatology with a once-and-for-all transformation at the end point of history, feminist eschatology, designed by women who have been in charge of repetitive tasks, daily clean-up, and nurture, regards social change for justice (especially for women) as a historical project that needs to be undertaken again and again. This concept of social change as conversion to each other and to the earth, rather than a flight into an endless and unrealizable future, Ruether claims, is more in keeping with the Jewish tradition of the Jubilee (cf. Leviticus 25:8-12) and with the finite nature of human and cosmic realities. In sum, collective feminist eschatology is suspicious of any eschatology that places the consummation of history in an "eternal now" (e.g., in neo-orthodox theology) or in a future realm at the end of history (e.g., in liberal and Marxist messianism) or beyond history (in apocalyptic and Christian messianism). It is focused exclusively on the present and emphasizes the struggle for justice as a never-ending task, to be renewed constantly, for the global community on earth.

Besides collective eschatology, feminist doctrine of the last things must deal with the fate of the individual as well, especially death and life beyond. Ruether formulates the central questions of individual eschatology with unflinching lucidity:

> But what of the sad insufficiencies of natural finitude, the un-controllable accidents and diseases that cut off people's lives before their time or condemn them to a half-life of undeveloped potential? What of all those who have suffered and died in misery because of social evils over which they had no control? What of the vast toiling masses of human beings who have had so little chance to live fulfilling lives through the centuries? What of the whole tragic drama of human history where so few have had opportunities for moments of leisure and happiness in the midst of oppressive labor? What even of those worthies who have made important contributions and lived full lives? Do their achievements live on only in our fading memories? Is there no larger realm of life where the meaning of their existence is preserved? These are the questions that have ever sparked the search for assurance of life beyond death.[31]

To all these questions and those related with the individual's destiny beyond death, Ruether says that the only appropriate answer is "honest agnosticism."[32] She stresses that our images and ideas of life after death are not revealed knowledge but "projections of our wishes and hopes."[33] With regard to death itself, she laments the widespread death-denying character of Western culture, which prevents us from accepting our finitude and limitations. What we know of death is that in dying, the life process of our organism and our consciousness, that is, our capacity to reflect on our life process, ceases. Does anything survive our death? Says Ruether:

> Our existence as an individual organism ceases and dissolves back into the cosmic Matrix of matter-energy out of which new centers of individual beings arise. It is this Matrix, and not the individuated centers of being, which is everlasting, which sub-sists underneath the coming to be and passing away of individ-ual beings.[34]

But what of the persistent concern about and affirmation of indi-vidual immortality? For Ruether, it is the symptom of the death-de-nying tendency of Western culture or, more precisely, of the male's desperate attempt to transcend mortality, to overcome his fear of death which haunts him as hunter of animals and killer of other human beings. It is ultimately an egoistic effort to absolutize personal or individual self as everlasting over against the total community of being.[35]

Feminist eschatology, on the other hand, is not concerned with the question of immortality since, based on women's birth and life-giving experience, it is able to view death as the final relinquishment of individuated ego into the great Matrix of being. Ruether understands this self-abandonment to the Matrix of being not only in an ontological sense of being united with the Matrix of being but also in a literal sense of giving one's body to the earth so that it becomes food for new beings to emerge from one's flesh and bones. To bury oneself in steel coffins, so that one cannot disintegrate into the earth, is "to refuse to accept this process of entering back into the matrix of renewed life."[36]

Were one to ask her what she means by saying that the great Matrix—which supports the matter-energy of our individualized beings and into which we are dissolved at death—is the "ground of all personhood," Ruether would reply that a precise explanation cannot be obtained, since the matter is beyond our imagination. This lack of clear and distinct explanation should not however bother us, she argues, because it is not our responsibility to know the eternal meaning of our life. Rather, our responsibility is

> to use our temporal life span to create a good and just community for our generation and our children. It is in the hands of Holy Wisdom to forge out of our finite struggle truth and being for everlasting life. Our agnosticism about what this means is then the expression of our faith, our trust that Holy Wisdom will give transcendent meaning to our world, which is bounded by space and time.[37]

Before concluding our exposition of Ruether's eschatology, it is necessary to mention another important aspect of her doctrine of the last things, namely, its ecological dimension. Given the connections among woman, body, and nature, feminism naturally leads to ecology, and an eschatology that does justice to woman, her bodily reality, and her full personhood would have to challenge the traditional theology of nature.

Feminist eschatology, according to Ruether, must question the understanding of humans as ontologically and morally superior to nonhuman beings, the right of the human to treat the nonhuman as private property to be exploited, the social structures with which males perpetuate their domination over females and nature, and the model of hierarchy of beings based upon the superiority of spirit over matter. It is important to recognize that one can no longer maintain a dichotomy between nature and history; indeed, nature itself is historical. It is furthermore necessary to recognize the continuity between human consciousness and the energy of matter throughout the universe, as well as the radical mutual interdependence between humans and ecology. An ecofeminist eschatology will have to incorporate these insights in order to emphasize the responsibility of humans to become the caretaker and cultivator of the whole ecological community upon which their existence depends.[38] This ecofeminist eschatology serves as a useful transition to Sallie McFague.

Sallie McFague

Well-known for her writings on metaphors and metaphorical theology, especially with reference to our understanding of God,[39] McFague has dedicated the last chapter of her most recent book, *The Body of God: An Ecological Theology,* to eschatology.[40] Though its central concern is to explore the metaphor of the world as the body of God and its implications for ecological theology, the work is of profound relevance for our theme of feminist eschatology. For one thing, McFague's critique of the classic model of organism enshrined in the phrase "the church as the body of Christ" and depicted by Leonardo di Vinci as the male figure with arms and legs outstretched to the four corners of the cosmos, and her proposal of the alternative model are deeply inspired by feminist thought, especially its epistemology. Such theory of knowledge, which she calls "attention epistemology," focuses on embodied differences and helps overcome the disdain for the body and the fear of different kinds of bodies.[41] In light of such an epistemology, the classic model of organism is perceived as hierarchical, anthropocentric (as well as androcentric), and universalizing, all characteristics regarded by feminism as derogatory toward women.[42]

For another thing, eschatology has always been concerned with the end of human history and the cosmos. The metaphor of the world as the body of God, McFague argues, can shed unexpected light on the possible shape of the new humanity in the eschatological age. This metaphor is derived not only from feminism, as has been noted above, but also from contemporary science, which postulates a "common creation story."[43] According to this theory, from one infinitely hot, infinitely condensed bit of matter (a millionth of a gram) some fifteen billion years ago, have evolved one hundred billion galaxies, each with its billions of stars and planets. This common creation story radicalizes both unity and difference. From unimaginable unity—the unity of nothing but one—has evolved unimaginable diversity. In the perspective of this common creation story, how would an ecofeminist eschatological imagination depict the new humanity and cosmos?

The significance of this cosmology, McFague points out, is fivefold. First, it suggests that the center of the cosmos cannot be human beings, since, after all, on the universe's clock, human existence has lasted but *a few seconds.* Anthropocentrism is delegitimized. Second, it stresses that the universe is an open-ended story, with a genuinely new future, not a static and closed Newtonian universe. Third, it shows that things, biotic and abiotic, exist in radical interrelatedness and interdependence; there is a cosmic genetic relatedness. Fourth, it emphasizes that the universe is a multilevelled organism in which the higher and more complex the level, the more vulnerable it is and dependent upon the level that supports it. Finally, the common story is a public one, available to all, susceptible of retelling by anyone and any religion. Hence, it is a meeting place for all religious traditions. An eschatology that is rooted in this common creation story would be, in McFague's view, characterized by the following features:

> a focus on gratitude for the gift of life rather than a longing for eternal life; an end to dualistic hierarchies, including human beings over nature; an appreciation for the individuality of all things rather than the glorification of human individualism; a sense of radical interrelatedness and interdependence with all that exists; the acceptance of responsibility for other forms of life and the ecosystem, as guardians and partners of the planet; the acknowledgment that salvation is physical as well as spiritual and hence, that sharing the basics of existence is a necessity; and, finally, the recognition that sin is the refusal to stay in our proper place . . . [44]

In sum, in this ecofeminist eschatology, humans are *decentered* as the point and goal of creation and *recentered* as God's partners in helping creation to grow and prosper as the body of God. This decentering and recentering also shifts the focus of eschatology. McFague recognizes that eschatology can and did mean a reflection on death and the afterlife, the "last things." However, in light of ecofeminism, it can also mean "the breaking in of new possibilities, of hope for a new creation. It can mean living from a vision for a different present based upon a new future."[45]

Of course, *Christian* eschatology should not be elaborated simply on the basis of feminist thought and the scientific theory of the common origin of the cosmos. It must be rooted also in the story of how God is embodied in Jesus or, as McFague calls it, the "Christic paradigm." This body of God in Jesus has both a shape and a scope. Its shape "includes all, especially the needy and the outcast"[46] who, in our nuclear, ecological age, are not only humans but natural world as "the new poor." Its scope is the "cosmic Christ," that is to say, the *direction* of creation is salvation itself, namely, the liberating, healing, inclusive love of God, and the *place* of salvation is the present physical world.[47]

In light of feminism, the common creation story, and the Christic paradigm, how does McFague elaborate eschatology? Here I will pass over her feminist critique of patriarchalism and androcentrism, since it is quite similar to Ruether's, and focus on her ecological theology and its impact upon eschatology.

Like Ruether's, McFague's eschatology moves away from concerns with the fate of the individual in death and beyond (individual eschatology) and concentrates on the welfare not only of humans but of the universe as such (collective eschatology with emphasis on the cosmos or ecoeschatology). Like Ruether, McFague shifts the focus of traditional eschatology from the future to the present, physical world, more specifically, to what humans must do as responsible stewards of creation. Thus, in her eschatology to date, there has been no discussion of individual eschatology as such; instead, there is a heavy emphasis on ethics.

In this context she argues that the eschatological vision, which acts both as critique of current dualistic, anthropocentric, androcentric, and individualistic paradigm and lure toward a holistic, cosmocentric, androgenic, and collective future, is characterized by five features.[48] First, eschatology must underscore both interdependence (the unity of each with all) and independence (the distinction of each from all). Hence no eschatological consummation should either erase all individuality or focus exclusively on individual happiness or eternal life apart from other humans and the cosmos. Second, this eschatology will decenter human beings as the goal and purpose of creation. In this sense, sin is the refusal to accept our place in the scheme of things, to accept one's proper limits so that other individuals of one's species as well as other species can also have needed space.[49] Third, ecofeminist eschatology will conceive salvation first of all as the fulfillment of all the basic, physical needs of the earth's creatures, of the bodies. One must not think of salvation or heaven in spiritual, otherworldly, atemporal, or nonspatial ways. Fourth, eschatology will involve an ethics of solidarity with the oppressed, who comprise not only humans but also nature, which we have made poor. Finally, in this vision of the new creation, human beings have a special vocation to bond with other human beings and other life forms in ways that will create a sustainable, wholesome existence for the rich variety of beings on our planet.

TOWARD AN ECOFEMINIST ESCHATOLOGY

As has been said, eschatology is still in its infancy, compared with other themes in feminist theology. Nevertheless, as elaborated by Ruether and McFague, it presents serious challenges and offers enriching possibilities to traditional eschatology. In this last section I will identify the contributions of an ecofeminist eschatology as presented by these two influential theologians and raise a few critical questions as well as indicate possible lines of development.

1. Feminist eschatology brings a different voice, long ignored or repressed, to the doctrine of the last things formulated, to date, overwhelmingly by males. In line with its theological method, it has performed a useful service by unmasking the androcentric character of allegedly universal truth-claims traditional eschatology made about death and the afterlife. For instance, it has shown how misogyny and disdain of the female body, even in the form of sublimation, have infected certain past affirmations about the resurrection of the body.

2. In general, feminist eschatology has succeeded in correcting certain unhealthy tendencies of past eschatologies, still operative in contemporary fundamentalist eschatologies.[50] For example, it has overcome the dualism that splits body and soul, the individual and society, nature and history, time and eternity. It has also undercut idle speculations about favorite eschatological themes such as dispensationalism, millennialism, rapture, the antichrist, the second coming, the signs of the end time, and so on, which have so long captivated popular imagination. It rightly refuses to offer a "reportorial eschatology," supplying the *"timetable, map, blueprint,* and *playbill* of the end."[51]

3. Feminist eschatology has also successfully blended the doctrine of the last things, usually considered as too remote to have immediate consequences for Christian living, with ethics and spirituality.[52] Such ethics and spirituality are, however, purified of their individualistic tendency and even their anthropocentrism, enshrined in the motto *memento mori* and in the spiritual *ars moriendi* tradition, and are given political and ecological dimensions. In so doing, it enriches the traditional understanding of sin and salvation by highlighting their social and ecological aspects.

4. Moreover, ecofeminist eschatology has made a valuable contribution to the burgeoning dialogue between theology and science. It has made creative use of recent cosmogonic hypotheses in astral and subatomic physics (e.g., the common creation story) not only to critique the traditional Christian anthropology based on the Babylonian, Hebrew, and Greek creation stories and develop a more adequate anthropology (e.g., the decentering of humans and their being assigned to their rightful place in the cosmic scheme of things[53]) but also to show their implications for eschatology.

For instance, Ruether argues that the heliocentric view destroyed the medieval notion of different kinds of "matter," mortal and immortal, upon which Christian eschatology, with its concept of immortal, "spiritual" body, had been based.[54] Similarly, the new physics, especially with its blurring of the distinction between matter and energy, raises questions about the familiar distinction in eschatology between the fulfillment of human history and that of the cosmos.

5. On the basis of their understanding of the place of humans in the universe and of their experiences as women, feminist theologians have been able to show how death is a natural part of the life process and thus to overcome the death-denying tendency of contemporary western culture (whether to be associated with the male's psychological makeup or not). As Ruether puts it, "in nature death is not an enemy, but a friend of the life process. The death side of the life cycle is an essential component of that renewal of life by which dead organisms are broken down and become the nutrients of new organic growth."[55]

6. Ecofeminist eschatology rightly rejects what Ruether calls "religious narratives of world destruction," that is, apocalyptic visions that predict armageddon, universal conflagration, and the total annihilation of the world from which the righteous alone can escape. Ruether acknowledges the important function of apocalypticism as a form of social protest of the oppressed against their oppressors. However, for her, it is fatally flawed by dualism (the opposition between "us and them", "God and Satan") and by its tendency to reify good and evil in identifying them with sectarian and tribal-national groups. Says she:

> Apocalypticism, like Platonic eschatology, is based on the fantasy of escape from mortality. Death itself is the "last enemy" to be overcome. The very nature of life of the biosphere, rooted in mortality and renewal through disintegration, is denied. Instead life and death are absolutized as opposites. One imagines that through destruction not only of the "enemy" humans, but the earth itself, one side, death, can be finally eliminated, and the other side, life, can be immortalized.[56]

Instead of attributing the destruction of the universe to God, feminist eschatology sees human agency as central to the threat of total extinction. The "four horsemen" of destruction are not supernatural beings but our own creations: human population explosion at the expense of plants and animals; environmental damage to air, water, and soil; the misery of growing masses of poor; and global militarization.

7. Lastly, ecofeminist eschatology has enlarged the notion of "communion of saints." The saints here, as McFague has shown well, are not restricted to humans but include all beings, biotic as well as abiotic. Furthermore, the "kingdom of God" is not simply a reality that comes into time but into *space* as well, because it is and must be embodied. In this way, heaven can and should be imagined in much more concrete and earthly fashion, and not as somewhere ethereal and opposed to the earth.

These are some of the ways, it seems to me, in which feminist eschatology has corrected certain imbalances of the traditional doctrine of the last things and enriched it with distinct voices. On the other hand, there are certain doctrines in traditional eschatology that are denied or dismissed without adequate justification.[57] Four of these deserve careful examination in particular.

First, regarding immortality. Ruether presents a "genealogy" of this doctrine in religions and philosophy, pointing out its rootedness in the male's primal fear of death (cf. Charlotte Perkins Gilman) and its deleterious effects on women and their bodies. Ruether's observations may be to the point from the psychological and social points of view, but as such they do not yet engage the philosophical foundations of this doctrine. This is not, of course, the place to enter into a discussion of these foundations, but it may be useful to mention one of the important insights of feminism, that is, its emphasis on the ontological unity of the human person against the body-soul dualism.

One of the common objections against the doctrine of immortality is derived from the way in which the brain and body are related. It is now commonly recognized that our mental life is bound up with brain structure and organized bodily energy. But to say that self-consciousness functions only in dependence on matter in an embodied manner does not by itself reduce self-consciousness to matter, a reductionism to which feminism is adamantly opposed. Nor is saying that there is continuity between matter and spirit tantamount to denying a qualitative difference between the two. Furthermore, it is quite possible to maintain the "immortality" of the human *person* without having recourse to the distinction, much less the separation, between body and soul.[58]

Second, even though Ruether is opposed to the doctrine of the immortality of the soul and the survival of the individual as individual beyond death, she does grant that the human person achieves a kind of survival by being dissolved back into what she terms the "cosmic Matrix of matter-energy" which alone is everlasting. Though Ruether refuses to explain in greater detail what she means by such a statement, it is fair to say that the position, which recalls the Buddhist conception of Nirvana and process thought's notion of immortality, is not free from difficulties.

For example, what is the difference between the cosmic Matrix of matter-energy and individual human beings (who are also matter-energy) that makes the former alone everlasting? Is it because there is a greater amount of matter-energy in the cosmic Matrix? But it is difficult to see how a quantitative difference can produce such an essential disparity as between immortality and mortality. Furthermore, McFague's point that "the body of God is not *a* body, but all the different, peculiar, particular bodies about us,"[59] and her insistence that her former "oceanic feeling of oneness with nature and God" has been replaced by "wonder at the particular, interest in detail, delight in difference"[60] would militate against Ruether's idea of the total dissolution of the individual into the cosmic Matrix with the resultant loss of self.

Third, Ruether dismisses linear eschatologies that place the consummation of human history either at the end of or beyond history. She urges that we should dedicate ourselves to the building up of a just and ecologically sustainable society in the present for our children and the next generation. While her critique of certain types of future-oriented eschatologies for their lack of concern for justice and social transformation is well taken, it is doubtful whether her overemphasis on the present has done justice to the transcendent dimension of Christian eschatology. Again, McFague's insistence on the radicalization of both immanence and transcendence can serve as a useful corrective here. While transcendence must be embodied, it cannot be reduced to immanence.[61] In like manner, while one should dedicate oneself to the betterment of society, one should not reduce the meaning of human history to raising children and producing a good and just society.

Finally, with regard to questions concerning the individual's fate after death, especially of "the vast toiling masses of human beings who had so little chance to fulfill themselves," Ruether commends, as we have seen, "honest agnosticism." While her reticence to give detailed descriptions of the beyond is admirable and while we have to be mindful of the analogical and imaginative character of our eschatological language, it is far from satisfactory to say, as she does, that "our images of life after death, individually and collectively, are not revealed knowledge, but projections of our wishes and hopes."[62] Such a position, besides putting us on the slippery road of Feuerbach and the "masters of suspicion," does not take seriously what has been revealed to us in the resurrection of Christ.

This last point brings me to indicate three lines of development that ecofeminist eschatology might consider. First, it is a consensus among contemporary eschatologists that the foundation upon which constructive thoughts about the future must be built is the resurrection of Jesus. Of course, a feminist critique must be applied, as has been done in various ways to our traditional christology, in order to remove whatever is injurious to the human dignity of women. But it is axiomatic that the story of Jesus, especially his death and resurrection (the "Christic paradigm") is the cornerstone of eschatology. Eschatology is derived from christology; it is a christology of the consummation of humanity and the cosmos. It is christology and anthropology conjugated in the future tense.[63] The starting point of this christological eschatology is the resurrection, not death. It is around this central fact that all other eschatological doctrines must be organized.[64] Only in this way can eschatology be Good News, especially for the oppressed, including women and nature, and the vast toiling masses of human beings who have had so little chance to live a decent life.

Second, while it is proper that ecofeminist eschatology lays the stress on collective eschatology and on the *eschaton,* it is necessary that it also deals with the *eschata.* Questions *are* still being asked about the meaning of death, the possibility of the afterlife, reincarnation, judgment, hell, heaven, and universal restoration. While mindful of Wittgenstein's injunction that "What cannot be spoken must be passed over in silence" (*Wovon man nicht sprechen kann, darüber muss man schweigen*), it is useful to remember that the Christian tradition does contain resources that enable us to speak, soberly yet concretely, about these realities. Of course, feminist theology can and should be brought to bear on our understanding of these realities. I have already indicated how our traditional theology of death and of the reign of God or heaven has been enriched by feminist thought. Furthermore, in my judgment, feminist insights on the unity of the whole cosmos and the inclusiveness of all reality can open up new possibilities for the two most controverted eschatological doctrines today, namely, reincarnation and *apocatastasis.*[65]

Finally, feminist theology would do well to retrieve the eschatologies contained in writings of women such as Mechthild of Magdeburg and Gertrude of Helfta, as well as in feminist science fiction. The former writings provide glimpses into how medieval women, despite the androcentric tendency of their age, succeeded in carving out for themselves a vision of eternal life that gave dignity to them as women (or more precisely, as virgins),[66] and the latter offer a subversive vision of the eschaton, a utopia that refuses to validate the status quo and emphasizes relationality and connectedness.[67]

NOTES

1. Note the extremely modest scope of this effort. Given the overwhelming abundance of literature on both eschatology and feminist theology, my intention is merely to explore what a feminist eschatology might look like by bringing certain central insights of feminist thought to bear on traditional eschatology. Such an attempt is, it is hoped, a useful exercise in theological imagination since, as will be shown later, feminist theologians have not paid much attention to this area of theology. In this essay I am using the term *feminist* to include also ecological themes, since the two theologians under study, Rosemary Radford Ruether and Sallie McFague, have tightly linked feminism with ecology. It is well-known that there are deep connections between feminism and ecology. Hence, the subtitle of the essay could have been "An Ecofeminist Eschatology."

2. See Elisabeth Schüssler Fiorenza, *Bread Not Stone: The Challenge of Feminist Biblical Interpretation* (Boston: Beacon Press, 1984), pp. 15-22.

3. See Hans Urs von Balthasar, "Umrisse der Eschatologie," in *Verbum Caro* (Einsiedeln: Johannes Verlag, 1960), p. 276. Von Balthasar is here repeating a remark by Ernst Troeltsch.

4. For a brief overview of recent trends in eschatology, see Peter C. Phan, *Eternity in Time: A Study of Rahner's Eschatology* (Selinsgrove: Susquehanna University Press, 1988), pp. 26-31, in which nine models of eschatology are discussed: consequent, supratemporal, existential, realized, anticipated, progressive, proleptic, hope, and political. For recent monographs on eschatologies, see Zachary Hayes, *Visions of a Future: A Study of Christian Eschatology* (Collegeville: The Liturgical Press, 1989); Tony Kelly, *Touching the Infinite: Explorations in Christian Hope* (Victoria, Australia: Collins Dove, 1991); D. Hattrup, *Eschatologie* (Paderborn: Bonifatius, 1992); D. Pokorny, *Die Zukunft des Glaubens: Sechs Kapitel über Eschatologie* (Stuttgart: Calwer, 1992); Hanz Schwarz, *Jenseits von Utopie und Resignation: Einführung in die christliche Eschatologie* (Wuppertal: Brockhaus, 1990); G. Panteghini, *L'orizzonte speranza: Lineamenti di Escatologia cristiana* (Padova: Messaggero, 1990); Geddes MacGregor, *Images of Afterlife: Beliefs from Antiquity to Modern Times* (New York: Paragon House, 1992).

5. Only a very small sample of representative works is offered here to give an idea of how these theological themes have been treated in feminist theology. On hermeneutics and methodology: Elisabeth Schüssler Fiorenza, *In Memory of Her: A Feminist Theological Reconstruction of Christian Origins* (New York: Crossroad, 1984); idem, ed., *Searching the Scriptures: A Feminist Introduction* (New York: Crossroad, 1994); Sandra M. Schneiders, *The Revelatory Text: Interpreting the New Testament as Sacred Scripture* (San Francisco: Harper, 1991); Pamela Dickey Young, *Feminist Theology/Christian Theology: In Search of a Method* (Minneapolis: Fortress, 1990). On the doctrine of God and the Trinity: Mary Daly, *Beyond God the Father: Toward a Philosophy of Women's Liberation* (Boston: Beacon Press, 1973); Sallie McFague, *Models of God: Theology for an Ecological, Nuclear Age* (Philadelphia: Fortress, 1987); Catherine Mowry LaCugna, *God for Us: The Trinity and Christian Life* (San Francisco: Harper SanFrancisco, 1991); Elizabeth A. Johnson, *She Who Is: The Mystery of God in Feminist Theological Discourse* (New York: Crossroad, 1993); Rebecca S. Chopp, *The Power to Speak: Feminism, Language, God* (New York: Crossroad, 1989). On christology: Rita Nakashima Brock, *Journeys by Heart: A Christology of Erotic Power* (New York: Crossroad, 1988); Patricia Wilson-Kastner, *Faith, Feminism and the Christ* (Philadelphia: Fortress, 1983). On ecclesiology: Letty M. Russell, *Church in the Round: Feminist Interpretation of the Church* (Louisville: Westminster/John Knox, 1993); Rosemary Radford Ruether, *Women-Church: Theology and Practice of Feminist Liturgical Communities* (San Francisco: Harper & Row, 1985); Elizabeth Schüssler Fiorenza, *Discipleship of Equals: A Critical Feminist Ecclesia-logy of Liberation* (New York: Crossroad, 1993). On anthropology: Micaela di Leonardo, ed., *Gender at the Crossroads of Knowledge: Feminist Anthropology in the Postmodern Era* (Berkeley: University of California Press, 1991); Mary Stewart Van Leeuven, ed., *After Eden: Facing the Challenge of Gender Reconciliation* (Grand Rapids, MI: W. B. Eerdmans Publishing Co., 1993); Uta Ranke-Heinemann, *Eunuchs for the Kingdom of Heaven: Women, Sexuality, and the Catholic Church,* trans. Peter Heinegg (New York: Doubleday, 1990). On ethics: Barbara Hilkert Andolsen, Christine E. Gudorf, and Mary D. Pellhauer, eds., *Women's Consciousness, Women's Conscience* (Minneapolis: Winston Press, 1985); Margaret Farley, *Personal Commitments: Beginning, Keeping, Changing* (San Francisco: Harper & Row, 1980). On spirituality: Joann Wolski Conn, ed., *Women's Spirituality* (New York: Paulist Press, 1980); Mary Jo Weaver, *Springs of Water in a Dry Land* (Boston: Beacon Press, 1992); Judith

Plaskow and Carol P. Christ, eds., *Weaving the Vision: New Patterns in Feminist Spirituality* (San Francisco: Harper & Row, 1989).

6. See his *Exegetische Versuche und Besinnungen,* vol. II (Göttingen: Vandenhoeck & Ruprecht, 1960), p. 100. Actually, Käsemann's exact words are: "Apocalypticism is the mother of all Christian theology." However, by apocalypticism he did not mean the late Jewish worldview as found in the book of Daniel, for instance, but the basic direction of the Christian faith toward the end of all history. This is also, as is well known, the thesis of Jürgen Moltmann.

7. See, for example, Anne E. Carr's *Transforming Grace: Women's Experience and Christian Tradition* (San Francisco: Harper & Row, 1988), and Catherine Mowry LaCugna, ed., *Freeing Theology: The Essentials of Theology in Feminist Perspective* (San Francisco: Harper, 1993) have no chapter on eschatology. This is somewhat surprising, especially in the case of the second book, since its stated purpose is to present "the essentials" of theology.

8. See Rosemary Radford Ruether, chapter 10, "Eschatology and Feminism," in *Sexism and God-Talk: Toward a Feminist Theology* (Boston: Beacon Press, 1983), pp. 235-58; idem, "Eschatology and Feminism," in Susan Brooks Thistlethwaite and Mary Potter Engel, eds., *Lift Every Voice: Constructing Christian Theologies from the Underside* (San Francisco: Harper, 1990), pp. 111-24 (a slightly expanded version of the first essay); Sallie McFague, "Eschatology: A New Shape for Humanity," in *The Body of God: An Ecological Theology* (Minneapolis: Fortress, 1993), pp. 197-212.

9. Karl Barth, *The Epistle to the Romans* (London: Oxford University Press, 1933), p. 314.

10. For a discussion of recent eschatology and its "physical style," see Zachary Hayes, *What Are They Saying about the End of the World?* (New York: Paulist Press, 1983).

11. See, for instance, his "Zur Theologie des Todes," *Synopsis. Studien aus Medizin und Naturwissenschaft* 3 (1949): 87-112, later expanded and published under the same title in *Zeitschrift für Katholische Theologie* 79 (1957): 1-44 and subsequently published as a separate book with an excursus on martyrdom, *Zur Theologie des Todes. Mit Einem Exkursus über das Martyrium* (Freiburg: Herder, 1958). Translated into English by Charles Henkey (New York: Herder and Herder, 1961).

12. For a study of Rahner's anthropology and eschatology, see Phan, *Eternity in Time.*

13. See especially *Gaudium et Spes,* numbers 33-45. For Vatican II's eschatology, see the entire chapter seven of *Lumen Gentium.*

14. For a brief history of the development of Rahner's eschatology, see Phan, *Eternity in Time,* pp. 34-39.

15. Sandra M. Schneiders, *Beyond Patching: Faith and Feminism in the Catholic Church* (New York: Paulist Press, 1991), pp. 15-25. Ann Loades, who edited *Feminist Theology: A Reader* (London: SPCK, 1990), speaks of three types of feminism: liberal, Marxist, romantic (p. 1). The liberal tradition is concerned with equality of civil rights for women as for men; Marxist feminism with economic autonomy; and romantic feminism celebrates the emotional and the natural and includes radical feminists who reject the male world altogether and those who advocate mutuality between women and men. Margaret Koch and Mary Stewart Van Leeuwen, following Karen Offen, distinguish three types of feminism: liberal, relational, and socialist (see *After Eden: Facing the Challenge of Gender Reconciliation,* pp. 21-25). Liberal feminism downplays

226 PETER C. PHAN

gender differences and emphasizes common humanity and individual rights; relational feminism highlights women's rights as *women* and the distinctive contributions of women. Socialist feminism focuses on the economic oppression of women. Despite their differences, these types of feminism are committed to the equality of women to men.

16. Denise Lardner Carmody, *Responses to 101 Questions about Feminism* (New York: Paulist Press, 1994), p. 5.

17. See Ruether, *Sexism and God-Talk: Toward a Feminist Theology,* pp. 235-58.

18. Ruether, *Sexism and God-Talk,* p. 240. She differentiates eschatological religion, which she identifies with Christianity, from natural religion (e.g., the Canaanite-Babylonian tradition) and from historical religion (e.g., the Hebrew religion). In her view, "Christian eschatology fuses the apocalyptic eschatology of post-biblical Judaism with the Platonic eschatology of the soul that separates itself from the bodily encumbrance through mortification and returns to its true home in heaven" (p. 244). Such eschatology, she notes, became gradually focused on the fate of the individual soul after death to the eclipse of the collective dimension present in millennial hope that was preserved in heretical sects and is now being revived in secular, revolutionary messianisms.

19. Ruether, *Sexism and God-Talk,* p. 235.

20. Thistlethwaite and Engel, eds., *Lift Every Voice,* p. 112.

21. Ruether, *Sexism and God-Talk,* p. 18. The positive formulation of this principle reads: "What does promote the full humanity of women is of the Holy, it does reflect true relation to the divine, it is the true nature of things, the authentic message of redemption and the mission of redemptive community" (p. 19).

22. See Charlotte Perkins Gilman, *His Religion and Hers: A Study of the Faith of the Fathers and the Work of Our Mothers* (New York: Century, 1923).

23. For a detailed exposition of Origen and Gregory of Nyssa, see Peter C. Phan, *Grace and the Human Condition* (Wilmington, DE: Michael Glazier, 1988), pp. 80-93; 177-89.

24. See his *De Instit. Virg.,* preface, quoted in Ruether, *Sexism and God-Talk,* p. 248.

25. Augustine, *The City of God,* 22.17. See also Jerome, *Epistle,* 108.23. For Ruether's exposition of this form of phobia of female sexuality, see *Sexism and God-Talk,* pp. 247-49.

26. See Ruether's critique of traditional mariology and alternative feminist construal in her *Sexism and God-Talk,* pp. 139-58.

27. Ruether, *Sexism and God-Talk,* p. 144. In Thistlethwaite and Engel, eds., *Lift Every Voice,* p. 120, she says: "So we see in Christian eschatology simultaneously a negation of the real sexual and maternal body of the woman, but also its appropriation, in spiritualized form, by the male celibate church leadership."

28. Thistlethwaite and Engel, eds., *Lift Every Voice,* p. 121.

29. For Ruether's exposition and critique of these messianisms, see her *Sexism and God-Talk,* pp. 82-85; 252-54.

30. Ibid., p. 254.

31. Thistlethwaite and Engel, eds., *Lift Every Voice,* p. 122.

32. Ibid.

33. Ibid.

34. Ibid. The same position was asserted in almost identical words in Ruether, *Sexism and God-Talk*, pp. 256-58. By "the cosmic Matrix" Ruether means the God/ess, the "mother-matter-matrix," as the dynamic source of being. This notion transcends the patriarchal conception of divinity. See *Sexism and God-Talk*, pp. 68-71.

35. In Rosemary Ruether, *Gaia & God: An Ecofeminist Theology of Earth Healing* (San Francisco: Harper San Francisco, 1992), p. 251, Ruether suggests that faced with the capacity of consciousness to roam through space and time and its utter dependence on mortal organisms, people and their religions strive to resolve this contradiction by imagining that consciousness is not really dependent on mortal organisms and that the mental self can survive, and even be strengthened by, the demise of the body. But, says she: "This concept of the 'immortal self,' survivable apart from our particular transient organism, must be recognized, not only as untenable, but as the source of much destructive behavior toward the earth and other humans."

36. Ruether, *Sexism and God-Talk*, p. 258.

37. Ibid.

38. See Ruether, *Sexism and God-Talk*, pp. 85-92; 259-64. Ruether makes use of the ecological traditions of Native American religion to criticize linear eschatologies that neglect the essential place of the environment in the future of humanity. She refers especially to the book by Vine Deloria, *God Is Red* (New York: Grosset and Dunlap, 1973). For Ruether's most recent development of ecofeminist theology, see her *Gaia & God*.

39. See her *Speaking in Parables: A Study in Metaphor and Theology* (Philadelphia: Fortress Press, 1975); *Metaphorical Theology: Models of God in Religious Language* (Philadelphia: Fortress Press, 1982); and *Models of God*. For a critical evaluation of these three works, see David J. Brommell, "Sallie McFague's 'Metaphorical Theology'," *Journal of The American Academy of Religion* 61 (Fall 93): 485-503.

40. McFague, *The Body of God*, pp. 197-212. It would be of great interest to compare and contrast this work with Ruether's *Gaia & God*.

41. See McFague, *The Body of God*, pp. 47-55.

42. For a correlation between oppression of woman and oppression of nature, see Gerda Lerner, *The Creation of Patriarchy* (Oxford: Oxford University Press, 1986) and Carolyn Merchant, *The Death of Nature: Women, Ecology and the Scientific Revolution* (New York: Harper and Row, 1980).

43. The term *common creation story* refers to the one creation story that all human beings, all other life forms and, indeed, everything that is, have in common. It is the story associated with the big bang theory of the beginning of the universe billions of years ago and its subsequent evolution. For a comparable account, see Ruether, *Gaia & God*, pp. 32-58.

44. McFague, *The Body of God*, p. 110.

45. Ibid., p. 198.

46. Ibid., p. 164.

47. Ibid., pp. 179-91.

48. Ibid., pp. 198-202. See also her essay "Cosmology and Christianity: Implications of the Common Creation Story for Theology," in Sheila Greeve Davaney, ed., *Theology at the End of Modernity* (Philadelphia: Trinity Press International, 1991), pp. 9-40.

49. For McFague's insightful analysis of "ecological sin," see her *The Body of God*, pp. 112-29.

50. For exposition and critique of fundamentalist eschatologies, see Zachary Hayes, "Fundamentalist Eschatology," *New Theology Review* 1 (May 1988): 21-35.

51. Gabriel Fackre, *The Religious Right of Christian Faith* (Grand Rapids, MI: Eerdmans, 1982), p. 88. For a broader context of fundamentalist eschatology, see Peter C. Phan, "Might or Mystery: The Fundamentalist Concept of God," in William M. Shea, ed., *The Struggle Over the Past: Fundamentalism in the Modern World* (Lanham, MD: University Press of America, 1993), pp. 81-102.

52. See Ruether, *Gaia & God*, part four (pp. 205-74), which retrieves the covenantal and sacramental traditions of biblical thought and Christian heritage for ecological spirituality and politics. An ecological spirituality, according to Ruether, must be built upon three premises: "the transience of selves, the living interdependency of all things, and the value of the personal in communion" (p. 251).

53. See McFague, *The Body of God*, pp. 99-112.

54. See Ruether, *Gaia & God*, pp. 35-36.

55. Ibid., p. 53.

56. Ibid., p. 83.

57. For a traditional statement of eschatology, see the document of The International Theological Commission entitled "De quibusdam quaestionibus actualibus circa eschatologiam" (1990). The Latin text is available in *Gregorianum* 73 (1992): 395-435. English translation in *Irish Theological Quarterly* 3 (1992): 209-43. For a critical study of this document, see Peter C. Phan, "Contemporary Context and Issues in Eschatology," *Theological Studies*, vol. 55, no. 3 (Sept. 1994): 507-36.

58. For instance, one can adopt Rahner's notion of *realsymbol* and apply it to the body. For a discussion of immortality and resurrection in Rahner, see Peter C. Phan, *Eternity in Time: A Study of Karl Rahner's Eschatology*, pp. 44-50; 170-76.

59. McFague, *The Body of God*, p. 211.

60. Ibid., p. 209.

61. Ibid., pp. 132-33.

62. Thistlethwaite and Engel, eds., *Lift Every Voice*, p. 122.

63. On this point, see Karl Rahner's remarks in his essay "The Hermeneutics of Eschatological Assertions," *Theological Investigations*, vol. 4, trans. Kevin Smyth (New York: Crossroad, 1982), p. 343: "Anything that cannot be read and understood as a Christological assertion is not a genuine eschatological assertion." For an elaboration of this point, see Phan, *Eternity in Time*, pp. 70-72.

64. This point is strongly made by Giorgio Gozzelino in his "Problemi e Compiti dell'escatologia contemporanea," *Salesianum* 54 (1992): 93-95.

65. See my "Contemporary Context and Issues in Eschatology."

66. For an overview of these writings, see Colleen McDannell and Bernhard Lang, *Heaven: A History* (New York: Vintage Books, 1988), pp. 100-107.

67. See Daphne Hamapson, *Theology and Feminism* (Oxford: Basil Blackwell, 1990), pp. 142-45.

List of Contributors

María Pilar Aquino, of Mexico, is Assistant Professor of Theological and Religious Studies at the University of San Diego, and was president of the Association of Catholic Hispanic Theologians in the U.S. (1993-1994). She is author of *Our Cry for Life: Feminist Theology from Latin America* and editor of *Aportes para una Theología desde la Mujer* (Madrid).

Anne M. Clifford is Associate Professor of Theology at Duquesne University. Her interests are in feminist theology and creation theology. She has published articles in *Systematic Theology: Roman Catholic Perspectives*, edited by Francis Schüssler Fiorenza and John Galvin, and in *Horizons* and the *Journal of Feminist Studies in Religion*. She is currently engaged in writing an introduction to feminist theology for Orbis Books.

Ann O'Hara Graff is now Assistant Professor of Theology at Seattle University, and for the past five years was at the Institute of Pastoral Studies at Loyola University in Chicago. Her areas of interest are ecclesiology, feminist studies, and cross-cultural studies. She has contributed articles to *Horizons*, *New Theology Review*, *Chicago Studies*, and several books.

Mary Catherine Hilkert has been Associate Professor of Systematic Theology at Aquinas Institute in St. Louis since 1984. She will join the theology faculty at the University of Notre Dame in 1996. Her primary areas of interest are theological anthropology, fundamental theology, and feminist theology. She is a contributor to *Freeing Theology: The Essentials of Theology in Feminist Perspective*, edited by Catherine Mowry LaCugna, and is author of *Naming Grace: Preaching and the Sacramental Imagination*, forthcoming.

Mary Ann Hinsdale is Associate Professor of Theology at the College of the Holy Cross. Her major areas of interest are ecclesiology, theological anthropology, hermeneutics, and feminist theory. Her publications include *Faith That Transforms* and *It Comes from the People: Community Development and Local Theology*.

Ada María Isasi-Díaz is Assistant Professor of Theology and Ethics at Drew University Theological School. She is author of *En la Lucha/ In the Struggle: Elaborating a Mujerista Theology*, co-author with Yolanda Tarango of *Hispanic Women: Prophetic Voice in the Church*, co-author of *God's Fierce Whimsy*, and co-editor of *Inheriting Our Mother's Gardens*.

Sally Ann McReynolds is Assistant Professor of Theology at St. Mary College in Kansas. Her interests are feminist methodology, liturgy, and social justice. She has published articles and reviews in *A Promise of Presence*, edited by Michael Downey and Richard Fragomeni; *The New Dictionary of Catholic Spirituality*, edited by Michael Downey; *Horizons,* and *The Way*.

229

Peter C. Phan, a native of Vietnam, is department chair and Professor of Systematic Theology at the Catholic University of America. He has published extensively in the areas of eschatology, patristics, and interreligious dialogue. One of his works, *Eternity in Time,* was given the Best Book Award by the College Theology Society in 1989.

Susan A. Ross is Associate Professor of Theology at Loyola University and was also Director of Women's Studies for the past three years. Her interests are sacramental theology and feminist thought. She has published articles in *Horizons, Journal of Religion,* and *Theological Studies.* She is currently working on a book on women, the body, and the sacraments.

Patricia L. Wismer was the chair of the Department of Theology and Religious Studies at Seattle University before her untimely death in 1993. Her particular areas of interest were theological anthropology, fundamental theology, and the problem of suffering. She took initiative in the design of both the women's studies program and the cross-cultural studies program at Seattle University.

Mary Ann Zimmer is provincial of the U.S. province of the Notre Dame Sisters. She is a Ph.D. candidate at Emory University, and her area of study is the relationship between popular religion and academic theology.

Index

231